INTERNATIONAL BUSINESS TRANSACTIONS

IN A NUTSHELL

Sixth Edition

By

RALPH H. FOLSOM

University Professor of Law
University of San Diego

MICHAEL WALLACE GORDON

Chesterfield Smith Professor of Law
University of Florida

JOHN A. SPANOGLE

William Wallace Kirkpatrick Professor of Law
The George Washington University

WEST
GROUP

ST. PAUL, MINN.
2000

TEXT IS PRINTED ON 10% POST
CONSUMER RECYCLED PAPER

We dedicate this book:

to Paris and the University of San Diego
Institute of International and Comparative Law

to the Escuela Libre de Derecho (Mexico) and
the University of Florida exchange program

and to all those who work to promote the
harmonization of international commercial law

*

III

PREFACE TO THE SIXTH EDITION

This sixth edition of **International Business Transactions in a Nutshell** is the fourth written by the three co-authors. The first two editions were authored by the late Professor Donald T. Wilson and published in 1981 and 1984. The third edition, in 1988, was the first undertaken by us and drew heavily on Professor Wilson's work. The third edition began to diminish extensive quotations and citations in favor of additional textual analysis of trends and doctrines. We added new chapters on International Trading of Goods, Doing Business in Nonmarket Economies, Doing Business in Developing Nations, and Regulation of Imports and Exports. Special emphasis was placed on the Convention on Contracts for the International Sale of Goods (CISG), ratified by the United States. The fourth edition was substantially altered to reflect changes from 1988 to 1991, including the Single European Act, the 1988 Omnibus Trade and Competitiveness Act, the alterations in nonmarket economies, and the movement toward greater economic integration in the Western hemisphere by the Canadian-United States Free Trade Agreement and the initial work toward a North American Free Trade Agreement and the initial work toward a North American Free Trade Agreement.

Because of the size of the fourth edition, further expansion to cover developments between 1991 and 1995 could be accomplished only if we split the former Nutshell in two. The fifth and sixth editions represent such a division, and the International Business Transactions Nutshell (6th edition) is published concurrently with the International Trade and Investment Nutshell (2nd edition).

This edition of the International Business Transactions Nutshell now focuses on the negotiation of business transactions, the documentary sale and use of letters of credit, currency issues, technology transfers, transactions in developing and nonmarket economies, dispute settlement, and the immunity of states and use of the act of state doctrine in commercial transactions. The International Trade and Investment Nutshell covers the commencement, insuring, operation and withdrawal of foreign investment, including business immigration, expropriation, government imposed restrictions on imports and exports, the GATT/WTO, and economic integration with an emphasis on the European Union and the North American Free Trade Agreement. The two Nutshells are intended to provide our readers with a broad introduction to the people and institutions who practice international business transactions, and the government and multilateral organizations which both encourage and restrict trade.

The changes since 1996 that are reflected in this sixth edition include the continued progress towards market economies by nations in transition from nonmarket economies, experience gained in the first half-dozen years of the NAFTA, the increasing use of various means of electronic commerce, and electronic letters of credit, the new international rules for standby letters of credit, and a partial survey of the UNIDROIT Principles of International Commercial Contracts.

These revisions reflect our value judgments as to what ought to be included in an introductory volume on a very broad subject which is constantly affected by movements in the world trading community. Our judgments will be familiar to those who have read or adopted our **International Business Transactions: A Problem-Oriented Coursebook**, originally published in 1987, and followed with a second edition in 1991, a third edition in 1995, and a fourth edition in 1999.

Our primary objective is to produce a Nutshell which law and business students, and professionals who are not specialists in international trade, will find helpful. We also hope to contribute to the general body of knowledge about the vast and intensely controversial field of international business transactions.

This Nutshell has been a collaborative effort. Each of us, however, has been primarily responsible for certain areas. Professor Folsom has been primarily responsible for the materials on negotiating international business transactions and technology transfers and licensing of intellectual property. Professor Gordon has been primarily responsible for the materials on doing business in market and nonmarket economies, foreign state immunity, and the act of state doctrine. Professor Spanogle has been primarily responsible for the materials on international trading of goods, financing international trade and dispute settlement.

We have been aided by colleagues at our own law schools and others both in this country and abroad, by student research assistants and by persons in practice. We welcome continued suggestions for the next edition.

RALPH H. FOLSOM
MICHAEL W. GORDON
JOHN A. SPANOGLE

December 1999

OUTLINE

OUTLINE

*

TABLE OF CASES

References are to Pages

A

B

TABLE OF CASES

C

G

H

I

J

K

L

M

N

O

P

T

U

V

TABLE OF CASES

*

INTERNATIONAL BUSINESS TRANSACTIONS

IN A NUTSHELL

Sixth Edition

*

INTRODUCTION

FROM BROCKTON AND BUR-BANK TO BANGKOK AND BEIJING

Representing a Boston client who sells goods to a buyer in Burbank creates relatively few issues which are not also present if the buyer is in Brockton (i.e., the same state as the seller, Massachusetts). Both sales are likely to involve a standard documentary sale transaction. Unlike a face-to-face transaction, the seller will not meet the buyer and hand over the goods simultaneously as the buyer hands over the money. Payment is likely to be required upon presentation of the *documents* by the seller to the buyer, not upon an inspection of the goods by the buyer after the goods have arrived. A letter of credit may be used to reduce risks and avoid a situation where either the seller or the buyer has possession of both the goods and the money at the same time. Use of a letter of credit adds to the transaction an issuing, and perhaps a second confirming, bank. The Boston seller may be willing to accept the letter of credit issued by a Brockton or Burbank bank, without confirmation by a bank in, or closer to, Boston. The sale to Brockton will be in dollars, just as will be the sale to Burbank. The parties will correspond in English.

1

Perhaps the most significant features unique to the Burbank purchase involve which state's law will apply and which state's court will be the appropriate forum if there is a conflict. But the rules of commercial law of Massachusetts and California are nearly identical. Both states have adopted the Uniform Commercial Code. The California lawyer passed a different bar exam than the Boston lawyer. But nearly all of the substantive law on each exam was the same, rooted in the common law and expressed in state legal systems containing many common features. The two lawyers studied the common law in their respective law schools, and they may even have gone to the same law school. Although a continent apart, the Massachusetts and California lawyers for the buyer and seller could exchange practices, and quickly function with little loss of efficiency and skill.

But what if the sale from Boston is not to Brockton, nor to Burbank, but to Bangkok? This international transaction will involve two different business and social cultures, and two different legal systems. The economy of Thailand is less developed than the United States and may present some problems unique to developing nations, such as a less efficient infrastructure at the port of entry for unloading the goods. Risk of damage thus is greater, and insurance rates will be higher. Customs officials might demand "unofficial" payments to admit the goods. As in the case of the sale to Brockton or Burbank, the sale to Bangkok probably will involve the use of a documentary sale with a letter of credit.

But the usage of documentary sales and letters of credit may differ in each nation. The meaning of commonly used commercial terms, such as c.i.f. or f.o.b., may have different meanings and place different risks on the parties in each nation. The parties may help resolve this by specifying the use of the International Chamber of Commerce Incoterms, which provide interpretations of commercial terms usually accepted by courts. Wanting assurance that the goods received are the same as the goods ordered, the Bangkok buyer may wish to have a third party inspect the shipment and certify that the goods shipped are the same as the goods ordered. The letter of credit in an international transaction is also more complex. If the Bangkok buyer uses a Bangkok bank as the issuing bank of the letter of credit, the Boston seller is almost certain to require that a United States bank confirm the letter of credit. The Boston seller does not wish to have to go to Bangkok to challenge the Bangkok bank if a conflict over the letter of credit arises. The Boston seller will prefer to go to a Boston bank to present the documents for payment, thus avoiding having to send the documents to an agent in Bangkok for presentation to a Bangkok bank. Additionally, letters of credit may be irrevocable or revocable. The Boston seller will insist on the irrevocable form, but practice in Bangkok might be to issue revocable letters. As in the case of rules applicable to the documentary sale, the parties may choose international rules generally accepted to govern letters of credit. They will almost certainly be the Uniform

Customs and Practice for Documentary Credits (UCP). They are also a product of the International Chamber of Commerce, as are the Incoterms noted above.

Not only will the contract for sale differ in our international sale, the contract for shipping the goods to Bangkok will differ. The greater distance to Bangkok will involve greater risks of loss during transportation. But that is true of the greater distance to Burbank than to Brockton in the domestic sale. If ocean transportation is used, shipments to either Burbank or Bangkok will likely transit the Panama Canal. However, the Boston seller can avoid any international issues in the sale to Burbank, such as transiting the canal, by shipping the goods across the continental United States to California. Selling to Bangkok does not offer that option. The shipment to Bangkok might be on a vessel with stops in several foreign nations before reaching Bangkok, creating additional and different risks. Furthermore, the laws and rules applicable to the shipment may differ. The United States applies its Carriage of Goods at Sea Act, based on the Hague Rules, while some other nations base their shipping laws on the Hamburg Rules or the Hague–Visby Rules.

A major difference in many international transactions involves the choice of *currency*. The Boston seller probably will insist on being paid in U.S. dollars, not Thai bahts. If Thai bahts are received by the Boston seller, it can not pay suppliers with them, nor give them to workers as salary. When the seller takes Thai bahts to a Boston bank, the bank may reject them because the bank is not familiar with them, and believed it will not be able to exchange bahts for U.S. dollars. If the bank is willing to accept the bahts, it may do so only with a substantial discount, causing a projected profit from the sale to become a loss. Even if the Thai currency is freely exchangeable, the rates of conversion from bahts to dollars might change between the time of the signing of the contract and the time of the exchange, causing either an unexpected gain or an unwelcome loss. Even if the Bangkok buyer agreed to pay in dollars, the Thai government might impose exchange restrictions prohibiting the removal of hard currency from Thailand.

Not only the currency but the *language* of the contract will have to be decided. Even if the contract terms are expressed in English, as preferred by the Boston seller, the Bangkok buyer may believe the contract terms say something quite different than the view of the Boston seller. While differences in the meaning of terms may also occur in the domestic transactions, the likelihood and magnitude of differences in the international transaction are likely to be more extensive.

If the sale from Boston is to Beijing rather than to Bangkok, the Boston seller will address most of the same issues as noted above with the sale to Bangkok, plus issues of dealing with a economy which possesses **nonmarket** economy characteristics. There are fewer nonmarket economies today than a decade ago, and many nonmarket economies are in a stage of transition to market economies. Thus there may be a question regarding the character or nature of the buyer's economy. It may be a nonmarket economy and also a developing nation, such as Cuba. It may be an advanced developing country (ADC) or newly industrializing country (NIC), but still be a nonmarket economy, such as China (if it is fair to characterize the PRC as beyond a mere developing nation). It may be a nonmarket economy trying to become a market economy, but having difficulty overcoming decades of central planning and government involvement in the production and distribution of goods. This is true of many nations in Eastern Europe and the former USSR. Or it may be a nonmarket economy which prefers to remain a nonmarket economy, but which finds it necessary to do business with market economies and opens the door to market economy characteristics only enough to achieve specific goals. That is the policy of Cuba.

Where the buyer is located in a nonmarket economy such as China, a major difference is that the purchaser may be the government rather than a private entity. Furthermore, the purchaser may not be the end user of the goods, but a centralized government agency, frequently called a foreign or state trading organization (FTO or STO). Most nonmarket economies have very strictly controlled currencies. The currencies tend to be nonexchangeable in international currency markets, and are usually artificial in value. They are sometimes so strictly controlled that they may not be removed from the country.

Unable to obtain scarce dollars from China, and unwilling to accept Chinese currency, the Boston seller may be asked to find Chinese goods to accept in exchange. This is *countertrade*, a modern variation of barter. The Boston seller receives goods instead of currency, and may have to search China for goods of value. The Boston seller might find goods it may use in its own operations. But if it is unable to use those goods in its own operations, it will have to market those goods. This additional and often complex aspect of what was to be a simple sale to Beijing involves two sales, and probably three contracts. The first sale is from the Boston seller to the Beijing buyer. The second sale is the purchase of goods by the Boston party from China. Two sales probably means the use of two contracts and two letters of credit. Because the two contracts are linked, there will have to be a third contract establishing the interrelationships between the parties. Often called the protocol contract, it may include penalties against the Boston seller if it does not find Chinese goods to purchase within a certain time period.

Countertrade has many faces. It includes the exchange outlined above, usually called "counterpurchase". More complex forms may appear if the Boston seller wants to establish a factory in Beijing, and in lieu of profits agrees to accept a percentage of the Chinese production—a form called "compensation" or "buy-back". In whatever face it appears, it is usually involuntary on the part of the United States seller or investor. Countertrade adds costs to the transaction, which will be passed on to the Beijing buyer. Often countertrade occurs because the foreign nation's products are not sufficient quality to be competitive in international trade. But sometimes traditional trade patterns tend to lockout such products even when they are very good quality, and countertrade may thus be a way of forcing open a market. Some countertrade is voluntary, especially the above noted compensation or buy-back forms. Whatever form countertrade assumes, it has been around for much longer than currency, and it will continue to play some role in international trade.

We have noted only a few differences in a commercial sale of goods where the seller and buyer are in different countries. There are many other new issues to confront. The differences noted above tend to be attributable to different legal and economic systems in the two nations. There also may be differences in the cultures of the two nations which affect the transaction. Misunderstandings of cultural norms may create minor embarrassments, or constitute serious improprieties. Either may result in lost business. If the Boston seller or its counsel has gone to Bangkok or to Beijing to negotiate or sign the contract, what conduct is expected? Do people greet each other by shaking hands, or is touching inappropriate? Is it proper to discuss business over breakfast? Should spouses be invited to a business dinner? Should one sit with legs crossed?

Are nominal gifts appropriate or distasteful? What transpires during the negotiations may involve one of the parties laws which attempt to govern moral conduct, such as the United States Foreign Corrupt Practices Act (FCPA), which prohibits many payments or gifts intended to influence foreign officials' decisions.

Our Boston seller may begin to sell sufficient products to Bangkok or Beijing that it decides to establish some form of agency or distributorship abroad. It may have experience with the use of agents or distributors in its sales to Brockton or Burbank. The buyer might have used an *agent* to represent it. The agent would not possess title to the goods, title would pass directly from the Boston seller to the buyer. The agent would be said to have had the goods "on consignment". Or the Boston seller might have used a *distributor*. The distributor takes title to the goods, and passes that title upon the sale to the buyer. The same decision between an agent or a distributor will have to be made when selling abroad, but the Boston seller may learn that there are quite different laws governing such sales. The foreign nation may have a special distributorship law, which reduces some of the seller's choices available in United States law. The foreign law is likely to favor the local distributor, especially regarding matters of the right to, and rights upon, termination. Even where there is no special distributorship law, the laws may be different. Those laws may be included among the many provisions of the local civil or commercial code, if the foreign nation has a civil law legal system. Establishing a foreign distributorship also may raise issues of trade restraints under the foreign law, when the distributor becomes the exclusive agent, or is limited to certain territory, or must sell at seller established prices.

Depending upon the form chosen for the sale of goods abroad, the Boston seller may become enough of an employer to be subject to the foreign nation's labor law. Labor law in many foreign nations differs dramatically from labor law in the United States. Nations are often protective of their workforce, and the Boston seller may encounter far stricter rules regulating the employment relationship, especially termination. A "once hired, can't be fired" rule is perhaps the most troublesome for employers. In addition to the foreign labor law, the Boston seller will have to deal with the movement of business persons across borders. Even a brief *business* visit to Bangkok or Beijing may require entry papers far more complex than a tourist visa. Much business is undertaken using tourist visas, but such use may create a risk if a contract is breached. As business persons cross borders for longer stays, visa requirements are likely to increase. But it is not only the immigration rules of Bangkok and Beijing which may appear to constitute an impenetrable maze to the Boston seller, it is also the United States immigration rules which create obstacles. The Boston seller may wish to bring Bangkok or Beijing business associates to Boston for training. That may require a business visa, or perhaps an education visa.

As our Boston client's trade evolves and increases, from an isolated sale, to occasional sales, and perhaps to the creation of a distributorship agreement, thought may be given to the manufacture of the products abroad. Manufacture abroad may follow the major step of creating a direct foreign investment (a subject of the International Trade and Investment Nutshell by the same authors), or perhaps by licensing a foreign producer in Bangkok or Beijing to manufacture the goods. Licensing production to a company in Brockton or Burbank would involve only the negotiation of the licensing agreement by the Boston licensor and the Brockton or Burbank licensee. But if the Boston seller licenses the production to a developing or nonmarket economy nation, i.e., parties in Bangkok or Beijing, the transfer of technology agreement may be subject to careful scrutiny by the host government. The Boston licensor will be most concerned with protecting its intellectual property, while the Bangkok or Beijing government may be more concerned with regulation of the transfer of technology. Even if the Bangkok or Beijing licensee is a privately owned enterprise, the government may mandate that all technology agreements be registered, and sometimes subjected to review for approval, to ensure that they do not include provisions considered detrimental to the economic development of the nation. Those concerns reach such issues as duration of the agreement, royalty amount, grant-back requirements, territory restrictions on sales, rejection of technology "adequately" available locally, and choice of law and forum. Not all developing nations and nonmarket economies have such requirements, which developed nations consider trade restrictive and which are generally inconsistent with contemporary rules on intellectual property, which focus more on protection of intellectual property than restrictions on its transfer.

The Boston licensor of the technology is very concerned about the existence and adequacy of laws protecting intellectual property in the foreign country. The Boston licensor has invested considerable time and money in developing its products, and wants the fullest protection offered by patent, trademark, copyright and trade secret laws. If the products are licensed to be manufactured by a Brockton or Burbank licensee, the Boston company is protected by a scheme of mostly federal law protecting intellectual property. But if the license is to Bangkok or Beijing, the licensor may confront very different views about rights to intellectual property. Such rights may not be recognized at all, because they are considered not subject to private ownership, but to constitute part of the national patrimony or the property of mankind. Even if intellectual property is acknowledged to be private property, if the foreign nation's gross national product depends to a sufficient degree on counterfeit production and exports that loss of such production may cause economic dislocations, it may refuse to adopt or actively enforce laws protecting intellectual property rights.

The above business transactions illustrate some of the differences in selling to or licensing the production of goods in foreign nations. These differences occur everyday in international business. The differences may create additional transactional costs. One transaction cost all business persons hope to avoid is the cost of resolving disputes. That is accomplished by avoiding them. But we are yet to find a way to assure all transactions will occur without conflict, and thus must be prepared to assume some costs of dispute resolution, and to understand the nature of dispute settlement in international transactions.

If a conflict arises between the seller and the buyer, the choice of law and choice of forum issues are very possibly extremely important to each party. It will come as no surprise to the Boston lawyer and client that the contract law of Thailand differs from that of Massachusetts much more than did the contract law of California. Furthermore, the legal system of Thailand, including procedural law, may have very different characteristics than the legal system of Massachusetts. But as more nations become parties to the Convention on International Sale of Goods (CISG), the applicable contract rules will be the same. While they may be the same, a Bangkok court will use a copy of the law in Thai, while a Boston court will use one in English. Different meanings to terms may result from different translations. Furthermore, the method of judicial interpretation in Bangkok will differ from that in Boston, far more so than judicial interpretation in

Brockton or Burbank. The Bangkok court will interpret the statutory provision, with some assistance from scholarly treatises, but with less attention to Thai cases then the Boston lawyer may expect. The Boston court is likely to focus on past Massachusetts decisions, and, if none are found, decisions of other states, which interpret the particular provision. Harmonization of law does not mean harmonization of the legal systems and therefore of methods of judicial interpretation.

Because of the very different attitudes towards dispute resolution, the parties may choose to include a provision in their contract for mandatory arbitration. Considered essential when dealing with some nations because of inefficient or corrupt judicial systems, arbitration is often chosen when judicial systems function honestly. Court back-logs, cost of litigation and more relaxed rules of evidence are often the reasons arbitration is used in a domestic setting, for example for disputes arising in the sale from Boston to Brockton, or Boston to Burbank. Those same reasons exist in the international setting, plus a sense of fairness provided by third party arbitration.

International litigation and arbitration add many new dimensions to the same issues when part of domestic litigation. Choosing Burbank (i.e., California) law rather than Boston (i.e., Massachusetts) law is a much less significant decision than choosing Bangkok (i.e., Thailand) law or Beijing (i.e., PRC) law rather than Boston law. The same is true in choosing a forum. Initiating a suit in a foreign country is likely to introduce us to different rules of subject matter and personal jurisdiction. Service of process in many foreign nations is a more formal process than in the United States, and is unlikely to be linked to personal jurisdiction so as to allow jurisdiction based on service. The extensive process of discovery in the United States is essentially non-existent abroad, and has few admirers sitting on the bench in foreign courts and asked to honor a U.S. court order for discovery in their nations. If the Boston seller is able to obtain jurisdiction over the Bangkok or Beijing buyer in a Boston court, and obtains a judgment, it may have little value unless the courts in Bangkok or Beijing will recognize and enforce the Boston judgment. Recognition and enforcement rules vary throughout the world. In the United States recognition and enforcement varies state-to-state, often confusing to foreign lawyers. But that variance from state-to-state in the United States is with respect to recognition of a judgment granted in a foreign **nation** rather than in a sister foreign state. Full faith and credit mandates recognition of sister state judgments. Thus the Boston judgment creditor will have an easier time enforcing the judgment in a Brockton or Burbank court, than in a Bangkok or Beijing court.

The participation of foreign officials in the transaction adds new dimensions beyond the possible questionable payments which may violate the Foreign Corrupt Practices Act. If the buyer is the foreign government, or an instrumentality of the government, special problems may arise if litigation over the contract ensues. What if the sale is canceled by the Bangkok or Beijing government agency, and the Boston seller sues, only to be confronted with a defense of sovereign immunity? The foreign government would be saying that it is the sovereign and is immune to suit anywhere. But that immunity is increasingly limited to *government* actions, rather than to *commercial* actions conducted by a government. Drawing the line between what is a government act and what is a commercial act is not easy. The United States, after decades of following the **absolute** theory of foreign state immunity, enacted the Foreign Sovereign Immunities Act (FSIA) in 1976, which adopts the **restrictive** theory—that foreign states are not immune when the transaction is commercial. That may help our Boston seller if the sales are commercial sales to foreign states, or to their agencies or instrumentalities.

A second defense our Boston seller may encounter when suing a foreign state is that the foreign act was an "act of state". The courts of one nation tend not to want to sit in judgment of acts of a foreign government which took place in the territory of that foreign government. This theory developed in case law, and unlike the above noted codification of state immunity theory in the FSIA, the act of state doctrine remains based in United States case law. That law has yet to clearly conclude whether or not a commercial action exception exists to the act of state doctrine. The doctrine as a whole has been partly restricted by the Supreme Court. Whatever the outcome of the commercial exception is, our Boston seller might be wise to insist on arbitration, or an express waiver of these defenses, in any contract to sell to the government in Bangkok or Beijing.

Even if the sale is to a private buyer, the government may interfere with the sale for such reasons as the scarcity of reserves which limits access to foreign currency, or the prohibition or limitation of entry of the products of the Boston seller into the nation. Would these reasons constitute **force majeure** and allow the buyer to avoid performance because of a frustration of performance? What if the buyer is an agency of the government and the purchase is canceled by order of the executive? Is the agency sufficiently separate from the executive to be entitled to present a **force majeure** defense?

Our Boston client has entered the world of international business transactions, and has learned quickly of the complexities of dealing with Bangkok or Beijing rather than Brockton or Burbank. It might decide not to deal with developing nations (Thailand) or nonmarket economies (PRC), but to sell to, or license or establish a direct foreign investment in, only those nations which are more developed and which are market economies. It may choose Brussels. In selling goods to a Brussels buyer it will not confront import licenses; it will receive a strong, convertible currency; and it will not be asked to accept countertrade. But it may have to deal in another language and, depending on the nature of the product, it may confront European

Union tariff and nontariff barriers absent in domestic U.S. sales. If the Boston company licenses a Brussels firm to make its products, it will have its intellectual property protected, but with some variations from the form of protection received in the United States. If it creates a subsidiary in Belgium it will not have to adopt a joint venture. But it will face civil law tradition corporate concepts and possibly some workers' rights not present in the United States. The company will have to learn something about dealing in an economically integrated market, in this case the European Union. The similarities with dealing in Brockton or Burbank are as prevalent as the disparities in dealing with Bangkok or Beijing. That is partly why a very large part of United States trade and investment abroad is with developed, market economy nations.

What follows in the chapters ahead is an introduction to some of the laws and policies, the organizations and entities, and the people that are involved in some of the activities that we believe are included in the term "international business transactions". Because that term includes, as noted above, the trade of goods across borders, licensing, foreign investment, the role of governments in the use of tariff and nontariff barriers, as well as such other areas as controls on exports, the taking of foreign property by governments, insuring foreign investment, the increasing implementation of bilateral and multilateral trade agreements, and forms and procedures of dispute resolution in all of these international business transactions, this 6th edition of the International Business Transactions Nutshell will share some of these areas with its companion volume, the 2nd edition of the same authors' International Trade and Investment Nutshell. This Nutshell focuses on the negotiation of business transactions, the documentary sale and use of letters of credit, currency issues, technology transfers, transactions in developing and nonmarket economies, business immigration, dispute settlement, and the immunity of states and use of the act of state doctrine in commercial transactions. The International Trade and Investment Nutshell covers the commencement, insuring, operation and withdrawal of foreign investment; expropriation; government imposed restrictions on imports and exports; the GATT/WTO; and economic integration with an emphasis on the European Union and the North American Free Trade Agreement. The two Nutshells are intended to provide a broad introduction to the people and institutions who practice international business transactions, and the government and multilateral organizations which both encourage and restrict trade.

CHAPTER ONE

NEGOTIATING INTERNATIONAL BUSINESS TRANSACTIONS

Sensitivity to negotiating in an international context is a valuable skill. An international business negotiation involves style and timing, as well as procedure and substance. Each of these features is discussed below. Procedure is the ingredient which is frequently underplanned, but is most often outcome determinative.

Negotiating styles differ from culture to culture and person to person. But at least two general styles may be observed in international settings: the adversarial-standoff style and the consensus building style. Each style can be effective in its own context.

NEGOTIATING BY CONTEST

The adversarial standoff style may be illustrated by reverting to medieval Europe and imagining two opposing armies drawn up in battle array. Although their common purpose is to secure agreement about who is to have what, they will bludgeon each other to achieve that agreement while parrying, shouting provocations, and carrying out diverting sorties along the way. This style is often counterproductive when negotiating an international business transaction. Its emphasis upon pressing maximum advantage to the point of conquest is frequently inappropriate when measured against other, more important factors. These factors include the efficient use of time, political and cultural differences, the volatility of international markets, currency exchange fluctuations, and expenses that must be paid by a client along the way to shaping a satisfactory international agreement. Moreover, the bad will engendered by this style may prejudicially color the opponent's judgment, in some cases killing the deal. In short, the adversarial-standoff style can have too high a cost for the "winner."

The adversarial-standoff style was used by representatives from the former Soviet Union in diplomatic and international commercial negotiations. Soviet negotiators attempted and sometimes successfully extracted the most from their negotiating opposite at the least cost to themselves. It should not be a surprise that this style involves the use of bluffs, threats, the ultimatum, rapid changes in previously "irrevocable" positions, procedural manipulations, purposeful ambiguity, repetitive demands, little or no desire for friendly interpersonal relations, and the impugning of a negotiating opposite's motivations. All of this occurs in the broader context of attempts to extract as much information as can be gained while revealing no information before agreement is reached on any point. For example, Soviet negotiators were known to enter a room with a large negotiating team that asks a seemingly endless stream of questions in exhausting detail, usually with multiple requests that answers be "clarified" with further information. The team then leaves the room, and an entirely new team arrives to ask further, and often the same, questions.

BUILDING A ROLLING CONSENSUS TOWARD AGREEMENT

The experienced United States negotiator, W. Averell Harriman, suggested that "You have to put yourself in the other fellow's shoes ... You also have to consider how to make it possible for him to make a concession ... But the idea that you can whip your negotiating opposite into agreeing with you is nonsense.... If you call a hand, you must recognize that you may lose it."

The consensus building style places an emphasis upon negotiators rapidly finding some kernels of agreement and expanding upon those areas with a view to building a momentum toward complete agreement. This momentum may overcome differences about how to resolve difficult issues. Because of each negotiator's underlying, often long-held and usually unexpressed images about the political, social and personal views held by a negotiating opposite, momentum stopped is not restarted easily in an international commercial setting. For example, in Europe, Americans are sometimes thought of as either spoiled, self-indulgent children or as gunslingers ready to start a war. Conversely, Churchill reportedly said that "The Germans are either at your throat or at your feet." The consensus building style's emphasis upon common ground helps to finesse such stereotypes as a "hidden dimension" in a negotiation.

One problem is that there may be no initial consensus about the reasons for negotiating at all. The United States went to the Paris Peace Talks to negotiate an end to the military conflict in Vietnam. The North Vietnamese went to the Talks to negotiate while the military conflict was being ended. Understanding why negotiating opposites are meeting with you is not always possible by considering only the explanation that is offered. In some countries, such as Japan, it is considered courteous to tell people what they want to hear. The key to the consensus building style is an advance determination of: (a) what your negotiating opposites really want; (b) what they really must have; (c) what they may offer in return; and (d) what they really cannot offer either because they lack authority to do so or because it would be unacceptable for enterprise, national or international reasons.

Because the consensus building style requires an advance strategy for moving toward complete agreement, the strategy must yield to negotiating opposites that which they absolutely must have in order to join in any agreement. For example, the Chinese require sufficient time and opportunity to adequately inspect and test purchased goods. Several Latin American countries require that foreign investments be structured as joint ventures and have regulated the level of royalty payments under licensing agreements. Some Islamic states cannot politically, and perhaps legally, countenance an agreement with persons doing business in Israel. Some nations cannot accommodate politically, and perhaps economically, an agreement that will have a negative effect upon the country's balance of payments. Unless these minimum requirements are acceptable beforehand, a consensus agreement is unlikely. Therefore, good practice demands that you research your opponents' goals, as well as the limits of their cultural, political, legal and business milieu. The timing of the indication of willingness to agree to such terms, however, should be carefully planned to facilitate the building of a consensus.

NEGOTIATING TEAMS

Negotiating teams are most often used with direct foreign investments, joint ventures and large licensing or sales transactions. Knowing in advance what minimum *quid pro quo* a negotiating opposite really must have in order to join in an international business agreement makes it easier to decide upon the persons who are necessary members of the negotiating team. Anyone who negotiates alone in an international setting runs a high risk of not appreciating all of the personal, cultural and linguistic meanings in any conversation, quite apart from the substance of whatever subject matter is under discussion. A team too large can be intimidating and suggest "imperialist" overtones; a team too small can be insulting and suggest "imperialist" overtones. The team, often of three people, should have one member with enough status or importance to convey a sufficient impression of sincerity of purpose and of respect for the dignity of those who will be the negotiating opposites. Specialists should be added as needed, perhaps in a capacity as part of an informal sub-committee. This is especially help-ful when technical engineering or scientific issues are anticipated. A savvy technical person is a must, and should give a briefing to the lawyer on techni-cal issues *before* the negotiations commence.

People who comprise the negotiating opposites may come from different, and perhaps unantic-ipated, quarters. In Japan, officials from a govern-ment ministry may participate in negotiations be-tween a United States investor and a Japanese national, and the national's banker may also join the talks. A lawyer may well not be a part of the Japanese negotiating team. In the early days of Western trade with the People's Republic of China, lawyers were not welcome. They sometimes partici-pated as "consultants" or "assistant vice-presi-dents." Negotiators in the former Soviet Union were often drawn from various Ministry of Trade Foreign Trade Organizations. Such people were ex-perienced in negotiating and often were specialists in various subject matter areas, e.g., petroleum ex-ploration.

It is always essential to understand the cultural background of negotiating opposites and the poten-tial for cross-cultural misunderstandings. Most cultures and foreign enterprises involve hierarchies which must be understood so as to properly evaluate the rank and power of negotiating opposites. Disclosure duties, for example, may vary as between cultures and within hierarchies. Also, past catastrophies of foreign companies or governments must be discovered and considered in advance. Large institutions will tend to over-compensate to avoid making the same disastrous mistakes twice.

Foreigners negotiating with United States lawyers would do well to review the empirical findings of Prof. Gerald R. Williams on American legal negotiating styles. See *Legal Negotiation and Settlement* (West Publishing Co. 1983). Prof. Williams analyzes the attributes of U.S. attorneys using two fundamentally different styles: cooperative versus competitive. These attributes are broadly similar to the two international negotiating styles described in this chapter: consensus building versus adversarial. Prof. Williams indicates that both the competitive and cooperative styles can be effective, but that cooperative United States legal negotiators are much more common and noticeably more likely to be effective in domestic negotiations.

ROLE PLAYING

All team members must know about and agree upon the negotiating strategy. However, it is inevitable that at some point in the negotiations an unplanned decision will have to be taken extemporaneously. Team members should agree in advance upon the person who will be the team's "voice" to make that decision. Other roles, such as the "compromiser" or the "diplomat", may be preassigned. A team which assigns the role of "hatchet man" to one of its members should remember the Chinese saying: "The nail which sticks up gets hit." Roles may be changed intentionally during a negotiation. One of the most interesting parts of any negotiation is an accurate assessment of the role being played by each negotiating opposite at any given moment.

TIMING

Understanding the overall timing framework for a successful negotiation is sometimes difficult for the United States attorneys and business executives. The phrase, "Life is long," may help to explain why it took the Vietnamese two years to agree about the shape of the negotiating table at the Paris Peace Talks. The Chinese and people from many other countries negotiate with a recognition that what cannot be settled today perhaps can be settled tomorrow or next week. Japanese are reluctant to do business with someone in whom they do not have sufficient trust and with whom they do not sense reciprocal feelings of friendship. (Remember this if considering the adoption of the adversarial standoff style of negotiations.) It may take weeks spent together on a golf course before such trust is engendered. People in other countries prefer not to negotiate during certain times of the year, e.g., Ramadan in Islamic nations. In some countries the

"weekend" is on days other than Saturday and
Sunday, those days being normal business days.
Some hours which in the United States are considered the normal business day (9:00 A.M.–5:00 P.M.)
are not considered appropriate for doing business in
other countries. In parts of Africa "noon" may be
any time between 10 a.m. and 2 p.m. The hours
between 2 p.m. and 5 p.m. are inappropriate for
doing business in Saudi Arabia.

IMPORTANCE OF PROCEDURE

It may be, and often is, that the procedure employed in international business negotiations is the
single most important cause of their success or
failure. The careful lawyer or executive will make
advance inquiry about whether contacts preliminary to the negotiation are advisable and about
which locations may be preferable for conducting
negotiations. Procedures calculated to facilitate the
building of personal relationships increase prospects
for a successful negotiation, especially in Asia. In
tough moments during a negotiation, courtesy alone
may keep a consensus momentum going. Enduring
courtesy is the essential lubricant of international
negotiations.

A negotiating opposite may not want to admit
that an apparent unwillingness to agree to a suggested point is caused by bureaucratic foot drag-
ging, lack of coordination, lack of technical understanding or simple confusion on its side. Procedures
that are flexible enough to allow time to work out

such problems may cultivate ego, avoid a loss of "face" and continue participation in the negotiations. For example, a negotiating opposite may be unwilling to let you know that failure to reach quick agreement is due to the fact that he or she, despite having a lofty sounding title or other credentials, does not have authority to make a final agreement or will not assume personal responsibility for the consequences of an agreement. The latter case occurs frequently in Japan. Some nations find it prudent to advertise publicly that only certain government agencies are authorized to carry out sales or purchases.

Procedures which cause surprise are intimidating and can engender hostility and distrust. Obvious examples include emotional displays used as smoke screens, changing the agreed agenda for negotiation, unannounced or late arrivals and departures of negotiating personnel, and retreating from agreements already made. The surprise introduction of a written document (such as an investor's initial proposal), the contents of which a negotiating opposite is asked to consider or even to read on the spur of the moment, often causes similar reactions. Taking minutes of a negotiation and preparing written summaries of points of agreement often speeds the consensus building process, but the surprise transmission of such documents to a negotiating opposite can work a greater and opposite effect. Of course, these procedures may be useful if negotiating by contest rather than consensus. Because the intimidating nature of a written document increases with its thickness, a one page summary of the contents stands a better chance of being read, especially by someone who need not consider the document.

IMPORTANCE OF CULTURE

Cultural and language differences between negotiating opposites accentuate the importance attached to procedure in international negotiations. Self-praise is deprecated in virtually all cultures. A story is told of one multinational investor in Africa who inserted certain "whereas" clauses into a negotiated agreement to the effect that the local government was unable to perform a task and that the investor possessed world wide management and technical success at the same task. An African newspaper published those "whereas" clauses as evidence of "imperialist attitudes."

Although giving gifts of modest value is appreciated in virtually all cultures, it is an expected occurrence between negotiating opposites in some countries. Certain gifts, such as books depicting the natural beauty of the investor's home area, are generally appreciated while more specialized gifts may be preferred in a particular country. For example, Johnny Walker Black Label Scotch is appreciated in Japan, but Red Label is valued in Thailand and Burma.

There is an almost universal cultural importance attached to sharing a meal with a negotiating opposite. Meal time affords a good opportunity for an investor to show an interest in and sensitivity about the host's culture. Unlike the United States, where business luncheons and dinners are common, in many cultures talking about business matters during a meal is considered impolite and is counterproductive.

There is considerable cultural diversity about the meaning of silence and delay in international negotiations. The common law rule that, under appropriate circumstances, "silence is acceptance" is not shared widely in many countries. In some countries silence may mean "no", while in other countries periods of silence are an acceptable and common occasion during which thoughts are arranged and rearranged. For example, an investor in Indonesia brought the final draft of a completely negotiated agreement to a counterpart for signature and, following some pleasant conversation, placed the agreement on the desk. In complete silence, the counterpart simply returned the document, unsigned, to the investor. The investor later learned that this day was not considered propitious in Indonesia for signing one's name. The agreement was signed the next day. Delays of days or even of months may not be signs that a negotiation is in difficulty, nor represent an attempt at increasing the costs of negotiating. Such delays may simply be the minimum time period in which a necessary consensus or authority is being achieved within a negotiating team.

An excellent analysis of cultural variables affecting international negotiations, known as LES-CANT, has been prepared by David A. Victor. See

International Business Communication (1992). LESCANT involves identification of the following cultural variables: Language; environment and technology; social organization; contexting (a measurement of explicit and implicit communications); authority conception; non-verbal behavior; and temporal conception. United States lawyers and business persons should consult the American Bar Association *Guide to International Business Negotiations: A Comparison of Cross–Cultural Issues and Successful Approaches (1994)*. This Guide covers cultural aspects of international business negotiations generally, and specifically with reference to 17 nations.

THE LANGUAGE OF NEGOTIATIONS

Differences in language skills between negotiating opposites raise some peril in every international business transaction. Each negotiating party prefers quite naturally to use the language whose nuances are best known. Words that have a clear and culturally acceptable meaning in one language may be unclear or culturally offensive in another tongue. The converse may be true as well. For example, the French word "détent" does not translate easily into the English language. The consequences of this translation difficulty have worldwide importance. Because some hand gestures and body movements are acceptable in one culture yet deeply offensive in another culture, they are rarely an appropriate communications aid in international negotiations.

For example, raising an open hand in the direction of another party can mean in North Africa that you hope that person will lose all five senses.

The use of interpreters substantially slows the pace of negotiations and may spawn further difficulties because the interpreter is one more fallible person taking part in the negotiations. Interpreting is exhausting work and rarely exact. During an international commercial arbitration in Los Angeles, a witness testified in German alongside a skilled interpreter whose job it was to translate the testimony into English. While the arbitrators waited, it required the interpreter's efforts, the efforts of a United States lawyer fluent in German, and the efforts of a German lawyer fluent in English, to produce an oral translation which all agreed was sufficiently accurate. Even assuming the availability of an accurate literal translation, a Japanese person saying "yes" in answer to a question may not be signifying agreement but may only mean, "Yes, I understand the question."

The peril of language difficulty can be equally acute in negotiations between a lawyer from the United States and a negotiating opposite who speaks the English language. Each party may be embarrassed to raise a language question. For example, in the middle of a telephone conversation between a lawyer from the United States and a negotiator in England, a London operator interrupted to ask if the lawyer was "through." Not wishing to terminate the conversation, the American answered, "No, I am not through". The operator disconnected the circuit, apologized, and once again dialed to get the call "through." A few minutes later the London operator came on the line again, interrupting the parties' conversation, to ask again if the United States caller was "through." Desiring to continue the conversation without further interruption, the American lawyer this time said "Yes, thank you", and the operator left the line connected.

Certain foreign enterprises require their negotiators to speak English when negotiating with Americans. The problem is that their English seldom tracks American English, and embarrassing moments occur when U.S. negotiators must delicately seek clarification of the opponent's words. Such clarifications must be undertaken with the utmost politeness and goodwill in order not to insult or intimidate the foreign party.

Even exceptionally able interpreters may have difficulty if a United States lawyer or executive uses American slang in communicating during an international negotiation. The American penchant for using "ball park" figures may not be shared or understood in countries where baseball is not a popular sport. Slow and distinct patterns of speech combined with simple declarative sentences will always facilitate international business negotiations.

LANGUAGE IN THE AGREEMENT

The person who controls the drafting of an international business agreement often drives the negotiations. United States lawyers will almost always seek to perform this leading role. The careful language normally used by American lawyers in commercial contracts may prove controversial. While legally trained persons in some countries share an affinity for written contracts that set out the full extent of every right and duty of each party, the practice in many other countries tends toward more generally worded agreements that leave it to the parties (e.g., in Japan) or to the courts (e.g., in Germany) to supply any necessary details. A detailed, exhaustively worded, draft contract which is introduced during negotiations with Japanese or Chinese persons may arouse distrust. To them, a contract relationship is perceived as something that is shaped mutually as understanding develops. A German negotiating opposite may not be willing to sign an exhaustively worded contract because German courts dislike such agreements. The German courts take the position that they know the law and do not need a contract to state what is known already.

This attitude may trap unwary parties. Chinese negotiators, for example, will resist bargaining on the details of a contract or joint venture, saying "All that is of course understood" or "a part of our law." They may even show resentment at attempts to detail business agreements. However, during performance at a later date, other representatives of a Chinese entity may not hesitate to say: "That is not written expressly in the contract and is not our duty." If a detail is important to the transaction, spell it out in the agreement. Many attorneys involved with Chinese business transactions have learned the hard way.

Permissible contract clauses in one country may be impermissible in another country and *vice versa*. For example, penalty clauses which are not legally enforceable in the United States are enforced routinely by French and, to a lesser extent, Italian courts. One-sided (adhesion) contracts may be fun for lawyers to draft, but they may serve only to raise suspicion by identifying the drafter as an adversary or to generate hostility and ill will. Draft adhesion contracts do not promote the consensus building style of international business negotiations. German courts will eviscerate an unfair adhesion contract without mercy.

One of the most frustrating features of international business agreements is the presence of texts in different languages, each of which is considered authoritative. Counsel to a United States enterprise will always seek to make English the sole language of the agreement, and sometimes succeed since English has become the predominant language of international business. Especially when negotiations have been conducted exclusively in English, time, expense, clarity and mutual understanding favor such a result. Even parties who do not natively speak English may use it as the language of agreement for these reasons. Agreements between Japanese and Indonesian businesses, for example, are often in English. But cultural pride (especially with French speaking negotiators) or fear of unfair dealing (especially with Chinese negotiators) may leave multiple texts in different languages the only acceptable solution once "agreement" is reached.

Another important linguistic feature of international transactions, particularly of concern to lawyers, is the existence of different language texts of relevant laws. In the European Union, for example, there are eleven official, authoritative texts for every treaty, regulation, directive, parliamentary report, etc. The NAFTA agreement is authoritative in English, French and Spanish. The nuances of languages can significantly affect the legality of any business transaction. Those same nuances can undermine any carefully constructed "consensus" international negotiators have worked hard to create.

PLANNING FOR RENEGOTIATION

An international business agreement, once achieved, must be monitored and maintained in good order. An agreement, particularly one spanning ten or twenty years, should be negotiated and written with a recognition that it may be renegotiated and rewritten after a few years. People live with unbalanced agreements only until such agreements can be changed. The foreign party may perform carefully and faithfully in accordance with a negotiated agreement, but other things may work to change a host country's attitude. For example, OPEC's rapid revision of the price of oil affected economic parameters of contract arrangements worldwide. The People's Republic of China routinely cancels or slows payment under multi-billion dollar contracts with foreign investors when currency reserves within the country become dangerously low.

Marked shifts in the political climate of a host country may bring marked changes in its government's attitude toward international business transactions. Marked change in the home country government attitude toward the host country may invite retaliation. Media discovery of contract terms unfavorable to a host country may focus local attention upon a foreign business. A foreign enterprise which is highly visible in a host country becomes an easy vehicle for venting local resentment against foreign investors.

Where plant, machinery and other assets are already "in place," renegotiation is one of several, relatively unattractive alternatives. One alternative may be expropriation. The unattractiveness of that choice, for example, led Occidental Petroleum Company and Belco Petroleum Company to renegotiate certain oil concession arrangements with the Peruvian government. The pressure of a suggested expropriation has prompted similar renegotiations in other countries. If the initial, negotiated agreement contemplates and institutionalizes a series of periodic (e.g., once yearly) discussions about "readjustments" of certain parts of the investment agreement in light of the parties' accumulated experiences, the prospect of an unanticipated and traumatic renegotiation may be lessened and the consensus continued.

CHAPTER TWO

INTERNATIONAL TRADING OF GOODS

INTERNATIONAL SALES LAW

The United Nations Convention on Contracts for the International Sale of Goods (1980)(hereafter CISG) governs the sale of goods between parties in the United States and parties in over forty other countries, unless the parties to the sale contract have expressly "opted out" of the Convention. CISG entered into force on January 1, 1988, thirteen months after the United States had ratified the Convention and deposited its instruments of ratification with the United Nations. As a self-executing treaty, no separate implementing legislation is needed. As federal law, it supersedes Article 2 the UCC where it is applicable. CISG is available to be used by private parties in ordinary commercial litigation before both federal and state courts in the United States.

At the time of ratification, the United States declared one reservation, a reservation under Article 95 that the United States is not bound by Article 1(1)(b). The effect of this reservation is that the courts of the United States are bound under international law to use CISG only when the places of business of both parties to the sale contract are each in different States, and both of those different States are Contracting States to CISG. Thus, CISG governs all contracts for the international sale of goods (unless the parties "opt out" under Article 6) between parties whose principal places of business are in the United States and other Contracting States.

As of Jan. 1, 1999, there were fifty-four Contracting States to CISG. In addition to the United States, they included: Argentina, Australia, Austria, Belarus, Belgium, Bosnia and Herzegovina, Bulgaria, Burundi, Canada, Chile, China, Croatia, Cuba, Czech Republic, Denmark, Ecuador, Egypt, Estonia, Finland, France, Georgia, Germany, Greece, Guinea, Hungary, Iraq, Italy, Latvia, Luxembourg, Lesotho, Lithuania, Mexico, Moldova, Mongolia, the Netherlands, New Zealand, Norway, Poland, Romania, the Russian Federation, Singapore, Slovakia, Slovenia, Spain, Sweden, Switzerland, Syria, Uganda, Ukraine, Uruguay, Uzbekistan, Yugoslavia and Zambia. The effect of the earlier ratification of Yugoslavia on its former constituent parts which are now independent states is not yet clear. It would be possible to argue that, as then constituent parts of States which adopted CISG, they are still bound by the Convention through the action of their previous governments, but the United Nations Treaty Section has taken the position that each state must make a positive indication of its intention to be so bound before it will consider them as a Contracting State. As of Jan. 1, 1999, only Macedonia had not done so. This position of the U.N. office may be followed by the United States courts or not. However, counsel should be cautious about assuming that such former constituent parts of Contracting States are still Contracting States after gaining independence.

Other states are expected to ratify or adopt CISG in the near future. This will increase the impact and effectiveness of CISG in unifying international sales law. A current and complete list of Contracting States to this Convention can be obtained by telephone from the U.N. Treaty Section.

A SHORT HISTORY OF THE DRAFTING OF CISG

CISG was drafted by the United Nations Commission on International Trade Law (UNCITRAL), and adopted and opened for signature and ratification by a U.N.-sponsored diplomatic conference held at Vienna in 1980. The mandate of UNCITRAL is the unification and harmonization of international trade law. The purpose of such unification is to reduce legal obstacles to international trade, and to promote the orderly development of new legal concepts to assist further growth in international trade. Although there are other international organizations engaged in similar work, the United Nations General Assembly created UNCITRAL in 1966 to establish a globally representative organization with representatives from all geographical regions and from all legal systems, including from both developed and less developed countries.

UNCITRAL consists of thirty-six member nations, but almost as many other nations usually attend meetings as observers, as do international organizations (e.g., ICC, IMF). Decisions are taken by consensus of both members and observers, not by vote. Thus, the process requires compromise and persuasion, rather than alignments; and the arguments are usually neither political nor dialectic, but are pragmatic, much as they should be in a well-taught law school seminar. The consensus requirement makes progress excruciatingly slow, but the difficulties in harmonizing systems from developed and less developed countries, from capitalist and socialist countries, and from common law and civil law legal systems are great. Further, the attainment of such consensus can help to promote wide acceptance of the results of UNCITRAL's product—as in the case of CISG.

In its first stage of work, UNCITRAL prepared four pieces of legislative work in its program on unification of international commercial law. One is CISG, discussed further below. A second is the Convention on the Limitation Period in the International Sale of Goods, adopted in New York in 1974. This Convention establishes a limitation period of generally four years, and attempts to bridge the difference between common law "statutes of limitation" (a procedural law approach to termination of rights of action) and the civil law "prescription periods" (a substantive law approach to such problems). A 1980 protocol aligned the provision of this convention on limitation periods with the provisions of CISG.

The third legislative work is the United Nations Convention on the Carriage of Goods by Sea of 1978, also called "the Hamburg Rules," which regulates international bills of lading. The Hamburg Rules are a revision of the Hague Rules (the Brussels Convention of 1924), and the Hague–Visby Rules. The primary difference is that the Hamburg Rules were significantly affected by the participation of less developed countries (LDCs) in their drafting. LDCs did not participate in the drafting of the Hague Rules in Brussels in 1924. The Hamburg Rules entered into force in 1992, and has twenty six Contracting States as of September 1, 1999.

In August, 1987, UNCITRAL issued the Convention on International Bills of Exchange and International Promissory Notes (hereafter CIBN), which was adopted by the United Nations General Assembly and opened for signature and ratification in 1988. This Convention establishes provisions for a new, optional, negotiable instrument which will be adaptable for use in the different domestic banking and legal systems—including under the Uniform Commercial Code (hereafter UCC), the British Bills of Exchange Act, and the civil law Uniform Law for Bills of Exchange (Geneva Conventions of 1930 and 1931). The United States signed this convention in 1988.

In its second stage of work, UNCITRAL has produced more model laws than conventions. As is discussed in Chapter 3, it has promulgated the U.N. Convention on Independent Guarantees and Stand-by Letters of Credit, which enters into force in January, 2000. In the 1990s, UNCITRAL published the Model Law on International Credit Transfers (1992) (an EU directive is based on this model law), the Model Law on Procurement of Goods and Services (1994) (four nations have enacted similar legislation), (the Model Law on Electronic Commerce) (Korea and Illinois have enacted similar legislation), and the Model Law on Cross–Border Insolvency.

In addition, UNCITRAL has adopted the UNCITRAL Model Law on International Commercial Arbitration (1985), which has been enacted in 28 nations and four states in the United States; and a Legal Guide on Drawing Up International Contracts for Construction of Industrial Works, which has been widely used in LDC development projects, even before its final adoption by UNCITRAL, because of its perceived balance, fairness and attention to detail. UNCITRAL is continuing its tradition of promoting unification in the area of financial transactions by preparing a Model Law on International Receivables Financing.

UNCITRAL is not the only international organization currently making proposals for the unification and harmonization of international law. The International Institute for the Unification of Private Law (UNIDROIT) held a diplomatic conference in Toronto in 1988 to adopt the Convention on International Lease Financing, which has eight Contracting States and entered into force in 1995, and the Convention on International Factoring, which has six Contracting States and entered into force in 1995. These two conventions, together with CISG and CIBN, may form an alternative source of law in international transactions for issues now analyzed under UCC Articles 2, 3 and 9. The OAS has also been active in this field on a hemisphere-wide basis.

In addition, UNIDROIT has prepared and issued in 1994 the Principles of International Commercial Contracts. The Principles are applicable to all contracts, not just sales of goods, and their provisions are set forth in more general terms. If CISG is the international analogue to UCC Article 2 in the United States law, then the Principles are the international analogue to the Restatement of Contracts in U.S. law. They are not intended to be adopted as a convention or enacted as a uniform model law. Instead, they are expected to be used by international commercial arbitrators, and even by judges where local law is ambiguous. Some of the specific concepts are discussed later in this chapter. The substantive rules of the Principles are often different from those of CISG, because the Principles were not drafted by official delegations of governments, and the individual drafters could adopt what they considered to be "best practices" in commerce.

CISG is the product of 50 years of effort by several organizations, all of which are still involved in the process of unification and harmonization of international commercial law. In 1930, the International Institute for the Unification of Private Law

(UNIDROIT) began preparation of a uniform law on international sales, using a committee of experts originally from England, France, Germany and Scandinavia, but later expanded. Drafts were produced in 1935, 1936 and 1939, but World War II intervened and prevented further development of the project. However, some basic principles were established by these early drafts, and continue in CISG: 1) the provisions should not be developed by selecting an existing system and amending it, or by putting together the existing rules of the different current legal systems, but by developing a new system which is internally consistent and includes modern provisions needed by businesses; 2) the provisions should apply only to international sales, and therefore not disturb existing traditions applicable to domestic sales; and 3) party autonomy should be fully protected.

In 1951, after World War II, UNIDROIT resumed preparation of a uniform law, and completed a final draft in 1963. In 1964, the government of the Netherlands convened a diplomatic conference which adopted two conventions: the Uniform Law on the International Sale of Goods (ULIS) and the Uniform Law on the Formulation of Contracts for the International Sale of Goods (ULF). The principal participants in the drafting of these two conventions were Western European nations, and they were criticized by many socialist and less developed countries as not adequately accommodating the interests of non-European parties. Only eight nations adopted ULIS, and seven adopted ULF. Although each convention came into force, they were not adopted widely enough to have much impact on world trade.

After the formation of UNCITRAL in 1966, that body carried out a survey of governments and concluded that ULIS and ULF would not be widely adopted. It therefore undertook to revise the texts of those two conventions to make them more acceptable to governments. Between 1970 and 1978, two new drafts for rules governing international sales, replacing ULIS and ULF, were prepared by a carefully balanced Working Group of UNCITRAL members, with many observers also participating. In 1978, UNCITRAL further modified, then adopted the new drafts, but consolidated them into a single text, issued in all official United Nations languages—so that there are six authoritative texts of CISG in six different languages—English, French, Spanish, Arabic, Chinese and Russian. However, one remnant of the prior ULIS—ULF division is incorporated into CISG. CISG Article 92 allows a Contracting State to declare, at the time of ratification or adoption, a reservation that it will not be bound by Part II of the Convention (Contract Formation) or by Part III of the Convention (Sale of Goods), which was the division between ULF and ULIS.

The United Nations General Assembly convened a diplomatic conference in Vienna in March—April of 1980, attended by delegates from 62 nations, which made a few further amendments of the text and then adopted the United Nations Convention on Contracts for the International Sale of Goods. The diplomatic conference did not authorize the preparation of any official commentary, although many legal scholars use the UNCITRAL Commentary, which was prepared for use at the diplomatic conference, but does not incorporate the changes made at the conference. Thus, it must be used carefully and with great discretion, preferably by persons already familiar with the history and development of the text.

Under Article 99(1), CISG entered into force on January 1, 1988, thirteen months after the deposit with the United Nations of instruments of ratification from ten Contracting States. The United States, along with China and Italy deposited its instruments of ratification of CISG with the United Nations on December 11, 1986.

UNCITRAL has placed the substantive sales law rules into the text of the Convention itself, so that the "private law" rules are part of the Convention, and are directly adopted by ratification. Thus, CISG is a "self-executing" treaty, and in the United States ratification of CISG meant the automatic adoption of the substantive provisions on sales, without any need for separate implementing legislation. The main purpose of CISG is to avoid conflicts of law problems, not to aggravate them. Thus, it is important that the scope of application of CISG be clear, both as to the circumstances where it does apply, and those where it does not.

THE SPHERE OF APPLICATION
OF CISG

The first six articles of CISG define its sphere of application. Article 1 requires that a sale of goods contract be both "international" and also bear a stated relation to a Contracting State before the contract can be governed by the Convention. In determining whether "a contract is for the international sale of goods," CISG does not define "contract," "sale," or "goods," but Article 1 does define "international." The transaction must be "between parties whose places of business are in different states." Neither the location of the goods themselves, nor the location of negotiations between the parties, is necessarily dispositive. Instead, the "place of business" of each party must be located, and be in a different State.

This "place of business" criterion will cause difficulty whenever one or both parties have more than one place of business. However, CISG Article 10(a) provides some help in such situations by specifying which "place of business" is to be considered. Unfortunately, Article 10(a) does not define what a "place of business" is, although the drafting history of the Convention suggests that a permanent establishment is required and that neither a warehouse nor the office of a seller's agent qualifies as a "place of business."

Article 10(a) does specify which one of multiple offices is to be used in determining the internationality of a transaction, but even this is subject to ambiguity—"the place of business is that which has the closest relationship to the contract *and* its performance" (emphasis added). Thus, where one office is more closely associated with the formation of the contract and a second office is more closely associated with a party's performance of its contractual obligations, there is an unresolved issue concerning which of those offices is the relevant "place of business." However, Article 10(a) does limit the usable facts in making a choice between multiple offices to those circumstances known to "the parties" before a binding contract is formed. This should permit well-advised parties to resolve possible ambiguities by stating in the contract which office of each party they believe to have "the closest relationship to the contract."

The Convention does not, however, govern all contracts for the international sale of goods, but only those contracts which have a substantial relation to one or more Contracting States—that is, States which ratified, accepted, approved or acceded to the Convention so as to become parties to the Convention. CISG Article 1 makes the Convention applicable to sales contracts where the places of business of the parties are in different States, and either (a) both states are Contracting States, or (b) only one State is a Contracting State and private international law choice-of-law rules lead to the application of the law of a Contracting State. Thus, CISG will govern a contract of sale between parties, where one party has its place of business in the United States and the other party has its place of business in France, China, Italy or any of the other Contracting States—*unless* the parties expressly "exclude the application of the Convention" under Article 6. This "opt-out" capacity is always available to the parties.

When it ratified CISG, the United States declared a reservation under Article 95 that it would not be bound by Article 1(1)(b). Thus, the United States' version of the Convention is that it is not applicable when a contract is between parties having places of business in different States and only one State is a Contracting State, even though choice-of-law rules lead to the application of the law of the Contracting State. A contract of sale between a United States party and another party in N, a non-Contracting State, will not be governed by CISG, even though United States law is applicable under usual choice-of-law rules. If United States law applies, but CISG does not, what law does govern the contract? Instead of CISG, United States law for domestic sales transactions would govern, which means the Uniform Commercial Code (UCC) is applicable in forty-nine states (all but Louisiana).

This reservation was included at the insistence of the United States delegation, because it was believed that the UCC is superior as a sales law to CISG. Therefore CISG was considered helpful to United States interests only where it provided a clear resolution of choice-of-law issues. It was believed that, if a court first had to resolve such choice-of-law issues and determined that United States law applied, it might as well apply the "best"

United States law—the UCC. The drafting history of the reservation indicates that the sales contract between a United States party and another party in N, a non-Contracting State, will not be governed by CISG, even if the litigation is in France, a Contracting State which has made no such reservation. For the purposes of interpreting Article 1(1)(b), the United States is not a "Contracting State."

CHOICE OF LAW CLAUSES

Under CISG Article 6, the parties may expressly determine not to be governed by ("opt out of") the Convention. However, if such a decision is made, care must be used in drafting such a statement of exclusion. A simple statement that a contract "shall be governed by New York law" is ambiguous, because a court could hold that the New York law concerning international sales is CISG, through federal pre-emption doctrines. Thus, if the parties decide to exclude the Convention, it should be expressly excluded by language which states that it does not apply *and* also states what law shall govern the contract. ("This contract shall not be governed by the United Nations Convention on Contracts for the International Sale of Goods, 1980, but shall be governed by the New York Uniform Commercial Code for domestic sales of goods and other New York laws.") Note that it is necessary to designate the law of a particular jurisdiction, in addition to CISG, in any choice of law clause because CISG, like any other single statute, will not furnish a complete legal regime.

If the parties can "opt out" of CISG, can they also "opt in" in circumstances not covered by Article 1? For example, can a sales contract between a United States party and another party in N, a non-Contracting State, be made subject to CISG by including a clause stating: "This contract shall be governed by the United Nations Convention on Contracts for the International Sale of Goods, 1980."

First, it should be noted that, although CISG Article 6 gives wide recognition to "party autonomy" (the ability of the parties to determine the terms of their deal), it only recognizes the ability of the parties *to exclude* the Convention. CISG itself has no provisions allowing adoption of the Convention through "party autonomy." Usually the United States courts try to recognize "party autonomy," especially in international transactions, and they have permitted the parties to select their own dispute resolution forum in a wide range of circumstances. However, difficulty arises under current United States law. The Convention does not apply through its own terms. The contract does not involve parties in two Contracting States, and the United States reservation makes private international law choice-of-law rules (including "party autonomy" rules) irrelevant as to whether CISG applies.

Under the *Erie* doctrine the relevant choice of law rules should be furnished by state law—the UCC, and, the UCC does limit "party autonomy." Under UCC § 1–105 choice of law provisions, parties may choose the law applicable to their contract from among those jurisdictions "having a reasonable relation to the transaction." Yet, the whole purpose of the United States' reservation was to limit the influence of CISG to transactions with Contracting States only.

The authorities are unanimous in believing that CISG will be applied in such a case, but provide no consistent rationale. The argument would certainly be based on the reasoning in *M/S Bremen v. Zapata Off–Shore Co.*, 407 U.S. 1 (1972), and the line of cases following it, in which the United States Supreme Court upheld the ability of parties to an international transaction to select their forum for dispute resolution. Those cases involved a forum selection clause rather than a choice of law clause, and neither the interpretation of a convention nor a sale of goods was involved, so the particular technicalities of CISG and the UCC were not analyzed. However, one federal appellate court has interpreted *Bremen* as controlling for choice of law clauses, but without any significant analysis of the differences. *Milanovich v. Costa Crociere, S.p.A.*, 954 F.2d 763 (D.C.Cir.1992). Thus the perception of *Bremen* is that the United States Supreme Court will uphold any party choice clause in any contract for an "international" transaction, under a general policy encouraging private contractual choice for dispute resolution in the context of international trade. A "strict construction" of the United States reservation under Article 95 might be construed as a limitation on that general policy. However, it may seem more likely that the courts will attempt to fulfill the parties' directions, but analytical difficulties remain.

There are many attorneys who will seek to "opt out" of CISG for all contracts under all conditions, simply because they do not understand it as well as they understand the UCC. However, such action may be a disservice to the clients' interests. There may be many circumstances when a seller of goods in an international transaction will be placed in a much more awkward position by the UCC and its "perfect tender" and "rejection" rules than it will be under the rules of CISG. In such transactions, automatic rejection of CISG should be resisted, unless the attorney is willing to write comparable seller-friendly rules into the contract as express terms of the contract. At least one author has stated that negotiating an international sales contract, or automatically opting out of CISG, without understanding how it affects the client's interests, constitutes malpractice.

OTHER SCOPE ISSUES

The Convention does not define "contract of sale," so that its application to some types of transactions is problematic. Known problems include "consignments," in which the "buyer" may return any goods which cannot be sold, barter transactions or "countertrade," in which goods are exchanged for other goods and not for money, and "conditional sales," in which the seller retains title to secured payment. Separate UNCITRAL reports on countertrade indicate that it may not be regarded as a contract of sale. CISG may cover the sales aspects of a conditional sale, but not its secured transaction aspects.

The Convention does have provisions addressing some known problem transactions. Article 3 expressly includes contracts for the sale of goods not yet produced, unless the "buyer" undertakes to supply "a substantial part" of the necessary materials. Sales involving a combination of goods and services are always a potential problem, and Article 3 includes such contracts unless "the preponderant part" of seller's obligation concerns "labour or other services."

The Convention also does not define "goods," but Article 2 does expressly exclude contracts for the sale of commercial paper, investment securities, ships, aircraft, hovercraft and electricity. The implications of these express exclusions on further construction of a definition of "goods" is unclear. Under the UCC, commercial paper and investment securities would be considered "intangibles," and not subject to a statute on sales of goods. UCC § 2–105(1). Express exclusions may be interpreted to include other intangibles not expressly excluded. Ships can be considered "immovables," and likewise excluded; but a more likely reason is that they are usually subject to registration and regulatory legislation—as are aircraft, etc. But timber to be cut, growing crops and railroad rolling stock are subject to the same conceptual and regulatory difficulties, and they are not expressly dealt with. Thus, the term "goods" is unclear, and Article 2 does not seem to help clarify it. The most important ambiguity may concern software, especially software that is "embedded" in goods.

On the other hand, CISG Article 2 expressly excludes international sales of goods to consumers, so that the Convention would not conflict with consumer protection laws, which are often "mandatory law." Execution sales and auctions are also expressly excluded, probably on similar reasoning. Further, CISG Article 5 provides that the Convention does not govern causes of action against the seller "for death or personal injury," even though arising out of a sales transaction, because any provisions on such causes of action would conflict with "mandatory law" of many jurisdictions.

One further limitation on the application of CISG is that its provisions do not govern all of the issues which may arise under a contract which is subject to the Convention. Under CISG Article 4, the Convention states that it governs "only the formation of the contract" and the "rights and obligations" of the parties to the contract. It does not govern the "validity" of the contract, or its effect on title to the goods, including presumably most rights and obligations of third parties to the contract.

The restriction concerning "validity" is likely to create more problems and litigation concerning CISG than any other provision. Originally created to avoid conflicts with regulatory law, the drafting history indicates that it also includes at least issues arising out of fraud, duress, illegality and mistake. Whether it also includes unconscionability, good faith, gross unfairness and the particular regulations of the form of disclaimers of warranty is debated by the authorities. One authority goes so far as to claim that the French law of force majeure governs the validity of a contract, an approach whose logic would ultimately allow wholesale displacement of the Convention by the substantive provisions of French law.

GENERAL PROVISIONS OF CISG

Articles 7–13 contain its "general principles." These provisions deal with interpretation of the Convention and filling gaps in its provisions (Article 7); interpretation of international sales contracts (Article 9); a few definitions (Articles 10 and 13); and a replacement for the Statute of Frauds (Articles 11 and 12). Article 7 is designed to assist in interpretation of the Convention itself, while Articles 8 and 9 are designed to assist in interpretation of the contract terms. Article 8 concentrates on statements and conduct by the parties themselves as indications of contract terms, while Article 9 concentrates on sources external to the parties, such as trade usage. The provisions of Article 10 concerning multiple business offices have already been discussed in relation to their impact on Article 1.

At first glance, CISG Article 7(1) appears to be a set of "pious platitudes," without any particular analytical content. However, it is intended to provide several inhibitions to the local courts of a State which will decide disputes under the Convention from applying local law to these international disputes, rather than the Convention. Thus, in interpreting the concepts stated in the Convention, such as "reasonable time," regard for the "international character" of the Convention is imposed upon courts to attempt to lead them to use international practice rather than domestic practice or precedent. This preference for international practice is stressed further by the directive "to promote uniformity of its application." The latter is intended to establish foreign decisions under CISG as more persuasive than local decisions on domestic sales law. Even the doctrine of "good faith," well-known in most local law, is muted. Although UCC § 1–203 imposes an obligation of good faith on each of the parties to a sale, CISG Article 7(1) only refers to good faith in relation to interpretation of the Convention, not of the contract, by courts.

Article 7(2) continues this approach in regard to supplementary principles of law, or "gap-fillers." Unlike the corresponding provision in the UCC, these supplementary principles are not to be gathered from United States domestic law, but either from "general principles" found within the Convention or international law or, if none can be found, from principles found in the law applicable under normal choice-of-law rules. The danger to uniform application is that local courts will discover many "gaps," no usable "general principles" derivable from the Convention, choose their own law as applicable, and easily fall back on their own familiar supplementary principles of law.

Article 8 attempts to establish rules for interpreting the contract itself, and its terms. It establishes a three-tier hierarchy: (1) Where the parties have a common understanding or intent concerning the meaning of a provision, that common understanding is to be used in any interpretation. (2) Where the understandings or intent of the parties diverge, and one party "knew or could not have been unaware" of the other party's intent, under Article 8(1) the latter party's interpretation prevails. And (3), where the parties were unaware of the divergence, their statements and conduct are each to be subjected to a "reasonable person" standard under Article 8(2). The Convention does not attempt to resolve the interpretation problems created if each party's understanding of the other's statements is possible under this "reasonable person" scrutiny. In evaluating party conduct and statements under Article 8(3), a court can look to the negotiating history of the contract and to the actual administration of the terms of the contract by the parties. (Termed "course of performance" in UCC § 2–208.)

Article 8(1) has been interpreted to require courts to consider subjective intent while interpreting both the statements and the conduct of the parties. *MCC-Marble Ceramic Center, Inc. v. Ceramica Nuova d'Agostino, S.p.A.*, 144 F.3d 1384 (11th Cir. 1998). Article 8(3) also can direct a court to a very different approach to contract interpretation than is usual in other U.S. contract cases. Its requirement that a court give consideration to all relevant circumstances is a clear direction to consider parol evidence even when there is a subsequent written agreement. It has also been suggested that both provisions can be used to promote the actual intent of the parties in the battle of the forms transaction, to avoid the "last shot" doctrine.

Article 9(1) allows the parties to include "any usage" to which they have agreed. The drafting history indicates that this paragraph refers only to express agreements to include usage, although the express agreement need not be written. Further, "any" usage may be so incorporated, including local ones, not just international usage. If so incorporated, usage is considered to be part of the express contract items, but is not the governing law of the contract. However, since Article 6 allows the express terms of the contract to carry the provisions of the Convention, agreed usages will prevail over CISG provisions where CISG is the governing law. The one exception to the last statement is Article 12, which is applicable only if one of the parties has its place of business in a Contracting State which has declared a reservation under Article 96. Under that reservation, which is considered to be "mandatory law" and may not be derogated by the contract terms, contracts must be evidenced by writing if so required by the local law of the Contracting State.

Article 9(2) concerns the incorporation of usages by implication. Both less developed countries (LDCs) and nonmarket economies (NMEs) sought to limit the application by implication of usage. Thus, if the parties do not expressly agree to incorporate a usage, it is available in interpreting the contract only if "the parties knew or ought to have known" of it, it must be a usage in international (not merely local) trade, it must be widely known to others in this international trade, and it must be "regularly observed" in that trade. This seems to set a very high standard for any party assuming the burden of proof, although the principle issue in litigation is likely to concern the delineation of the specific "trade" involved.

Article 11 provides that a contract for the international sale of goods is enforceable, even though it is not written, and may be proven by any means. Thus, there is no equivalent in the Convention of the common law Statute of Frauds. However, Articles 12 and 96 allow a Contracting State to declare a reservation that the local law of that Contracting State shall govern the form requirements of the sale contract "where any party has his place of business in that State." Such a reservation may be declared at any time, but it is applicable only to the extent that the domestic law of the State making the reservation "requires contracts of sale" to be in writing. The United States has not made this declaration, so its Statute of Frauds provisions in UCC § 2–201 are not applicable to contracts under the Convention. However, the local law of parties from other States may be applicable if they have the required local legislation. The former Soviet Union was the strongest proponent of the Article 96 reservation, and the Russian Federation, Belarus and the Ukraine made this declaration when they adopted the Convention.

If the Article 96 reservation has been declared, the parties may not agree otherwise under Article 10. This gives the local law the effect of "mandatory law" under the Convention. However, it should be noted that a telex or a telegram can be used under Article 13 to satisfy the "writing" requirement. Further, a telex or a telegram qualify as a "writing" regardless of the formal requirements of the local law. Articles 12 and 96 only make unenforceable those contracts which are "other than in writing" (a Convention term), and Article 13 then defines "writing," as used in CISG, to include a telex or telegram.

CONTRACT FORMATION

The contract formation provisions (Articles 14–24) form a separate "part" of CISG—Part II. Under Article 92 a Contracting State may declare a reservation at the time of ratification that it will not be bound by Part II, even though it is bound by the rest of CISG. This is an historical appendix to the Convention, arising out of the separation between ULF and ULIS. It is not expected to be used, since most of the States which adopted ULIS also adopted ULF.

Although every first-year American law student studies about "offer, acceptance and consideration," those three elements of contract formation are not present in other legal systems. Civil law emphasizes the agreement process, and does not include a "consideration" requirement. An examination of most commercial transactions will show that there is no real issue concerning consideration in most of them. An examination of most "consideration" cases will show that few of them are commercial contracts— rather, they are aunts attempting to induce nephews not to smoke. Thus, it should not be surprising to learn that CISG has no requirements of "consideration" in its contract formation provisions.

As was discussed in the previous section, the writing requirements of the Statute of Frauds are also not applicable, unless one of the parties has a place of business in a Contracting State which has declared a reservation under Article 96. Further, the "integration" concepts of the parol evidence rule are not applicable under Article 8(1).

Part II of CISG focuses on "offer" (Articles 14– 17) and "acceptance" (Articles 18–22). In Convention terminology, under Article 23 a contract "is concluded" (becomes binding) "when an acceptance of an offer becomes effective." There is no need for consideration, and no formal requirements.

Article 14 defines "offer" with three requirements. First, it must be "a proposal for concluding a contract," which is a standard provision. Second, it must indicate "an intention to be bound in case of acceptance," which will distinguish an offer from a general sales catalogue or advertisement or a purchase inquiry. Article 14(2) elaborates this concept by making proposals addressed to the general public presumptively not offers "unless the contrary is clearly indicated." Third, an offer must be "sufficiently definite." This provision is directed toward only three contract terms: the description of the goods, their quantity and their price. Other terms can be left open, but not those three. The criteria for judging definiteness are somewhat ambiguous. The offer is definite enough if the goods are "indicated," which does not seem to require that they be described with any particularity. Similarly, an offer *is* definite if it "expressly or impliedly fixes or makes provision for determining the quantity and the price," but it is not clear whether failure to meet that criterion requires a finding of indefiniteness.

This provision seems more restrictive than the comparable UCC provision on open, or flexible, price contracts (§ 2–305), and was so intended because many civil law states do not recognize such contracts. Article 55 might seem to be helpful, but its provisions may be available only where a contract has already been "validly concluded," which assumes a valid offer. The Convention language is flexible enough, however, to authorize most forms of flexible pricing. Thus, the contract does "make Provision for determining the price" where the price is to follow an index specified in the contract, or has an escalator clause or is to be set by a third party. Arguably, the latter would include "lowest price to others" clauses. The principal problem not resolved under the foregoing analysis may be only the order for a replacement part in which no price is stated. It is here that Article 55 is certainly useful. The offeror may have "implicitly" agreed to pay seller's current price for such goods, and Article 55 fixes the price as that generally charged at the time the contract is "concluded."

Open quantity contracts, such as those for requirements, output and exclusive dealings, may cause less difficulty. In each such contract, there arguably is a "provision for determining the quantity" through facts which will exists after the parties become bound, even if the precise number cannot be fixed in advance. However, in view of the requirements of CISG Article 14, it is usually preferable to include either estimated quantity amounts or minimum quantity amounts, to assure that there is a fixed or determinable quantity provision.

Assortment is a final problem concerning "definiteness." (Compare UCC § 2–311.) However, a clause which permits either the buyer or the seller to specify a changing assortment during the period of the contract would seem to make a provision for determining both quantity and type of goods. The major hurdle in such cases is the requirement that the offer "indicate the goods" and be "sufficiently definite." But Article 14(1) does not require that the offer "specify" the goods, and so clauses which allow later selection of assortment are presumably authorized, if the parties take care in describing the type of goods from which the assortment will be selected. In a case involving aircraft engines, where seller's offer stipulated one set of engines if a Boeing aircraft were selected by the buyer, and a different set of engines if Airbus was selected, the court held that this was not an offer under CISG Article 14. Thus, a contract was not concluded even though a Letter of Intention had been signed by the parties.

One of the consequences of the abandonment of the "consideration" requirement is that the traditional common law analysis of the revocability of an unaccepted offer has no foundation without the consideration doctrine. The traditional common law doctrine made an offer revocable at will until accepted, unless there was an agreement supported by consideration to keep it open (such as an option). In German law, an offer is binding unless the offeror states that it is revocable. These two approaches are opposites, and the compromise adopted by CISG uses neither of the approaches.

Under Article 16, an offer originating under the Convention is revocable unless "it indicates" that it is not revocable. In adopting this position, the Convention rejects both the common law rule that an offer is always revocable and the German civil law rule that an offer is not revocable unless it is expressly stated to be revocable. This basic concept is similar to that used in creating a "firm offer" under UCC § 2–205, but no "signed writing" is required. There are two ways in which an offer can become irrevocable under Article 16: through the offeror's statements and through reasonable reliance by the offeree. (Promissory estoppel rides again?) However, such an irrevocable offer must also meet the Article 14 requirements, including the fixed or determinable price, quantity and assortment terms discussed above.

An offeror can indicate that an offer is irrevocable "by stating a fixed time for acceptance or otherwise." The first reference seems relatively clear, and would include a statement that an offer will be held open for a specified period and no longer. But, what is included in "or otherwise"? For example, does it include a statement that an offer will *lapse* after a specified period? That does not necessarily waive the offeror's right to withdraw the offer earlier, but the delegates at the Diplomatic Conference could not agree on how their language applied in that hypothetical case. The criteria for irrevocability of an offer after reasonable reliance by an offeror under Article 16(2)(b) seem to follow United States caselaw and the Second Restatement of Contracts, Section 87.

Article 18(1) defines "acceptance" as either a statement or "other conduct" by an offeree "indicating assent to an offer." Silence is not necessarily acceptance, although the negotiations and other prior conduct of the parties may establish an implicit understanding that lengthy silence followed by affirmative conduct is acceptance. But in *Filanto v. Chilewich Int'l Corp.*, 789 F.Supp. 1229 (S.D.N.Y. 1992), the first CISG case decided by a United States court, the court used the prior relations of the parties, including exchanges of draft contracts, to find that a lengthy failure to object by one party to a proposed final draft of the other party, followed by the beginning of performance by the proposing party, was an acceptance which created an express "agreement in writing" for purposes of the Federal Arbitration Act.

The *Filanto* decision has been criticized many times. In part, the decision seems to state that there can be a contract to arbitrate which is separate from the sales contract and is separately formed. The concept that the dispute resolution clause can create valid obligations, when no sales contract was ever formed to support it, seems contrary to CISG Art. 8(1). The antecedents of such an analysis are all in arbitration cases and not in sales cases. But, the law governing formation of an arbitration contract should not be different from the law governing formation of the underlying sales contracts. The decision's determination that the silence of one party is acceptance relies on past conduct, without indicating which actions were referenced. Filanto and a recent German decision both represent judicial hostility to the possible return under CISG to the "last shot" doctrine in the "battle of the forms" transaction, discussed below.

Article 18(2) determines when an "indication of acceptance" is effective for "concluding" the contract. Thus, along with Articles 16(1) and 22, it forms the Convention's analog to "the mailbox rule"—except that the CISG rules are different. At common law, "the mailbox rule" passed the risk of loss or delay in transmission of an acceptance to the offeror once the offeree has dispatched the acceptance. It also chose that point in time to terminate the offeror's power to revoke an offer and to terminate the offeree's power to withdraw the acceptance. Under CISG Article 18(2), however, an acceptance is not effective until it "reaches" (is delivered to) the offeror. Thus, risk of loss or delay in transmission is on the offeree, who must now inquire if the acceptance is not acknowledged. On the other hand, the offeror's power to revoke under CISG Article 16(1) is terminated upon dispatch of the acceptance—which is the common law rule. However, the offeree's power to withdraw the acceptance terminates only when the acceptance reaches the offeror. Thus, an acceptance sent by a slow transmission method allows the offeree to speculate for a day or two while the offeror is bound. A telex will release the offeree from the acceptance.

Even though Article 18(1) states that acceptance by conduct alone is possible, the remaining paragraphs of Article 18 seem to imply that in the usual case the offeree must notify the offeror that acceptance by conduct is forthcoming. Article 18(3) indicates that acceptance by conduct without notice is possible only when that procedure is allowed by the offer, by usage or by the parties' prior course of performance. If so allowed, the acceptance by conduct, such as shipping the goods without notice, is effective upon dispatch of the goods, rather than upon their delivery to the offeror. However, notification of the acceptance may reach the offeror indirectly through third parties, such as banks or carriers.

The traditional analysis of the CISG approach to the "battle of the forms" is quite different than that of the UCC, and closer to the common law "mirror-image" analysis. Under Article 19, if the buyer's purchase order form and the seller's order acknowledgment form differ as to any material term, there is no offer and acceptance. Instead, there is an offer, followed by a rejection of that offer and a counter offer (usually the seller's order acknowledgement form). The rejection of the original offer terminates it under CISG Article 17. Thus, the parties do not "conclude" a contract by exchanging forms, and if one party reneges on its obligations, before performance, it probably is not bound to perform.

However, the vast majority of transactions involving exchanges of such forms are performed by the parties, despite the lack of a contract formed by the exchange of forms. Once the goods have been shipped, accepted and paid for, there has been a transaction, and a contract underlying that transaction has been formed by the parties—what are its terms? To put the same question in a different way, is the seller's shipment of the contract "conduct" by the seller which accepts the terms in the buyer's purchase order? Or, is the buyer's acceptance and payment for the goods "conduct" which accepts the terms in the seller's order acknowledgement form? The common law analysis would make the terms of the form last sent to another party controlling, since that last form (usually seller's) would be a counter offer and a rejection and termination of all prior unaccepted offers. This is the "last shot" principle, and CISG Articles 17, 18(3) and 19 seem to follow it.

But see the *Filanto* case, discussed above, which used prior conduct of the parties to find a contract where exchanges of forms was followed by one party's silence. There is also a German decision in which an additional term in the "acceptance" limited buyer's ability to notify seller of defects in the goods. That was held to be a non material additional term, despite the language of CISG Art. 19(3). Professors Honnold and Van Alstine have suggested that courts can avoid the mirror-image and last shot doctrines by seeking the actual intent of the parties under CISG Art. 8(1). Such an approach would follow the analytical pattern used in *MCC-Marble*, supra. All of these authorities seem to agree that the mirror-image and last-shot doctrines should not be resurrected, and that there are more sophisticated analytical tools to resolve the battle of forms under CISG.

In summary and in comparison to the UCC, CISG reduces the flexibility of the parties by prohibiting some open price terms; CISG expands the "firm offer" concept and applies it to more offers; and in the battle of the forms, CISG may delay the formation of a contract through the "mirror image" rule, and may use the "last shot" principle to make the offeree's (usually seller's) terms control the transaction. However, on the last points, both the courts and the authors who have written on the subject have suggested ways of avoiding this traditional analysis.

SELLER'S OBLIGATIONS

Under CISG Article 30 the seller is obligated to deliver the goods and any related documents and to transfer "the property in the goods" to the buyer. In addition, the seller is obligated to deliver goods which conform to the contract as to quantity, quality and title.

Some of these obligations are governed by domestic law, and not the Convention, because under Article 4(b) the Convention "is not concerned with" the effect of the contract on "the property in the goods sold." Domestic law, therefore, determines whether "the property" passes from seller to buyer at the "conclusion" (formation) of the contract, upon delivery, or at some other time; whether a certificate of title is required; and whether seller may retain title as security for the purchase price or other debts.

"Delivery" under CISG is a limited concept, relating to transfer of possession or control of the goods. The CISG draftsmen did not attempt to consolidate all the incidents of sale—physical delivery, passing of risk of loss, passing of title, liability for the price, and ability to obtain specific performance, etc.—into a single concept or make them turn on a single event, as has been done in many sales statutes. Instead, they followed the format of the UCC in providing separate provisions for each of these concepts.

As to the place of delivery, CISG recognizes four distinct types of delivery terms: (1) delivery contracts in which the seller must deliver to the place specified in the contract; (2) shipment contracts, in which the contract "involves carriage of the goods", but does not require delivery to any particular place; (3) sales of goods at a known location which are not expected to be transported; and (4) sales of goods whose location is not known or specified, and which are not expected to be transported. CISG Article 31.

In delivery contracts, seller may be obligated to deliver the goods to buyer's place, or to a sub-buyer's place, or to any location specified. However, it should be noted that CISG has no provisions directly describing seller's duties in such contracts, for they are expressly excluded from Article 31, and all interpretation left to contract terms only. The goods must be conforming when delivered, not merely when shipped, unless performance is excused by force majeure under CISG Articles 79 and 69.

In a shipment contract, seller has no obligation to deliver the goods to any particular place, but it is clear that transportation of the goods by an independent third party carrier is involved. Since the goods are to be "handed over" to the carrier and not to the buyer, transactions involving carriage by the buyer seem excluded from this provision. It is not clear, however, whether the reference to a carrier must be express (such as through commercial terms like "FOB" or "CIF") or whether they can also be implied from the facts (the goods and seller are located in State A and buyer plans to use or resell them in State B). Thus, it is preferably for the sale of contract to specify expressly whether carriage of the goods by a third party is intended or not.

The shipment contract may require seller to take more than one action to accomplish its obligation of "delivery." First, under Article 31(a), the seller must transfer ("hand over") the goods to a carrier—the first carrier. Second, under Article 32(3), depending upon the sale contract terms, seller must either "effect insurance" coverage of the goods during transit or, at buyer's request, give buyer the information necessary to effect insurance. Third, under Article 32(1), if the goods are not "clearly identified to the contract" by the shipping documents or by their own markings, seller must notify buyer of the consignment specifying the goods. Finally, the contract may require seller to arrange for the transportation of the goods, in which case seller must contract for "appropriate" carriage under "usual terms" under Article 32(2).

Where carriage of the goods is not "involved," the buyer may or may not be told where the goods are or will be. Absent a contrary provision in the contract, in such a transaction if buyer is told the location of the goods he is expected to pick them up at that location; otherwise at seller's place of business. Under Article 31(b) and (c), the seller's obligation under CISG is to put the goods "at buyer's disposal" at the appropriate place. The Convention is not clear as to whether this requires notification to buyer, but it would require notification to any third party bailees to allow buyer to take possession.

Where the delivery of the goods is to be accomplished by tender or delivery of documents, Article 34 merely requires that the seller conform to the terms of the contract. The second and third sentences of Article 34 establish the principle that a seller who delivers defective documents early may cure the defects until the date due under the contract, if possible, and buyer must take the cured documents, even though the original tender and cure has caused damage to buyer.

The time requirements for seller's performance are stated in Article 33. They all relate to the contract terms: the goods or documents must be delivered on or before a stated or determinable date set in the contract, within a stated or determinable span of time specified in the contract, or, if no date or span of time is set, within a "reasonable time." "Reasonable time" is not defined, and will depend on trade usage, but at least it precludes demands for immediate delivery.

The Convention has no provisions concerning seller's duties in regard of export and import licenses and taxes, but leaves the determination of these incidents of delivery to the contract terms, or usage. Where these issues are not covered by the contract terms or usage, the authorities give conflicting analyses as to what rules may be derived from the general principles of CISG.

CISG Article 35 obligates the seller to deliver goods of the quantity, quality, description and packaging required by the contract. In determining whether the quality of the goods conforms to the contract, the Convention eschews such separate and independent doctrines as "warranty" and "strict product liability" from the common law analysis, as well as "fault" or "negligence" from civil law. Instead, CISG focuses on the simpler concept that the seller is obligated to deliver the goods as described in the contract, and then elaborates on the connotations of that contractual description. This approach, however, produces results which are comparable to the "Warranty" structure of the UCC, and also follows the pattern of UCC interpretation long urged by Professor John Honnold.

Thus, Article 35(2)(a) and (d) require that the goods be fit for ordinary use and properly packaged (comparable to UCC § 2–314), 35(2)(b) requires that they be fit for any particular use made known to the seller (comparable to UCC § 2–315), and 35(2)(c) requires that they conform to any goods which seller has held as a sample or model (comparable to UCC § 2–313(1)(c)). Each of these obligations, however, arises out of the contract, so that the parties may "agree otherwise" and limit seller's obligations concerning quality (comparable to "disclaimers of warranty" under UCC § 2–316(2)).

There are no conditions on the imposition on seller of the obligation of fitness for ordinary use. All the contracts governed by CISG will be commercial contracts, so that there is no need for the UCC limitation to "merchant" seller. One issue not expressly resolved is whether the "ordinary use" is defined by seller's location or by buyer's location, if "ordinary use" in each is different. Although it has been argued that the standards of buyer's location govern, an alternative analysis is that any such disparity in usage means that neither usage is international in scope, and therefore neither usage can qualify as "ordinary." Instead, any use not recognized as "ordinary" in international trade must be analyzed under the criteria for fitness for a "particular purpose."

The obligation of fitness for a particular purpose arises only if buyer makes the particular purpose known to seller (expressly or impliedly) at or before the "conclusion of the contract," and buyer also relies on seller's skill and judgment, and such reliance is reasonable. There is no express requirement that buyer inform seller of buyer's reliance but only of the particular purpose. More importantly, there is no requirement that buyer inform seller of any of the difficulties which buyer may know are involved in designating or designing goods to accomplish this particular use. However, it is likely that courts can avoid any abuse of these gaps in the statute by the "reasonable reliance" criterion. The assignment of burdens of proof on such issues is not clear.

Seller is relieved of any of the obligations under Article 35(2) against defects in quality whenever buyer is aware or "could not have been unaware" of a defect at the time the contract is "concluded." However, knowledge gained at the time of delivery or inspection of the goods will not affect seller's obligation. The "could not have been unaware" language is the subject of much dispute among common law and civil law authorities. Most common law authorities consider it to be "subjective" and relate to buyer's actual state of mind, rather than to impose "constructive knowledge" on buyer for items he should have learned.

Under CISG Art. 35, a seller is generally not obligated to supply goods that conform to the public laws and regulations in the buyer's state. However, there are at least three exceptions to this general rule. First, if those laws and regulations are identical to those in the seller's state, the goods must conform to them. Second, if the buyer informs the seller about the laws and regulations in its state, the goods must conform to them. And, third, if the seller knew or should have known of the laws and regulations in the buyer's state due to special circumstances, such as having a branch office in buyer's state, then the goods must conform to them. See *Medical Marketing Int'l, Inc. v. Internazionale Medico Scientifica, S.R.L.,* 1999 WL 311945 *(E.D.La.1999).*

Under CISG Article 36(1) these obligations begin under CISG "at the time when the risk [of loss] passes to the buyer"—a concept explored in depth later—but how long do they continue? Although the less developed countries sought a statutory provision requiring "a reasonable time" for the duration of such obligations, such a provision was not included. Instead, Article 36(2) defers to the contract, and speaks of long term obligations of quality which arise from a "guarantee ... for a period of time." However, it is clear that any nonconformity concerning the quality of the goods which exists at the time the risk of loss passes is actionable, even if discovered later. Thus, the buyer is still able to recover for any nonconformity which becomes apparent long after delivery, but the buyer may have to prove that the defect was present at delivery and was not caused by buyer's use, maintenance or protection of the goods.

CISG Article 40 seems to create another obligation on seller—the obligation to notify buyer of any nonconformity known to seller, or of which "he could not have been unaware." If seller does know of a defect and does not notify, then seller may not be able to rely on buyer's failure to inspect the goods quickly or notify seller of any discovered defects. Thus, even though buyer may lose its right to rely on a nonconformity because buyer did not inspect the goods "within as short a time as is practicable" under Article 38, or did not under Article 39 notify seller of any defects, specifying the nature of the defects, within a reasonable time after it discovered or "ought to have discovered" them, buyer's right to rely on the nonconformity revives if seller, in turn, knew of the nonconformity and did not notify buyer of it.

Can seller exclude these obligations concerning the quality of the goods by terms in the contract—and, if so, how? CISG Article 6 states that the parties may, by agreement, derogate from any provision of the Convention, and Article 35(2) supports that ability to limit obligations concerning the quality of the goods. However, it is also clear that the standard formulation in domestic contracts—disclaiming implied warranties—will be inapposite, since the CISG obligations are neither "warranties" nor "implied." New verbal formulations must be found, which deal directly with the description of the goods and their expected use.

The major unresolved issue is the extent to which local law regulating disclaimers will impact on the international contracts governed by CISG. Such local law covers a spectrum from prohibitions on disclaimers in printed standard terms to the "how to do it manual" set out in UCC 2–316. There seems to be agreement that the former raises a question of "validity," and therefore governs contracts arising under CISG; and that the UCC provisions do not raise questions of "validity," and therefore do not govern CISG contracts. The distinction drawn seems to depend upon whether the local public policy prohibits conduct completely, or allows it but only within certain conditions. See Hartnell, "Rousing the Sleeping Dog: The Validity Exception to the CISG," 18 Yale Int'l L. 1 (1993). Whether the United States courts will accept such a distinction is conjectural at this point. However, they should, at the least, draw a distinction between UCC provisions, which require language to be "conspicuous" and those provisions which require a particular linguistic formula, such as use of the word "merchantability." As is shown above, the latter is inapposite under CISG.

Seller's obligation under CISG Article 41 concerning title to the goods under CISG is to deliver the goods not only free from any encumbrances on their title, but also free from any claim of a third party. Thus, like UCC § 2–312, seller is obligated to transfer "quiet possession" of the goods. Although the obligation is very broad, it probably is not breached by claims which are frivolous on their face or by state restrictions on use of the goods. The parties may derogate from the terms of these provisions of CISG by agreement, but buyer's knowledge that the goods are subject to a bailee's lien does not necessarily imply such an agreement. Instead, buyer may expect seller to discharge the lien before tender of delivery.

In addition to good title and "quiet possession," seller is obligated to deliver the goods free from patent, trademark and copyright claims assertable under the law of the buyer's "place of business" or the place where both parties expect the goods to be used or resold. This obligation is, however, subject to multiple qualifications. First, seller obligations arise only with respect to claims of which "seller knew or could not have been unaware." Second, seller has no obligation with respect to intellectual property rights or claims of which buyer had knowledge when the contract was formed. Third, seller is not liable for claims which arise out of its use of technical drawings, designs or other specifications furnished by buyer, if seller action is in "compliance with" buyer's specifications. It is clear that this provision applies when seller is following specifications required by the contract, but its application is not clear when seller is merely following "suggestions" of buyer as to how best to meet more general contract provisions. Fourth, seller is excused from these obligations if buyer does not give notice of breach under Article 42—unless seller knew of the claim, which knowledge may be required under Article 41(1) in order to create liability initially. Finally, it has been argued that mistake of law will excuse seller, or at least that seller has performed its obligations concerning intellectual property rights if it has relied on trustworthy information of a lawyer that there are no such rights which might be infringed by use or resale of the goods, because seller could not then "know" of the possible claims of infringement.

REMEDIES FOR SELLER'S BREACH

If seller breaches any of its obligations, buyer has three basic types of remedies: specific performance, "avoidance" of the contract, and an action for damages. In addition, there is a potential self-help remedy under Article 50. All this is roughly comparable to the remedies available to an aggrieved buyer under the UCC. The difficulty facing the drafters of the Convention is illustrated by two facts: First, specific performance is the preferred remedy at civil law, while the action for damages is preferred at common law. Second, at civil law, a finding of "fault" is usually required for imposition of any recovery of damages, while the common law aggrieved party need show only "nonconformity." CISG had to bridge both gaps.

As to specific performance, CISG Article 46 gives buyer who has not received delivery a right to specific performance, subject to two qualifications: buyer must not have resorted to an "inconsistent" remedy, and buyer should not bring its action for specific performance in a common law court. This provision gives buyer the right to seek specific performance, rather than damages, but does not force him to do so. Thus, any preference for this remedy must arise from buyer's perspective, not from the court's. Even in civil law jurisdictions, buyers will often prefer damages and purchase of substitute goods, because of the expense and delays inherent in litigation. Even if the court prefers specific performance, buyer can terminate this option by declaring the contract "avoided," which is an inconsistent remedy.

Where the goods have been delivered, but are not conforming to the contract, buyer may require specific performance in the form of delivery of conforming substitute goods only if the nonconformity amounts to a "fundamental breach." Likewise, buyer may require seller to repair the goods only if that is reasonable, "having regard to all the circumstances." While no one quite knows what a "fundamental breach" is, it is defined in Article 25 as a breach whose results "substantially deprive [the aggrieved party] of what he is entitled to expect under the contract," unless the results were both foreseen and unforeseeable. Honnold's suggested illustrations include the machine which does not operate when delivered, and the concept clearly requires more than the common law "nonconformity."

As to "avoidance of the contract," which is comparable to "cancellation of the contract" at common law and under UCC § 2–106(4), CISG permits buyer to use this remedy only if there has been a "fundamental breach" by seller, regardless of when the breach occurs. Thus, CISG does not adopt the distinctions between "acceptance of the goods," rejection and "revocation of acceptance" contained in the UCC (§§ 2–601, 606, 608, 612). Also note that "avoidance of the contract" under CISG is a different concept than "avoidance" under the UCC (§ 2–613). The drafting history of CISG indicates that "fundamental breach" seems to impose a stricter standard on buyer than the "substantial impairment" test of the UCC (§§ 2–608, 612). However, there is no indication that the drafters contemplated the old English "fundamental breach" test, which required that the breach "go to the root" of the contract, but which was repudiated by the House of Lords in 1980. *Photo Production Ltd. v. Securicor Transport Ltd.*, [1980] 1 All Eng.Rep. 556.

Given the uncertainties of the "fundamental breach" test, it will be very difficult for buyer, or buyer's attorney, to know how to react to any particular breach—and whether "avoidance" (cancellation) of the contract is permissible or not. In-

correct analysis could put buyer in the position of
making a fundamental breach through its response.
CISG Articles 47 and 49(1)(b) attempt to cure these
uncertainties by offering buyer a method of formu-
lating a supposedly strict standard for performance.
Buyer may notify seller that performance is due by
a stated new date (after the contract date for performance), and seller's failure to perform by the
new date is a fundamental breach. (Derived from
the German *Nachfrist* notice.) However, this *Nachfrist* provision seems to be available only for nonde-
livery by seller, not for delivery of nonconforming
goods, and avoidance is available only if seller does
not deliver during the additional period allowed by
the notice. Further, it is not clear whether seller's
delivery of nonconforming goods during the additional period precludes avoidance or not. In other
words, must the quality of a late delivery by seller
meet a strict standard of "nonconformity", or the
"fundamental breach" test? Finally, in regard to
certainty in application, how long an additional
period must buyer give seller? Article 47 requires
that it be "of reasonable length," but unless there
is a custom on this issue buyer has no certainty that
the period given in the *Nachfrist* notice is long
enough, especially if long distances are involved. In
one German decision, the buyer fixed an additional
period of 11 days under CISG Art. 47(1), which was
"too short to organize carriage by sea." The buyer's
declaration of avoidance seven weeks after delivery
of the non-conforming goods was approved by the

court because seller had offered only a partial delivery of the conforming goods in the interim.

Even if buyer seeks to "avoid the contract" after a "fundamental breach" by seller, seller has a right to "cure" any defect in its performance before avoidance is declared under CISG Article 48(1). If seller's nonconforming tender is early, seller may cure by making a conforming tender up to the delivery date in the contract, whether the nonconformity would create a fundamental breach or not. However, there is still an issue concerning whether seller's right to cure survives buyer's actual declaration of "avoidance of the contract." The language of the statute indicates that it will be very difficult to sustain a finding of fundamental beach where seller has made a timely offer of cure. If seller's tender or offer of cure is made after the delivery date in the contract, seller still has a right to cure through late performance, but only if it can be done "without unreasonable delay," inconvenience or uncertainty of reimbursement expenses. Must performance offered as cure meet a strict "nonconformity" test, or is it still subject to the "fundamental breach" test? CISG has no provisions on this issue. Thus, the entire thrust of these CISG provisions on buyer's remedies is to require cooperation between the parties in resolving disputes over timeliness of delivery and quality of goods.

Thus, for buyer to have any remedy for nonconforming goods tendered by seller, buyer must inspect the goods in "as short a [time] as is practicable" (Article 38); notify seller of the nonconformity "within a reasonable time" (Articles 39, 49); and permit seller to attempt to cure any nonconformity, if the cure does not cause "unreasonable delay" or "inconvenience" (Article 48). There has been more litigation over the effectiveness of such notices than over any other single issue. In one case, where buyer notified seller that the goods (shoes) had "poor workmanship and improper fitting," the court held that the notice was defective. Apparently it was not specific enough.

In addition, for a fundamental breach permitting avoidance, the buyer must determine and be able to prove that the result of the nonconformity is "substantially to deprive him of what he [was] entitled to expect under the contract" (Article 25). If the goods are properly rejected, buyer can still get its money back, even if it has already paid for the goods, under the restitutionary provisions of Article 81; but it must also return the goods "substantially in the condition which he received them" under Article 82(1).

In addition to rejection of the goods through "avoidance" (cancellation) of the contract, the aggrieved buyer has one other informal remedy which appears to give it the power of self-help. Under CISG Article 50, the buyer who receives nonconforming goods "may reduce the price" it pays to seller. There is no requirement of prior notice to seller, and there is little guidance on how to determine the amount of the reduction, or what evidence of diminution in value should be sent to seller. The provision, therefore, seems best suited to deliveries which are defective as to quantity, rather than quality, although at least one author has suggested that it is available only for defective quality. A buyer attempting to use this self-help remedy *must* allow seller to attempt to cure, if seller so requests. This type of self-help provision is familiar at civil law, and also appears in the UCC (§ 2–717), but seems not widely used by common law attorneys. If the buyer resells the defective goods, the resale price is evidence of their value at the time of delivery.

CISG Articles 74–78 provide the aggrieved buyer with an action for damages, and damages can be available when the contract has been "avoided" (cancelled) and also even when seller has successfully cured defects in its performance. There is no requirement that buyer prove seller was at "fault" as a prerequisite to damage recovery. Both direct and consequential damages are recoverable; and expectancy, reliance and restitutionary interests are all protected. Consequential damages are limited in the familiar manner that losses may not be recovered, which were neither actually foreseen nor should have been foreseen. However, this may not be the same as the common law *Hadley v. Baxendale* test, because recovery is available if the loss suffered is foreseeable as a "possible consequence of the breach." The aggrieved buyer must take "reasonable measures" to mitigate its damages under Article 77. Incidental damages relating to interest are covered separately in Article 78.

Where similar goods may be purchased in the market, the most usual measures of the aggrieved buyer's damages are either (1) the difference between the price of "cover" (substitute goods actually purchased) and the contract price, or (2) the difference between the market price for the goods and the contract price. The Convention provides for the recovery of each of these measures of damages, but if buyer does purchase cover only the first measure is available. The Convention gives no guidance on how to determine whether any particular purchase by buyer is a purchase of cover, or is ordinary inventory build-up. Where the market price differential is used, the market price is to be measured at the time of "avoidance" (cancellation), unless buyer has "taken over" the goods before cancelling, in which case, the market price is measured at the time of "taking over."

Note that the seller of goods may be in a significantly better position under CISG than under the UCC, if the buyer claims a relatively minor fault in the goods. Although seller has a right to cure any defects under either statute, this right under the UCC has either time limitations or expectation requirements not stated in CISG. Rejection merely because of a tender which is not "perfect" seems to be available under the UCC, but is definitely not available under CISG. Thus, the seller is less likely to find the goods rejected for an asserted minor non-conformity, and stranded an ocean or continent away, without any effective legal remedy.

BUYER'S OBLIGATIONS

Buyer has two primary obligations in a sale contract under Article 53: to pay the price, and to take delivery of the goods. The former duty is the more important of the two. In addition, there are several derivative preliminary duties which Professor Honnold refers to as "enabling steps."

Unless the sale contract expressly grants credit to buyer, the sale is a cash sale, and payment and delivery are concurrent conditions. Further, payment is due when seller places the goods, or their documents of title, "at buyer's disposal according to the contract." CISG Article 58(1). If the sales contract involves carriage of the goods, seller may ship the goods under negotiable documents of title and demand payment against those documents under Article 58(2), even though no particular method of payment was actually agreed upon by the parties. In such circumstances, buyer still has a right of inspection before payment. If, however, buyer has expressly agreed to "pay against documents" (such as through the use of CFR or CIF term), the buyer has agreed to pay upon tender of the documents, regardless of whether the goods have yet arrived, and without inspection of the goods. Article 58(3).

If buyer is to pay against "handing over" of the documents, or handing over the goods, the place of "handing over" is the place of payment. Otherwise, the place of seller's business is the place of payment, unless the contract provides otherwise. Article 57. Such a provision requires buyer to "export" the funds to seller, which is a critical issue when buyer is from a country with a "soft" currency, or with other restrictions on the transfer of funds. In addition buyer has an obligation to cooperate and take all necessary steps to enable payment to be made, including whatever formalities may be imposed by buyer's country to obtain administrative authorization to make a payment abroad. Article 54. Failure to take such steps may create a breach by buyer even before payment is due.

In addition to the payment provisions, Article 55 addresses the problem of open-price contracts, an issue discussed previously in this chapter. Professor Honnold believes that Article 55 permits initial indefiniteness of the price, and allows a court to enforce such contracts at "the price generally charged at the conclusion of the contract." However, most other writers conclude that the Article 55 provisions are available only for supervening indefiniteness of a contract which initially had a method of determining the price. Such a situation arises often when an index adopted by the contract is no longer calculated or published. However, the Article 55 solution would be to adopt the price charged when the contract was initially formed, which seems unduly harsh towards the seller. To avoid this possibility, sellers using flexible pricing contracts will wish to provide many fall-back indices, in case some should fail.

The buyer's second obligation, to take delivery, also poses duties of cooperation. It includes a duty to make the expected preparations to permit seller to make delivery and may include such acts as providing for containers, transportation, unloading and import licenses. Article 60.

RISK OF LOSS

The basic rule, under CISG and domestic law, is that buyer bears the risk of loss to the goods during their transportation by a carrier, unless the contract provides otherwise. Article 67. The contract will often contain a term which expressly allocates the risk of loss, such as "FOB" or "CIF," and such terms supersede the CISG provisions. If there is no such delivery term, under CISG the risk in a shipment contract passes to buyer when the goods are "handed over" by the seller to the first carrier. They need not be on board the means of transportation, or even pass a ship's rail—any receipt by a carrier will do. Further, they need not be "handed over" to an ocean-going or international carrier—possession by the local trucker who will haul them to the port is sufficient. However, if the seller uses its own vehicle to transport the goods, seller bears the risk until the goods are handed over to an independent carrier, or to buyer.

Where the contract requires that the seller deliver the goods to buyer at buyer's location, or that seller provide part of the transportation and then "hand the goods over to a carrier at a particular place," seller bears the risk of loss to that location or particular place. Thus, in a contract between a Buffalo, N.Y., seller and Beijing, China, buyer: (1)

in a shipment contract (FCA Buffalo), the risk would pass to buyer when the goods were delivered to the first carrier in Buffalo; (2) in a destination contract (DES Beijing), the seller would bear the risk during transit, and the risk would not pass to buyer until the goods were delivered in Beijing; and (3) in a transshipment contract (FAS New York City), the seller would bear the risk from Buffalo to "along side" a ship in New York harbor, and buyer would bear the risk thereafter.

If the goods are not to be transported by a carrier (e.g., when buyer or an agent are close to seller and will pick up the goods), the risk passes to buyer when he picks them up or, if he is late in doing so, when the goods are "at his disposal" and his delay in picking them up causes a breach of contract. Article 69. The goods cannot, however, be "at his disposal" until they have first been identified to the contract.

In most situations, title and risk are treated separately. Thus, manipulation of title through the use of documents of title, such as negotiable bills of lading, is irrelevant and has no effect on the point of transfer of risk of loss. However, under Article 68, if the goods are already in transit when sold, the risk passes when the contract is "concluded." This rule reflects a use of "title" concepts in risk allocation, even though it may be practically impossible to determine whether damage to goods in a ship's cargo hold occurred before or after a sale contract was signed.

Just as title and risk are treated separately, so also breach and risk are treated separately. If seller is in breach of contract when the goods are shipped, these basic risk of loss rules are not changed, which is contrary to the position of UCC § 2–510. Thus, a breach by seller, whether it is a "fundamental beach" under Article 25 or not, is irrelevant to determine risk allocation or the point when the risk of loss passes to buyer. However, if seller does commit a fundamental breach in shipment contract, further damage to the goods during transit will not deprive buyer of its right to avoid the contract under CISG Article 79. Likewise, a nonfundamental breach in a shipment contract, plus damage in transit, will not create a right for buyer to avoid the contract.

REMEDIES FOR BUYER'S BREACH

The preferred remedy for an aggrieved seller, if buyer should breach, is a cause of action for the price, which is seller's functional equivalent of an action for specific performance. A cause of action for damages, but not the price, is distinctly secondary. In addition, seller may wish to reclaim the goods if they are delivered or obtain some protection for them if they are rejected.

As to seller's recovery of the price, CISG Article 62 gives the seller an unqualified right to require buyer to pay the price, but no CISG article expressly states that the seller has a cause of action for payment of the price. Of course, there are implicit conditions on this right, first, that seller has itself performed to the extent required by the terms of the contract (Article 30) and, second, that payment of the price is due (Article 58). However, if seller has an action for the price, it may be an action "for specific performance" under Article 28? If it is an action for specific performance, then an aggrieved seller would have to meet the requirements of UCC § 2–709, as well as CISG Article 62, before a United States court would order buyer to pay the price rather than damages. However, if an action for the price does not require the entry of a "judgment for specific performance," then CISG Article 28 would seem to be inapplicable; and seller need meet only the requisites of CISG Article 62. On the issue of the applicability of Article 28, Professors Honnold and Farnsworth publicly disagree, so the question would seem to be open at this time.

If an unpaid seller is unable (for any reason) to obtain the price, can he get his goods back from the defaulting buyer, *after* delivery, by "avoiding" the contract and seeking to reclaim them? Such reclamation is difficult at common law (see, e.g., UCC §§ 2–507 and 2–702). The Convention, however, seems to allow such reclamation, because Article 64, which gives seller the power to declare the contract "avoided," does not distinguish between pre-and post-delivery situations and Article 81 requires "restitution ... of whatever the first party has supplied" after avoidance. This analysis, however, is available only so long as third parties (buyer's creditors and trustees in bankruptcy) are not involved, for CISG does not affect title to the goods and third party rights (Article 4), and does not require a court to order "specific performance" which it would not order under its own law. (Article 28).

As to damages, CISG Articles 74–78 provide the unpaid seller (as well as an aggrieved buyer) with an action for damages and the general principles are the same as in the discussion of buyer's remedies for seller's breach. The most usual measures of an unpaid seller's damages are either (1) the difference between the contract price and the resale price if the goods were actually resold or (2) the difference between the contract price and the market price for the goods at the time of avoidance of the contract. The Convention provides for recovery of each of these measures of damages, but if seller resells the goods only the first measure is available. The major practical problem concerning unpaid sellers is that the "lost volume" seller is not adequately protected by the above two measures of damages. However, the CISG provisions which establish these measures state that they are not exclusive, and the basic principles of Article 74 specifically include recovery of lost profits, should allow a court to grant full protection to the lost volume seller. One U.S. court has awarded "lost profits" damages, correctly measuring it by subtracting from the contract price only those variable costs saved by the termination of the sale. *Delchi Carrier SpA v. Rotorex Corp.*, 71 F.3d 1024 (2d Cir.1995).

A Buyer who rejected goods after they have been received must take "reasonable" steps to preserve them (Article 85), which may include depositing the goods in a warehouse at seller's expense. Article 87. If seller has no agent in buyer's location, a buyer who rejects goods which have been "placed at his disposal at their destination" must take possession of them "on behalf of the seller" if this can be done without payment of the price (i.e., through paying for a negotiable bill of lading) and without "unreasonable inconvenience" or expense. After such a taking of possession on behalf of seller, buyer must again take "reasonable" steps to preserve them. If the goods are perishable, a rejecting buyer in possession may have to try to sell them and remit any proceeds to seller, less buyer's expenses of preserving and selling them. CISG does not, however, contain any provisions which require a buyer in possession who has rejected the seller's tender to follow seller's instructions, such as to resell on seller's behalf, whether seemingly reasonable or not.

THE UNIDROIT PRINCIPLES OF INTERNATIONAL COMMERCIAL CONTRACTS

The UNIDROIT Principles for International Commercial Contracts represent a different approach to unification and harmonization of international commercial law. CISG and its comparable conventions in other fields attempt to regulate the law of specific subjects in international transactions, and only by adopting rules which can gain "concensus" approval of national governments.

Thus, this approach is much like that of the National Conference of Commissioners on Uniform State Laws (the drafters of the UCC). UNIDROIT (The International Institute for the Unification of Private Law in Rome) has proposed something quite different, which is the equivalent of a "Restatement of Contracts" for international commercial contracts. It is not limited as to types of such contracts and will not be proposed for ratification as a convention, and so does not need approval of any national government.

In transactions to which CISG is applicable, the courts will usually apply the rules of CISG. However, where CISG is silent or ambiguous, courts are instructed by CISG Art. 7(2) to consult the "general principles" of international commercial law, and the UNIDROIT Principles are one source of such general principles. Further, in non-sale of goods contracts, the Principles are also available for consultation. In addition, it is expected that arbitrators may use the Principles in the absence of any choice of law by the parties, or that the parties themselves may expressly choose the Principles as the law to govern their contract. Finally, the drafters hoped that the Principles might serve as a model law, especially for LDCs. Note that, in all these uses, the effectiveness of UNIDROIT's Principles depend upon their persuasive value.

To promote maximization of their persuasive value, UNIDROIT assembled individual experts and requested that they draft the Principles to reflect current trade practices. These practices could be reflected either in conventions, such as CISG, or in private contracts, such as general conditions or (international) standard form contracts in use by industry. Where there was no existing common trade practice, the drafters were instructed to formulate solutions which are best adapted to international commercial transactions, whether they were in fact part of any existing legal regime or not. Thus, they do not necessarily represent the national rule of a majority of states.

The principles were drafted over a period of 20 years, and were adopted by UNIDROIT's Governing Council in May, 1994. They are more comprehensive than CISG. For example, they include new provisions on how a contract may be formed, on confirmation of documents, on contracts with open term clauses, on negotiations in bad faith, on the duty of confidentiality, on merger clauses, on use of standard forms, and on the battle of the forms. There are also new concepts proposed, such as "gross disparity" as an element of the analysis of validity and "hardship" as an element of excuse of performance. There are provisions on payment, not only be "cheque," but also by funds transfers and other methods and on the currency to be paid in the absence of specification.

This Nutshell cannot provide a detailed, comprehensive description of the Principles, but it will provide three examples as illustrations of their approach to three known problems: the battle of the forms, the unilateral use of standard form contracts, and excuse of performance by changed circumstances.

In the battle of the forms, Art. 2.22 of the Principle eschews the "mirror-image" and the "last-shot" traditional rules. Instead of the mirror image rule, it provides that a contract is concluded where the parties reach an agreement on all the terms of the contract, except for those incorporated in "standard terms." There will be a problem in identifying what terms are standard terms in the modern world of computer-generated contract clauses inserted into electronic communications between the parties, but this provision will at least make sense of the transaction involving exchanges of printed forms. It also attempts to deal with the standard use of clauses which insist that no agreement is formed unless that form's terms are accepted ("my way or the highway" clauses). If such a clause is contained in the standard terms, it is ineffective, but its use in "non-standard terms" would prevent the formation of the contract. Thus, the rationale of the Principles' provision is that, where the parties agree on terms which they are willing to raise individually and negotiate, they should be bound to a contract.

What are the terms of that contract? Instead of adopting the traditional "last shot" doctrine, or even the modified "first shot" doctrine of the UCC, the Principles adopt the "knock-out" rule. The terms of the contract include (1) the "non-standard" terms, which presumably have all been expressly agreed upon by the parties; (2) those standard terms which are "common in substance," unless objected to; and (3) the default rules of the Principles. Thus, the rationale of the Principles is that, where the parties agree on terms which they are willing to raise individually and negotiate, those agreed terms are the terms of the contract. The identification of which terms are "standard terms" in an electronic communication environment will become an increasingly more difficult and important issue. The status of "conflicting terms" will be easy to resolve, but the status of "additional terms," especially in an electronic environment, may be more difficult. Is silence or omission of relatively pervasive terms (but not quite "usage") either an implied conflict or an implied objection? For large corporations, the tactical efforts may well change from universal use of clauses stating "I accept only on my terms" before the contract is concluded, to universal broad-based objection clauses sent after the contract is supposedly concluded.

Where there is use of a standard form by only one party, there is no "battle" of forms, but such forms may be one-sided. Under Art. 2.20 of the Principles, a standard term is not "effective" if the "other party could not reasonably have expected it." A term is a standard term if it was prepared in advance for general and repeated use. Thus, the Principles relates such terms to the expectations of the non-drafting, and presumably non-reading party, adopting as a norm the prevalent conduct today that standard terms are rarely read.

However, the Comments to the Principles indicate that the non-drafting, non-reading party is bound to many, but not all, terms which are standard in an industry. One example in the Comments of a "surprising" term would be a standard term in a travel agency tour package contract that the agency is not liable for the hotel accommodations, but is merely an agent of the hotelkeeper; after it had advertised that it was selling a complete tour package. Other examples include choice of forum clauses which choose courts or arbitral tribunals which are located outside the jurisdiction of the immediate parties to the contract. Thus, unexpected terms can be surprising *either* because of their content *or* their manner of presentation. This resembles the unconscionability doctrine, but there is less emphasis on finding both "harsh terms" and an "unfair surprise" in the contracting process.

The Principles provide two distinctly different paths for asserting excuse from performance by changed circumstances. One is labelled "Force Majeure" and the other is labelled "Hardship." These two paths are not the equivalent of the common law doctrines of impossibility and impracticability. Instead, the concepts in the Principles have civil law foundations.

The *force majeure* provisions in Art. 7.1.7 are similar to those in CISG Art. 79, and include the use of the concept "impediment." The non-performance must be due to an impediment which the non-performing party "could not control" and "could not reasonably be expected to have taken . . .

into account." Thus, complete impossibility seems to be required for excuse under these provisions, and mere impracticability is not sufficient. The non-performing party must give notice "of the impediment", and is liable for a failure to notify, but the Principles do not specify when the notice must be given.

The "hardship" provisions in Arts. 6.2, however, are completely different from any concepts in CISG or in the common law. Hardship occurs when "events fundamentally alter" the cost or value of a promised performance. Illustrations include a ten-fold increase in prices of products to be supplied or a 99% decline in the currency of payment, but there may be a consensus that a 50% change is sufficient to trigger the application of the doctrine. This would be in line with many of the "price unconscionability" cases in the U.S.

However, under the Principles, "hardship" does not by itself excuse performance. Instead, under Art. 6.2.3, the effect of hardship is to compel renegotiation of the contract, if the disadvantaged party so requests. If the attempt to renegotiate fails, either party may seek intervention by "the court." Which courts would have such jurisdiction is left unstated. Also, whether intervention by an arbitral tribunal is available as an alternative is not expressly stated. A court which finds the hardship criteria to be satisfied can "adapt" the contract so as to restore its "equilibrium," or may even terminate the contract.

COMMERCIAL TERMS

Where the goods are to be carried from one location to another as part of the sale transaction, the parties will often adopt a commercial term to state the delivery obligation of the seller. Such terms include F.O.B. (Free on Board), F.A.S. (Free Alongside) and C.I.F. (Cost, Insurance and Freight). These terms are defined in the UCC (§§ 2–319, 2–320), but the UCC definitions are seldom used intentionally in international trade. In fact the UCC definitions are becoming obsolescent in domestic trade also, because the abbreviations used are now associated primarily with water-borne traffic, and the statutory terms do not include the new terminology associated with air freight, containerization, or multi-modal transportation practices.

In international commerce the dominant source of definitions for commercial delivery terms is "Incoterms," published by the International Chamber of Commerce (I.C.C.) and last revised by them in 1990. Incoterms is an acronym for International Commercial Terms, and provides rules for determining the obligations of both seller and buyer when different commercial terms (like F.O.B. or C.I.F.) are used. They state what acts seller must do to deliver, what acts buyer must do to accommodate delivery, what costs each party must bear, and at what point in the delivery process the risk of loss passes from seller to buyer. Each of these obligations may be different for different commercial terms. Thus, the obligations, costs, and risks of seller and buyer are different under F.O.B. than they are under C.I.F.

There are other sources of such definitions, in addition to the UCC and Incoterms, such as the American Revised Foreign Trade Definitions (1941). It has been widely used in Pacific Ocean trade, but may be replaced by the more recently revised Incoterms.

Since the I.C.C. is a non-governmental entity, Incoterms is neither a national legislation nor an international treaty. Thus, it cannot be "the governing law" of any contract. Instead, it is a written form of custom and usage in the trade, which can be, and often is, expressly incorporated by a party or the parties to an international contract for the sale of goods. Alternatively, if it is not expressly incorporated in the contract, Incoterms could be made an implicit term of the contract as part of international custom. Courts in France and Germany have done so, and both treatises and the UNCITRAL Secretariat describe Incoterms as a widely-observed usage for commercial terms. This description should allow Incoterms to qualify under CISG Article 9(2) as a "usage ... which in international trade is widely known to, and regularly observed by, parties to" international sales contracts, even if the usage is not global.

Although the UCC has definitions for some commercial terms (e.g., F.O.B., F.A.S., C.I.F.), these definitions are expressly subject to "agreement otherwise." Thus, an express reference to Incoterms will supercede the UCC provisions, and United States courts have so held. Such incorporation by express reference is often made in American international sales contracts, especially in Atlantic Ocean trade. If there is no express term, and the UCC is the governing law rather than CISG, Incoterms can still be applicable as a "usage of trade" under UCC § 1–205(2). The UCC criteria for such a usage is "a practice.... having such regularity of observance ... as to justify an expectation that it will be observed with respect to the transaction in question." A usage need not be "universal" nor "ancient," just "currently observed by the great majority of decent dealers." UCC § 1–205, Comment 5.

Incoterms gives the parties a menu of thirteen different commercial terms to describe the delivery obligations of the seller and the reciprocal obligations of the buyer to accommodate delivery. They include:

1) EXW (Ex Works)

2) FCA (Free Carrier)

3) FAS (Free Alongside Ship)

4) FOB (Free On Board)

5) CFR (Cost and Freight)

6) CIF (Cost, Insurance and Freight)

7) CPT (Carriage Paid To)

8) CIP (Carriage and Insurance Paid To)

9) DAF (Delivered at Frontier)

10) DES (Delivered Ex Ship)

11) DEQ (Delivered Ex Quay)

12) DDU (Delivered Duty Unpaid)

13) DDP (Delivered Duty Paid)

There are several types of divisions which one may make of these thirteen different terms. One is a division between the one term which does not assume that a carrier will be involved (EXW), and all the twelve other terms. A second division is between those six terms which require the involvement of water-borne transportation (FAS, FOB, CFR, CIF, DES and DEQ) and those six other terms which are applicable to any mode of transportation, including multi-modal transportation (FCA, CPT, CIP, DAF, DDU, and DDP). The UCC has none of the latter six terms, although the types of transactions they are designed for arise routinely, and can be handled under the UCC designations "F.O.B. place of shipment," "C. & F.", "C.I.F.," and "F.O.B. named place of destination."

The twelve terms requiring transportation can also be divided into "shipment contract" terms (FCA, FAS, FOB, CFR, CIF, CPT, and CIP) and "destination contract" terms (DAF, DES, DEQ, DDU, and DDP.). The UCC and CISG both use this terminology. CISG Art. 31. The underlying concept is that, in shipment contracts seller puts the goods in the hands of a carrier and arranges for their transportation, but transportation is at buyer's risk and expense. (UCC § 2–504). On the other hand, in destination contracts seller is responsible to put the goods in the hands of the carrier, arrange their transportation, and bear the cost and risk of transportation. Unfortunately, many aspects of transportation usages have changed since 1952, and the UCC concepts do not always fit the practices now described in Incoterms.

The I.C.C. suggests that these thirteen commercial terms be divided into four principal categories, one for each of the different first letters of the constituent terms, E,F,C and D. The "E" term (EXW) is where the goods are made available to buyer, but use of a carrier is not expressly required. All other terms require the use of a carrier. The "F" terms (FCA, FAS, FOB) require seller only to assume the risks and costs to deliver the goods to a carrier, and to a carrier nominated by the buyer. The "C" terms require seller to assume the risks and costs to deliver the goods to a carrier, arrange and pay for the "main transportation" (and sometimes insurance), but without assuming additional risks due to post-shipment events. Thus, under "C" terms, seller bears risks until one point in the transportation (delivery to a carrier), but pays costs to a different point in the transportation (the agreed destination). The "D" terms (DAF, DES, DEQ, DDU and DDP) require the seller to deliver the goods to a carrier, arrange for their transportation, and assume the risks and costs until the arrival of the goods at an agreed country of destination.

Incoterms are periodically revised, lately about once every ten years. The last revision was in 1990 and is set forth in I.C.C. Publication No. 460. In the latest revision, the I.C.C. included references to electronic messages and to new types of transport documents, such as air waybills, railway and road consignment notes, and "multimodal transport documents." The I.C.C. explained that these changes were needed because of "the increasing use of electronic data interchange (EDI)" and "changed transportation techniques," including "containers, multimodal transport and roll on-roll off traffic."

However, other changes were made in the 1990 Revisions that were not explained. Many commercial delivery terms have incorporated payment and inspection obligations as part of their definitional scheme, particularly the concept of "payment against documents" which precluded post-shipment inspection of the goods before payment. Under prior versions of Incoterms, these obligations and disabilities had been expressly stated in the definition of such terms as CIF and C & F. In the 1990 Revision of Incoterms, all references to payment terms and post-shipment inspection terms have been deleted, leaving only a standard provision that buyer must pay for any *pre*-shipment inspection. These deletions are not explained.

These deletions leave a gap, which must be filled from some other source of information. There are at least three sources of such information. One such source of payment and inspection terms is the prior versions of Incoterms, such as the 1980 Revision, when the definitions included terms on payment and inspection. The definitions in the 1990 Revision of Incoterms refer to "the usual transport document," and it can be argued that this reference incorporates the standards established in definitions from prior versions. Further, the deletions are not explained, except to indicate a desire not to impede the introduction of the use of EDI messages to handle transportation arrangements. On the other hand, the 1990 Revision establishes several new terms, for which this approach will be ambiguous; and this approach, over time, could be used to impede the use of EDI technology. However, some carryover use of such payment and inspection terms should be expected.

A second source of payment and inspection terms is national law, such as the UCC. In Sections 2–319 to 2–323, the UCC provides "default rules" for a number of commercial terms. Under prior versions of Incoterms, these default rules were not applicable if the parties selected Incoterms, because the parties had "agreed otherwise." Now, however, that analysis may no longer stand. The parties have agreed that Incoterms will pre-empt UCC terms, where applicable; but Incoterms no longer has payment and inspection provisions, so the payment and inspection provisions of the UCC definitions may no longer be pre-empted. There are difficulties with this analytical approach. One is that many of the Incoterms commercial terms no longer correspond to their UCC namesakes. A second is that the parties, by nominating Incoterms, may have intended to bypass all aspects of the statutory definitions and substitute customary definitions. Nevertheless, some use of the UCC and other definitions from national law should be expected, as a source of information to resolve the legal issues created by the deletion of the payment and inspection provisions in the Incoterms definitions.

If neither prior versions of Incoterms nor specific definitions in national law are deemed to be acceptable sources of information, then the general provisions of national law, whether contained in the UCC or CISG, give virtually no provisions for interpretation of the commercial terms, except to allow a court to consult customs and usage of trade. Custom and usage therefore can be a third source of such terms. However, custom and usage must be proven as matters of fact, usually by expert testimony; and the proof must surmount several legal hurdles to be accepted by a court. And the use of experts and surmounting of legal hurdles was exactly what the parties thought they were avoiding by incorporating Incoterms into their contract. It is possible that those expectations may now be violated, at least as to payment and inspection terms. Thus, use of Incoterms definitions may subject the users to problems of proof of custom and usage that may not arise for the UCC definitions.

The following is a brief discussion of each of the Incoterms commercial terms.

Under the Incoterms Ex Works (EXW) commercial term (including Ex Factory and Ex Warehouse), the seller needs only to "tender" the goods to the buyer by placing them at buyer's disposal at a named place of delivery. Thus, seller has no obligation to deliver the goods to a carrier or to load the goods on any vehicle. Seller must also notify buyer when and where the goods will be tendered, but has no obligation to arrange for transportation or insurance. The risk of loss transfers to buyer at the time the goods are placed at its disposal. Seller will normally provide a commercial invoice or its equivalent electronic message, but has no obligation to obtain a document of title or an export license. The Incoterms definition has no effect upon either payment or inspection obligations under the contract, except to require buyer to pay for pre-shipment inspection. The Incoterms risk of loss provision is contrary to the default rules of both the UCC (§ 2–509) and CISG (Art. 69), which delay passing the risk until buyer's receipt of the goods, both because seller is more likely to have insurance and because seller has a greater ability to protect the goods.

Under the Incoterms Free Carrier (FCA) commercial term, the seller is obligated to deliver the goods into the custody of a carrier, usually the first carrier in a multi-modal transportation scheme. The Incoterms definition of "carrier" includes freight forwarders. Seller has no obligation to pay for transportation costs or insurance. Usually the carrier will be named by, and arranged by, the buyer. However, seller "may" arrange transportation at buyer's expense if requested by the buyer, or if it is "commercial practice" for seller to do so. But, even under such circumstances, seller may refuse to make such arrangements as long as it so notifies buyer. Even if seller does arrange transportation, it has no obligation to arrange for insurance coverage during transportation, and need only notify buyer "that the goods *have been* delivered into the custody of the carrier" (emphasis added). The risk of loss transfers to buyer upon delivery to the carrier, but buyer may not receive notice until after that time. The seller must provide a commercial invoice or its equivalent electronic message, any necessary export license, and usually a transport document that will allow buyer to take delivery—or an equivalent electronic data interchange message. The Incoterms definition has no provisions on either payment or post-shipment inspection terms under the contract.

This FCA term is the Incoterms commercial term which is most comparable to the UCC's "F.O.B. place of shipment" term under § 2–319(1)(a). However, there are two levels of confusion. One is that Incoterms has an "FOB" term which is different, and the UCC "F.O.B." term is more likely to be compared with the Incoterms "FOB" term. The other is that the obligations under FCA and the UCC "F.O.B. place of shipment" term are, in fact, different. The norm under the UCC's "F.O.B." is for seller to arrange transportation, while seller need do so under FCA only in special circumstances. (UCC §§ 2–319, 2–504.) Further, if seller does ship, under UCC § 2–504 seller usually must also arrange insurance coverage, unless instructed otherwise by buyer. Under Incoterms FCA, seller does not seem ever to have any obligation to arrange for insurance coverage. Traditionally, under both the

1980 version of Incoterms FAS and the UCC "F.O.B. place of shipment" term, there is no implied special payment or inspection terms, no implied requirement of payment against documents or payment before inspection. This would also seem to be a preferable interpretation of the current Incoterms FCA term.

Under the Incoterms Free Alongside Ship (FAS) commercial term, the seller is obligated to deliver the goods alongside a ship arranged for and named by the buyer at a named port of shipment. Thus, it is appropriate only for water-borne transportation, and seller must bear the costs and risks of inland transportation to the named port of shipment. Seller has no obligation to arrange transportation or insurance for the "main" (or water-borne) part of the carriage, but does have a duty to notify buyer "that the goods *have been delivered* alongside the ship" (emphasis added). The risk of loss will transfer to the buyer also at the time the goods are delivered alongside the ship. Seller must provide a commercial invoice and usually a transport document that will allow buyer to take delivery, or the electronic equivalent of either. But seller has no obligation to provide an export license, only an obligation to render assistance to buyer to obtain one.

The Incoterms definition has no provisions on either payment or post-shipment inspection terms under the contract. Under the UCC (§ 2–319), the term "F.A.S. vessel" requires the buyer to pay against a tender of documents, such as a negotiable bill of lading, before the goods arrive at their destination and before buyer has any post-shipment opportunity to inspect the goods. UCC § 2–319(4). Otherwise, the UCC "F.A.S." term is similar to the Incoterms "FAS" term, including obligating the seller only to deliver the goods alongside a named vessel and not obligating the seller to arrange transportation to a final destination.

However, the definition of FAS in the prior 1980 version of Incoterms provided that payment against documents was not required under an FAS contract, while the 1980 Incoterms did contain such payment provisions in its definitions of other commercial terms. Thus, it is more likely that the current version of Incoterms FAS is not intended to require payment against documents, to restrict inspection before payment, or to be used with negotiable bills of lading.

Under the Incoterms Free on Board (FOB) commercial term, the seller is obligated to deliver the goods on board a ship arranged for and named by the buyer at a named port of shipment. Thus, this term is also appropriate only for water-borne transportation, and seller must bear the costs and risks of inland transportation to the named port of shipment, and also of loading the goods on the ship (until "they have passed the ship's rail"). Seller has no obligation to arrange transportation or insurance, but does have a duty to notify buyer "that the goods *have been delivered* on board" the ship (emphasis added). The risk of loss will transfer to the buyer also at the time the goods have "passed the ship's rail." The seller must provide a commercial invoice, or its equivalent electronic message, any necessary export license, and usually a transport document that will allow buyer to take delivery—or an equivalent electronic data interchange message.

The Incoterms definition has no provisions on either payment or post-shipment inspection terms under the contract. The UCC does define "F.O.B.," but it is not a term requiring water-borne transportation. Thus, as has been discussed above, the UCC "F.O.B." is more closely linked to the Incoterms FCA term. But the UCC also has a term "F.O.B. vessel," which does relate only to water-borne transportation, and therefore is most closely linked to the Incoterms FOB term. Under the UCC, the term "F.O.B. vessel" requires the buyer to pay against a tender of documents, such as a negotiable bill of lading, before the goods arrive at their destination and before buyer has any post-shipment opportunity to inspect the goods. UCC § 2–319(4). Otherwise, the UCC "F.O.B. vessel" term is similar to the Incoterms "FOB" term, including obligating the seller only to deliver the goods to a named ship's rail and not obligating the seller to arrange transportation to a final destination.

However, the definition of FOB in the 1980 version of Incoterms provided that payment against documents was not required for an FOB contract, while the 1980 Incoterms did contain such payment provisions in its definitions of other commercial terms. Thus, it is more likely that the current version of Incoterms FOB is not intended to require payment against documents or to restrict inspection before payment, unless such a term is expressly added or there is a known custom in a particular trade. In addition, it is more likely that negotiable bills of lading are not intended to be used with Incoterms FOB shipments, unless the parties specify "payment against documents" in the sale contract.

Under the Incoterms Cost, Insurance and Freight (CIF) commercial term, the seller is obligated to arrange for both transportation and insurance to a named destination port and then to deliver the goods on board the ship arranged for by the seller. Thus, the term is appropriate only for water-borne transportation. Seller must arrange the transportation, and pay the freight costs to the *destination port*, but has completed its delivery obligations when the goods have "passed the ship's rail" at the *port of shipment*. Seller must arrange and pay for insurance during transportation to the *port of destination*, but the risk of loss transfers to the buyer at the time the goods pass the ship's rail at the *port of shipment*. Seller must notify buyer "that the goods have been delivered on board" the ship to enable buyer to receive the goods. Seller must provide a commercial invoice, or its equivalent electronic message, any necessary export license, and "the usual transport documents" for the destination port.

The Incoterms definition has no provisions on either payment or post-shipment inspection terms under the contract. However, it does require that the transportation document "must ... enable the buyer to sell the goods in transit by the transfer of the document to a subsequent buyer ... or by notification to the carrier," unless otherwise agreed. As is explained below in the materials on bills of lading, the traditional manner of enabling buyer to do this, in either the "payment against documents" transaction or the letter of credit transaction, is for seller to obtain a negotiable bill of lading from the carrier and to tender that negotiable document to buyer through a series of banks. The banks allow buyer to obtain possession of the document (and control of the goods) only after buyer pays for the goods. Thus, buyer "pays against documents," while the goods are at sea, and pays for them before any post-shipment inspection of the goods is possible. This transaction should still be regarded as the norm under Incoterms CIF, and the definition of the term in the 1990 version does refer to the use of a negotiable bill of lading.

The 1980 version of Incoterms was more precise on these obligations, requiring buyer to "accept the documents when tendered by the seller ... and pay the price as provided in the contract." The implication from this provision, as explained above, was that buyer had no right to inspect the goods before this payment against documents. The UCC also has a definition of "C.I.F." which requires the buyer to "make payment against tender of the required documents." UCC § 2–320(4). The UCC "C.I.F." term is otherwise similar to Incoterms CIF, in that it requires seller to deliver to carrier at the port of shipment and bear the risk of loss only to that port, but to pay freight costs and insurance to the port of destination.

The Incoterms Cost and Freight (CFR) commercial term is similar to the CIF term, except that seller has no obligations with respect to either arranging or paying for insurance coverage of the goods during transportation. Under the CFR term, the seller is obligated to arrange for transportation to a named destination point and then to deliver the goods on board the ship arranged for by the seller. Thus, the term is appropriate only for water-borne transportation. Seller must arrange the transportation and pay the freight costs to the *destination port*, but has completed its delivery obligations when the goods have "passed the ship's rail" at the *port of shipment*. Seller has no express obligation to arrange or pay for insurance on the goods during transportation, and the risk of loss transfers to the buyer at the time the goods pass the ship's rail at the *port of shipment*. Seller must notify buyer "that the goods *have been delivered* on board" the ship (emphasis added) to enable buyer to receive the goods. Seller must provide a commercial invoice, or its equivalent electronic message, any necessary export license, and "the usual transport document" for the destination port. As with CIF, the Incoterms CFR definition has no provisions on either payment or post-shipment inspection terms under the contract. However, it does require that the transport document "must ... enable the buyer to sell the goods in transit by the transfer of the document to a subsequent buyer," which has traditionally meant use of a negotiable bill of lading and payment against documents. Both the UCC and prior versions of Incoterms regarded this term as requiring payment against documents while the goods were still at sea, thus restricting port-shipment inspection of the goods before payment. These provisions should still be regarded as the norm under Incoterms CFR.

The Incoterms Carriage and Insurance Paid To (CIP) and Carriage Paid To (CPT) commercial terms are similar to its CIF and CFR terms, except that they may be used for any type of transportation, including multimodal transportation, and not just for waterborne transportation. Under the CIP term, seller is obligated to arrange and pay for both transportation and insurance to a named *destination* place. However, Seller completes its delivery obligations, and the risk of loss passes to the buyer, upon delivery to the first carrier at the place of *shipment*. Thus, the term is appropriate for multimodal transportation. The CPT commercial term is similar, except that seller has no duty to arrange or pay for insurance coverage of the goods during transportation.

Under both CIP and CPT, seller must notify buyer "that the goods have been delivered" to the first carrier, and also give any other notice required to enable buyer "to take the goods." Under both, seller must also provide a commercial invoice, or its equivalent electronic message, any necessary export license, and "the usual transport document." A list of acceptable transport documents is given, and there is no requirement that the document enable buyer to sell the goods in transit. There are no payment or post-shipment inspection provisions in the Incoterms definitions, and the UCC does not define these terms. Further, the Introduction to Incoterms contrasts CIP and CPT with CIF and CFR, indicating that there is no requirement to provide a negotiable bill of lading with CIP or CPT terms. Thus, unless the parties expressly agree to a "payment against documents" term, it is more likely that the CIP or CPT commercial terms are not intended to require payment against documents or to restrict inspection before payment.

Incoterms provides five different commercial terms for "destination" or "arrival" contracts. Two of them, Delivered Ex Ship (DES) and Delivered Ex Quay (DEQ) should only be used for waterborne transportation. The other three, Delivered At Frontier (DAF), Delivered Duty Unpaid (DDU) and Delivered Duty Paid (DDP), can all be used with any type of transportation, including multimodal transport. In all of them, seller is required to arrange transportation, pay the freight costs and bear the risk of loss to a named destination point. Although these definitions have no provisions on insurance during transportation, since seller bears the risk of loss during that event, seller must either arrange and pay for insurance or act as a self-insuror during transportation. There are also no provisions on payment or post-shipment inspection, but there is no requirement for use of a negotiable bill of lading, and delivery occurs only after arrival of the goods.

Thus, there is no reason to imply a "payment against documents" requirement if none is expressly stated. On the other hand, the parties are free to agree expressly on both a destination commercial term and a payment against documents term.

Under the Incoterms DES commercial term, delivery occurs and the risk of loss passes when the goods are placed at buyer's disposal on board ship at the named destination port. To be "at buyer's disposal", the goods must be placed (at seller's risk and expense) so that it can be removed by "appropriate" unloading equipment. However, the goods need not be cleared for importation by customs officials; that is buyer's obligation. [Under the UCC, the term "ex ship" requires seller also to unload the goods.] Under the DEQ commercial term, the goods must be placed at buyer's disposal on the quay or wharf at the named destination port. However, the parties who use a DEQ term should further specify either "Duty Paid" or "Duty Unpaid," because both DEQ (Duty Paid) and DEQ (Duty Unpaid) terms are in use. If "Duty Paid" is specified, or there is no specification, seller must "pay the costs of customs formalities ... duties, taxes ... payable upon ... importation of the goods, unless otherwise agreed."

In both DES and DEQ shipments, seller must notify buyer of the estimated time of arrival of a named vessel at a named destination port. Also, in both DES and DEQ shipments, seller must provide buyer with a commercial invoice or the equivalent electronic message, "a delivery order and/or the usual transport document", and an export license. For DEQ shipments, seller must also provide an import license, unless otherwise agreed.

Under the Incoterms DAF commercial term, which is most appropriately used with rail or road transportation, delivery occurs and the risk of loss passes when the goods are placed at buyer's disposal at a named place at the frontier, but before the customs frontier of the importing country. Under the DDU commercial term, delivery occurs and the risk of loss passes when the goods are placed at buyer's disposal at "the agreed point at the named point of destination" in the country of importation. However, seller has no obligation to pay import duties or charges. Under the Incoterms DDP commercial term, delivery occurs and the risk of loss passes when the goods are placed at buyer's disposal at the named place in the country of destination, cleared for importation into that country. Seller must pay all import duties and charges and complete customs formalities at its risk and expense. The only UCC destination term is "F.O.B. destination," § 2–319(1)(b), which seems similar to "DDU," but without much of the detail and precision.

In each of these terms DAF, DDU and DDP, seller must notify buyer of the dispatch of the goods and give any other notice necessary for buyer "to take the goods." In each type of shipment, seller must provide a commercial invoice or its equivalent electronic message. In a DAF shipment, seller must also provide "the usual document or other evidence of the delivery" and an export license. In a DDU shipment, seller must also provide a "delivery order and/or the usual transport document" and an export license. In a DDP shipment, seller must provide the delivery order or transport document and both an export license and an import license.

INTERNATIONAL ELECTRONIC COMMERCE

The recent phenomenal growth of E Commerce caught the legal regimes of the world unprepared. None was ready for the legal problems caused by the new forms of contract-making, payment, performance and information exchange. They have done their best to adapt traditional rules to new transaction patterns, but each legal regime has adapted in a different manner. Thus, there is little consistency in the rules applicable to E Commerce transactions which cross national borders.

Such a lack of consistency is not new, but the problems are magnified by two other aspects of E Commerce. One is that the parties often do not know when an E Commerce transaction is in fact across national boundaries. A website with a ".com" address may literally be located anywhere in the world. Thus, the website address of each party, which may be the only information each has of the other, may not reveal the transborder nature of the transaction. The second aspect is that screens are small, and the amount of writing on a screen is limited, so long, sophisticated contracts with lots of form-pad clauses are "out" in E Commerce. In particular, most E Merchants believe that too many other terms have priority over choice of law and choice of forum clauses, so they do not appear in the terms of many E Commerce contracts. Thus, a second potential device for revealing the transborder nature of the transaction is usually missing.

The new contracts issues created by E Commerce include how to satisfy requirements for agreements in writing and signatures, authentication and attribution without personal contact, security and integrity of electronic messages, and express and implied terms and conditions for both commercial and consumer contracts. It also raises jurisdiction issues, ranging from choice of law to presence in a jurisdiction for purposes of being sued in a civil action to presence in a jurisdiction for purposes of regulation by public authorities. The public authorities not only wish to prevent fraud and deception by E Merchants, but also to regulate privacy, intellectual property and taxation issues, among others. In all these areas, there are very few statutory rules or decided cases; and, where there are, the existing rules and approaches to E Commerce differ from one legal regime to another.

Thus, there is a perceived need, not only for statutory rules to facilitate E Commerce, but for such rules to be similar across national borders, since it is not usually clear where the parties are located. Promoting similar rules could be accomplished by either an international multilateral treaty or proposed model legislation. Because the practices of E Commerce are still developing, UN-CITRAL (the organization which developed CISG) has also developed a Model Law on Electronic Commerce, which it adopted in 1996. The Model Law is a minimalist approach to legislation, seeking to facilitate E Commerce transactions and not to regulate them. This Model Law is now available to all legal regimes for enactment to provide guidance for E Merchants and their customers.

In its general provisions, the UNCITRAL Model Law provides equality of treatment for paper documents and electronic messages. It provides that "data messages" are not to be denied legal effect because they are electronic, and that any "writing" requirement is satisfied by a data message which is accessible for subsequent reference. Legal requirements for a "signature" are met by a data message if there is a method which is "reasonable for the circumstances" to identify both the identity of the person sending the message and that person's approval of the message. An electronic data message is allowed to satisfy evidentiary requirements, and an evidentiary requirement for "an original document" is satisfied by an electronic data message whose information integrity can be assured, and whose information can be displayed. Finally, record retention requirements may be satisfied for data messages by appropriate electronic retention.

The UNCITRAL Model Law also contains more specialized rules, which may be varied by agreement between the parties. These rules concern contract formation, attribution of messages, and acknowledgment and time of receipt of data messages. As to attribution, a message is deemed to be sent by a designated originator if it is sent either by an authorized person or by a machine that is programmed by the originator to operate automatically. The addressee of the data message is authorized to rely on it as being from the originator if either an agreed-upon security procedure has been used or the originator enabled the actual sender to gain access to a message identification method.

A major problem with electronic data messages is that they get lost much more often than messages sent through the U.S. Post Office. Thus, acknowledgment of receipt of electronic messages is much more important to the parties than is acknowledgment of paper-based messages, and the parties often stipulate in their agreements that data messages must be acknowledged. If they so agree, under the UNCITRAL Model Law, acknowledgment can be accomplished either by the method agreed upon or, where no specific acknowledgment method has been agreed, any communication or conduct can be sufficient. Even where the parties have not agreed to require acknowledgment, the originator of a data message may unilaterally require it by stating in the body of the message that it is conditional on acknowledgment. Such a message is deemed "never been sent" until acknowledgment is received. Receipt of a message generally requires that the message enter an information system outside the control of the originator or its agents.

There are other provisions in the UNCITRAL Model Law which are specific to the contracts for the carriage of goods and to transportation documents. These provisions generally permit electronic data messages to replace bills of lading and way-bills, even where local statutes require a writing on a paper document. They also provide that legal rules which compel the use of paper documents in carriage contracts are satisfied by such data messages.

The UNCITRAL Model Law on Electronic Commerce has been enacted by the Republic of Korea, Singapore and the state of Illinois, as of September 1, 1999. Further enactments are expected. In the United States, the National Conference of Commissioners on Uniform State Laws has adopted two different proposed uniform acts to facilitate electronic commerce. One is the Uniform Electronic Transactions Act (UETA), which is similar in scope and substance to the UNCITRAL Model Law. It applies to all types of electronic messages and contracts, and seeks to validate and facilitate their use at a very basic level. The second is the Uniform Computer Information Transactions Act (UCITA) which applies primarily only to software licensing transactions, and incorporates very detailed provisions concerning every aspect of the transaction. Its format is similar to UCC Article 2 on sales of goods, and at one time was intended to be UCC Article 2B, until it was rejected by the American Law Institute as not sufficiently balanced.

UCITA also rejects many of the concepts in both the UNCITRAL Model Law and UETA. Thus, the Uniform Commissioners have proposed two different uniform acts whose provisions conflict on such basic terms as authentication and attribution. The introduction and adoption of differing state, national and international legislation with conflicting provisions to govern E Commerce is likely to create difficulties for all the participants in a transaction where the location of the parties is unknown. These difficulties are likely to grow as more non-U.S. parties participate in E Commerce, and a greater proportion of such transactions are across national boundaries.

THE "PAYMENT AGAINST DOCUMENTS" TRANSACTION

How does the "payment against documents" transaction work? When buyer and seller are forming their contract for the sale of the goods, seller will insist that buyer "pay against the documents", rather than after delivery and inspection of the goods themselves. Such a payment term must be bargained for and expressed in the sales contract. It will not normally be implied.

Seller will then pack the goods and prepare a commercial invoice. If the commercial term requires it (e.g., under a "CIF" term) seller will also procure an insurance certificate (another form of contract) covering the goods during transit. Seller then delivers the goods to the carrier, which issues a negotiable bill of lading as a combination receipt and contract. This bill of lading will commonly require carrier to deliver the goods only "to seller or order"—i.e., only to seller or a person seller may designate by an appropriate endorsement.

Under the terms of the bill of lading contract, in return for payment of the freight charge, carrier promises to deliver the goods to either (1) the named "consignee" in a "straight" (or non-negotiable) bill of lading, or (2) the person in possession ("holder") of a properly indorsed "order" (or negotiable) bill of lading. The order (negotiable) bill of lading should be used in the payment against documents sale, so that the buyer is able to obtain delivery of goods *only if* buyer has physical possession of a properly endorsed bill of lading. Such a bill of lading controls access to and delivery of the goods, so that the bill of lading is also a "document of title."

Further, if it is a negotiable bill of lading, it also controls the right to obtain the goods from carrier. Thus, a negotiable bill of lading delivered by seller to the collecting banks will assure buyer and seller that: (1) the goods have been delivered to carrier, (2) they are destined for buyer and not some third party, and (3) the collecting banks can control carrier's delivery of the goods to buyer by simply retaining possession of the order bill of lading. In other words, when a bank undertakes to collect funds from the buyer for the seller, it receives from seller a "document of title" (the bill of lading), issued by carrier which gives the bank control of carrier's delivery of the goods. Buyer cannot obtain possession of the goods from a carrier without physical possession of the negotiable bill of lading, so after the banks have received that piece of paper from seller, they can obtain payment (or assurances that buyer will pay them) before buyer receives the ability to obtain the goods from carrier.

Once the seller has obtained a negotiable bill of lading to his own order, how does he obtain payment? First, he attaches a "draft" to it, together with an invoice and any other documents required by the sales contract. Then he uses the banking system as a collection agent. A "draft" (sometimes also called a "bill of exchange") will usually be a "sight draft," which is payable "on demand" when presented to buyer. The draft is drawn for the amount due under the sales contract, and it is payable to seller's order.

At the bank, the seller endorses both the draft and the negotiable bill of lading to Seller's Bank, and will also transfer the other documents to it. If no letter of credit is involved in the transaction, the bank will usually take these documents only "for collection," although it is also possible for the bank to "discount," or buy, the documents outright and become the owner.

To understand the collection transaction by the banking system, consult the flow chart on page 118. Seller's Bank is required to send the draft and its accompanying documents for presentment to the buyer which is usually done by sending them through "customary banking channels." Seller's Bank deals with "for collection" items individually, without assuming that they will be honored, and therefore without giving seller a provisional credit in the seller's account until the buyer pays the draft.

The draft, with its attached documents, will pass through "customary banking channels" to Buyer's Bank (the "presenting bank"), which will notify the buyer of the arrival of the documents. Buyer's Bank will demand that the buyer "honor" the draft which means paying the amount of a demand draft, or "accepting" (promising to pay later) a time draft. The buyer may require the bank to "exhibit" the draft and documents to it to allow the buyer to determine whether they conform to the contract. The buyer has three banking days after the notice was sent to decide whether to "honor" the draft, if mere notice is sent. However, if the draft and documents are exhibited directly to the buyer, the buyer must decide whether to honor the draft or not by the close of business on that same day, unless there are extenuating circumstances.

Buyer must "pay against the documents" and not the goods themselves, which is why it is preferable to specify the terms of the documents in the original contract for the sale of goods. Once buyer has paid, or arranged to pay, Buyer's Bank, it will obtain possession of the bill of lading and only then will it be entitled to obtain the goods from carrier. Buyer never sees the goods, only the documents—so it inspects the documents rigorously to determine that they comply exactly with the requirements of the sale contract. Substantial performance by seller in the tender of documents is not acceptable.

DIAGRAM OF AN INTERNATIONAL DOCUMENTARY SALE

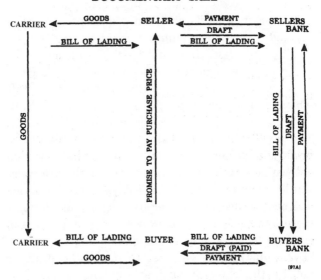

An international sale of goods involving payment against documents is diagramed on this page.

Note the risks to each party. If the seller ships conforming goods, it will be paid before the documents or the goods are released to the buyer. Thus, seller will not lose control of the 'goods without being paid for them. If buyer pays Buyer's Bank, the proceeds are remitted immediately and automatically to seller's bank account in seller's nation.

What can go wrong from the seller's point of view? Seller has shipped the goods to a foreign buyer without being paid before shipping them, and with no guarantee of payment from anyone other than the buyer. The buyer may refuse to pay the sight draft, with documents attached, when it arrives. This would give the seller a cause of action, but often it is usable only in the buyer's jurisdiction, which means bringing a suit abroad with its extra expense, delay and uncertainty. In particular, a plaintiff could feel that it will be the target of discrimination in the courts of another nation.

The seller would still have control of the goods, because after dishonor of the draft the bill of lading will be returned to the seller. However, the goods would now be at a foreign destination—one at which the seller has no agents, and no particular prospects for resale. In addition, if the seller wished to bring the goods back to its base of operations (and normal sales territory), it would have to pay a second transportation charge, and this may be substantial in relation to the value of the goods. Thus, the dishonor of the draft and rejection of the goods by the buyer can create economic circumstances where seller's only rational option is a distress sale in buyer's nation. This risk to seller is inherent in the payment against documents transaction, unless seller requires that buyer also procure the issuance of a letter of credit. (See Chapter 3 for a complete description and discussion of the letter of credit transaction.)

On the other hand, for its payment of the price, buyer has a document from carrier entitling it to delivery of the goods, an insurance certificate protecting buyer against casualty loss and perhaps an inspection certificate warranting that the goods conform to the sale contract. In other words, buyer should receive what it bargained for—delivery of conforming goods or insurance proceeds sufficient to cover any loss. However, without the ability to inspect the actual goods before payment, buyer cannot be absolutely assured that they conform to the contract.

What can go wrong from the buyer's point of view? There are *at least* six problems which could arise:

(a) The goods could be lost or stolen.

(b) The carrier could stow the goods or operate so negligently that they are damaged in transit.

(c) The goods shipped could be non-conforming to the sales contract. The non-conformity could range from (1) the seller shipping scrap paper to (2) the labelling on the packaging being incorrect (which can cause problems with customs agents in both countries).

(d) The bill of lading and attached draft could be stolen and presented to buyer by a thief—with any necessary indorsements having been forged.

(e) The goods could fail to conform to the bill of lading, so that the documents state that goods of a particular description will be delivered, and the goods actually delivered are of a different description.

(f) The bill of lading could be forged—and no goods were shipped.

Some of these problems are recognized and dealt with in the standard handling of the "payment against documents" transaction. For example, insuring the goods against loss or theft is standard practice in the CIF transaction. Other problems, such as payment before inspection, make buyers feel unprotected, and they have searched for devices within the transaction which can afford them more protection. Such a device, in common use in modern transactions, is the Inspection Certificate.

Three of these problems are uniquely related to any transaction using a bill of lading, and will be considered in the materials below:

(a) The loss of the bill of lading, followed by the forgery of a necessary indorsement and carrier's misdelivery (delivery of the goods to the wrong person under a bill of lading).

(b) The misdescription of the goods by the shipper and in the bill of lading followed by carrier's delivery of goods which do not conform to the description in the bill of lading.

(c) The forgery of a complete bill of lading by shipper without carrier's knowledge.

BILLS OF LADING

As to regulation of the transfer of the bill of lading, UCC Article 7 would appear to regulate these relationships, but in fact, except for intrastate transactions, the UCC is preempted by federal law. The Federal Bill of Lading Act (formerly called the Pomerene Act), 49 U.S.C.A. §§ 80101–80116, governs the transfer and transferability of all bills of lading generated to cover both international and interstate shipments. The form and content of bills of lading are also governed by the Harter Act, 46 U.S.C.A. §§ 190–196, and the Carriage of Goods by Sea Act, 46 U.S.C.A. App. §§ 1300–1315. With this multiplicity of statutes governing the terms of the bill of lading and its use, conflicting concepts from overlapping statutes should be expected. Congress has recently recodified the Federal Bill of Lading Act. It did not intend to change the substance of the Act, but it did reorganize, reword and consolidate the prior provisions and change all the section numbers.

The Federal Bill of Lading Act governs all interstate and international shipments which use a bill of lading issued by a common carrier. By its terms, the statute governs the bill of lading if the goods are shipped from the United States to another country. The word "carrier" is not defined, so it is not clear whether documents issued by freight forwarders are covered. Further, the term "bill of lading" is not defined, so it is not clear whether air waybills or inland waterway documents are included.

There are two different types of bills of lading—a "straight," or non-negotiable, bill of lading, and an "order," or negotiable, bill of lading. (These are also known in the trade as "white" and "yellow" for the different colors of paper on which they are often printed.) Each usually represents the shipper's contract with the carrier, and will set forth the terms of that contract expressly or incorporate a carrier's terms and tariffs by reference.

MISDELIVERY

A non-negotiable, or "straight," bill of lading is issued to a named person, the consignee. Under a non-negotiable bill of lading, the carrier obligates itself to deliver the goods at the destination point to the consignee named in the bill of lading. 49 U.S.C.A. § 80110. Possession of the actual straight bill of lading does not confer rights over the goods or against the carrier to a person in possession of the paper who is not the consignee. Further, indorsements on such a straight bill of lading are irrelevant to making the bill negotiable or to giving rights to the indorsee. In short, the carrier is liable to the consignee of a straight bill of lading for misdelivery if it delivers the goods to anyone but the consignee or a person whom the consignee delegates to receive them. Thus, straight bills of lading are not appropriate for a "payment against documents" transaction, and the case reporters are full of litigation where an attorney tried a short-cut using a straight bill of lading as the "easy" way to do this transaction—and sacrificed the client's interests. Straight bills of lading are also called "air waybills," "sea waybills" and "freight receipts," depending upon the intended method of main transportation for the goods.

An "order," or negotiable, bill of lading is issued to a named person "or order." This allows the named person (the consignee) to indorse the bill of lading to "order" delivery of the goods to others. If possession of the bill of lading is transferred to a third party, and the bill of lading is indorsed to that third party (either specially or in blank), then the third party becomes a "holder" of the bill of lading. Under a negotiable bill of lading, the carrier obligates itself to deliver the goods to the "holder" of the bill of lading at the destination point. 46 U.S.C.A. § 80110. Thus, possession of the negotiable bill of lading becomes crucial. The carrier must see the actual bill of lading both to determine who has possession and to determine to whom the indorsements run.

Therefore, possession of the actual negotiable bill of lading, properly indorsed, does confer rights over the goods and against the carrier to the person in possession of the paper, the "holder." The original consignee may indorse the negotiable bill of lading either "in blank" by a bare signature ("Ralph Folsom") or by a "special indorsement," which specifies the name of the intended holder ("Deliver the goods to Michael Gordon, or order. Ralph Folsom"). 46 U.S.C.A. § 80104. Under a blank indorsement, any person in possession becomes a holder, and is entitled to demand delivery from the carrier. Under a special indorsement, only the named indorsee can become a holder, and only that person can demand delivery from the carrier or indorse the bill of lading to another party so as to make it a holder. Thus, the special indorsement protects the interests of the parties from thieves and forgers much better than a blank indorsement.

In short, the carrier is liable to the holder of a negotiable bill of lading for misdelivery if it delivers the goods to anyone but the holder. 49 U.S.C.A. § 80111. In this sense the negotiable bill of lading is a "document of title," because possession of it, properly indorsed, controls title to the document, title to the goods, and the direct obligation of the carrier to hold the goods and deliver them to the holder of the document. For this reason, the negotiable bill of lading is appropriate for a "payment against documents" transaction. The collecting banks can use their possession of such bills of lading to control title to both the goods and the document until they have collected the price from the buyer. Some other commercial nations have only "straight" bills of lading and not negotiable bills of lading, but most commentators believe the United States' system is preferable.

The holder of the bill of lading does not have absolute title to the goods in all cases, but nearly so. If the shipper is not the owner of the goods, for example if the goods have been stolen at gunpoint from the "true owner," then no holder of the bill of lading will have title because the shipper's claim of title was void. However, if the owner voluntarily parted with the goods but was defrauded by the shipper (a "cash sale" in which the check bounces later), then the shipper obtains voidable title (UCC § 2–403) and can pass good title to a holder of the document who purchases it in good faith for value without notice. 49 U.S.C.A. § 80105. The rights of such a good faith holder for value are also superior to any seller's lien or right to stop delivery of the goods in transit.

Under the Federal Bill of Lading Act, as under the UCC, any forgery of a necessary indorsement is not effective to create or transfer rights, whether the forgery is perfect or inept. Further, any unauthorized signature by an agent is treated as a forgery, as long as it was made without actual, implied or apparent authority. The protection is illustrated in the situation where a thief steals a negotiable bill of lading from the holder who was in possession of the document under a special indorsement. As such, the holder's indorsement is necessary to transfer rights to the document or goods to any other party. Without that indorsement, the thief is not a holder and has no rights to the document or goods. If the thief forges the holder's signature, that forgery is ineffective, and the thief is still not a holder and still has no rights. If the thief transfers the document to another party, that party also is not a holder and cannot obtain rights under the document without the holder's signature. *Adel Precision Products Corp. v. Grand Trunk Western R. Co.*, 332 Mich. 519, 51 N.W.2d 922 (1952). The carrier is still obligated to deliver the goods only to the holder, the victim of the theft.

Thus, if a collecting bank or other party takes the document under a special indorsement, it is protected from loss from theft of the paper and forgery, and even from unauthorized transfer by an agent.

If the carrier does deliver to the forger, or to someone who received the document from the forger without the holder's indorsement, the carrier is liable for misdelivery under 49 U.S.C.A. § 80111. The forger is also liable, if he can be found. The person who received the goods and other transferees have all made warranties under 49 U.S.C.A. § 80107 that they had "a right to transfer the bill and title to the goods," when they had no such rights or title.

The concept is that each person who takes the bill of lading should "know your indorser." If the goods are misdelivered, the party most easily found is the one who received the goods, and that party is liable. That party then has a warranty action against its transferor—and it is the person involved most likely to be able to find that transferor. The transferor, in turn, has a warranty action against its transferor—and so on back up the chain of transfers. This is not very efficient, but the purpose is to push liability back up the chain of transfers to the person who took from the forger, or even to the forger himself. (In the meantime, the holder collects from the misdelivering carrier, which collects from its insuror.)

Collecting banks which transfer the document for value can be subject to this warranty liability. If the buyer pays, and those funds are transmitted to the forger, then the collecting banks have received value. However, such banks have at least three potential escape valves. One is to disclaim such warranty liability when indorsing the negotiable bill of lading. The statutory warranties do not arise if "a contrary intention appears." Thus, an indorsement "XYZ Bank Prior indorsements not guaranteed" would clearly disclaim liability for such a warranty. A second avenue is to claim that the bank is only holding the document "as security for a debt," for the statute exempts such holders from warranty liability. The difficulty with this avenue is that a collecting bank does not pay the seller until after it receives payment, so it never becomes a creditor, secured or otherwise. The third avenue is the I.C.C. "Uniform Rules for Collection" (1978), which provide that banks have no obligation to examine documents, other than to verify that they "appear to be as listed in the collection order." (Article 2.) That may indicate a corporate, blanket "contrary intention" under the statute. Any bank found to have warranty liability can pass this liability back to its transferor, as long as it can identify that transferor.

MISDESCRIPTION

The carrier in a shipment transaction has no privity with the contract between buyer and seller for the sale of goods, and therefore has no obligation to deliver goods that conform to the sale contract. However, the goods are described in the bill of lading which constitutes part of the carriage contract. Thus, the carrier does have an obligation to deliver goods which conform to the description in the bill of lading. Under the Federal Bills of Lading Act, a carrier is liable for any failure to deliver goods which correspond to the description in the bill of lading, either as to quantity or as to quality. 49 U.S.C.A. § 80113. This obligation is owed the owner of the goods under a straight bill of lading and to the holder of a negotiable bill of lading.

The problem with this obligation is that the carrier usually does not know what it is carrying, since the goods are often in containers. Thus, the carrier knows that it received a container which was labelled "100 IBM word-processing computers." It will not, and is not expected to, open the container to check whether it contains computers, or to count how many items there are in it. Even if it opened the container, it would not be expected to check whether each computer is in working order. Even if it did so check, it is not likely to have the expertise to determine whether each computer can perform the necessary routines to be a word processor. Thus, the carrier is not expected to warrant the description and capability of packaged goods given to it to transport.

To solve this problem, carriers are allowed, under the Federal Bills of Lading Act, to effectively disclaim their obligations to deliver goods which conform to the description. 49 U.S.C.A. § 80113(b).

Appropriate disclaimer language is set forth in the statute, and includes:

"contents or condition of contents of packages unknown",

"said to contain", and

"shipper's weight, load, and count".

Other language conveying the same meaning can be used; the statutory linguistic formulas are not required.

The disclaimers are not effective if the carrier knows that the goods do not conform. The protection is available only to the uninformed carrier. However, when goods are loaded by a carrier, the carrier is obligated to count the number of packages and is expected to note the condition of the packages. The carrier is also obligated to "determine the kind and quantity" (but not the quality) of any bulk freight that it loads. For bulk freight, even where it is loaded by the shipper, the carrier must still determine the kind and quantity of the freight if the shipper so requests and provides adequate facilities for the carrier to weigh the freight. In situations where the carrier must count packages or weigh the goods, disclaimers (such as "shipper's weight, load, and count") will not be effective.

Thus, what is established is a system in which the carrier is responsible for checking some quantity terms, the number of cartons and the weight of a shipment. These are items which the carrier is likely to check in any event, to be certain that some cartons are not inadvertently left behind, and to determine the appropriate freight charge. However, the carrier is not required to check most quality terms, such as what goods are in a container and whether they are in operating condition or not. In the latter case, it can truthfully say that it has received 100 cartons "said to contain" IBM word processing computers, without opening the cartons; but it does need to count the number of cartons. The intersection of these rules arises when the carrier accepts a sealed container supposed to contain 2000 tin ingots weighing 35 tons, and issues a bill of lading for a container "said to contain 2000 tin ingots." If the container is empty, weighs less than a ton and the carrier does not weigh it, the carrier's disclaimer is not likely to protect it. *Berisford Metals Corp. v. S/S Salvador*, 779 F.2d 841 (2d Cir.1985).

According to the statutory provision, all of these disclaimers are effective only if the seller loads the goods. 49 U.S.C.A. 80113(b)(1). This restriction seems appropriate for disclaimers of the "shipper's weight, load, and count" variety, but seems inapposite for disclaimers of the "said to contain" or "contents or condition of contents of packages unknown" variety. There are cases which require shipper actually to load, however, in the sense that the carrier is liable for misdescription despite "shipper's weight, load and count," if carrier issues a bill of lading and the shipper has in fact never loaded anything on board the carrier's cars. See, e.g., *Chi-*

cago and N.W. Ry. Co. v. Stephens Nat. Bank, 75 F.2d 398 (8th Cir.1935).

THE FORGED BILL OF LADING

If the carrier issues a bill of lading for which there are no goods, the carrier is likely to be liable to the holder. However, suppose the carrier never issued any bill of lading. Instead, a person unrelated to the carrier created (forged) the bill of lading, with no authority from the carrier. The buyer who purchases such a forged bill of lading has paid funds to a forger, probably through a series of banks, and finds that the carrier has no goods to deliver. There is no misdelivery or misdescription claim against the carrier, for there never were any goods delivered to the carrier for it to redeliver or to describe. If the carrier did not issue the bill of lading and its "signature" is a forgery or unauthorized, that signature is not "effective," and carrier will not be liable on the bill, absent some sort of actionable negligence.

The forger is liable for the fraud, if he can be found. Unlike the forged indorsement situation, there is no one who has received any goods, for there never were any goods to deliver. However, like the forged indorsement situation, each party that transferred the bill of lading for value makes warranties to later parties, and the first warranty is that "the bill is genuine." 49 U.S.C.A. § 80107. If the bill of lading itself is forged that warranty is breached. Thus, all parties who transferred the bill and received payment funds can be liable to breach of warranty actions against them by later parties. The concept is that the last person to purchase the bill will "know its indorser," and be able to recover against its transferor. That transferor can, in turn, recover against *its* transferor, and so on up the chain of transfers, until the loss falls either on the forger or upon the person who dealt with and took the bill from the forger.

Collecting banks which have transferred the document for value can be subject to this warranty liability, but have the same three potential escape values discussed under forged indorsements. (1) A disclaimer of warranty through making "a contrary intention appear." (2) A claim that the bank is holding the document only "as security for a debt." (3) The limitation in the I.C.C. Collection Rules that banks need examine only the appearance of the documents. Each of these approaches has analytical difficulties, as is discussed above, but they may indicate a corporate, blanket intention to disclaim the statutory warranties implicitly. Any bank which is found to have warranty liability can pass this liability back to its transferor, as long as it can identify and find that transferor.

ELECTRONIC BILLS OF LADING

The Federal Bills of Lading Act does not define "bill of lading" and does not require that it be written on a piece of paper or signed by anyone. Thus, use of electronic bills of lading would seem to be a technical possibility. However, all of the primary rules of the federal law are filled with an implicit assumption that the bill of lading is a paper document. The references to indorsement (in blank or to a specified person), transfer by delivery and "person in possession" (holder) make sense only in a paper document transaction.

However, telecommunications technology can provide electronic messages which perform the main functions of the bill of lading: as a receipt, transport contract and document of title. Thus, several types of bill of lading equivalents are currently in use, but most of them are used only as receipts for the goods generated by the carrier. Their utility is enhanced where a "straight," or non-negotiable, bill of lading (or waybill) does not need to be presented to a carrier to obtain possession of the goods. Unfortunately, the Federal Bills of Lading Act requires the carrier to deliver the goods only to a person who "has possession of the bill," even under a straight bill of lading (49 U.S.C.A. § 80110(a)(2)), and makes the carrier liable for damages if it does not take and cancel the bill when delivering the goods. 49 U.S.C.A. § 80110(c). These requirements are often ignored by carriers in practice, and the parties merely exchange printed forms, but the statutory requirements do inhibit the acceptance of electronic bills of lading in the United States.

Despite these requirements, the Interstate Commerce Commission now authorizes the use of uniform electronic bills of lading, both negotiable and non-negotiable, for both motor carrier and rail carrier use. These have been authorized since 1982 and 1988 respectively. There is an assumption that such electronic bills of lading merely communicate information about the goods, the shipper and the consignee. There are no provisions defining the rights and obligations of the parties to the electronic bill. Thus, the bills do not allow for further sale or rerouting of the goods in transit, or for using the bills of lading to finance the transaction. Under the regulations, negotiable uniform electronic bills of lading must "provide for endorsement on the back portion," but there is no explanation of how an electronic message has a "back portion," or how "endorsement" is to be effected.

There have been several programs to create electronic carrier-issued international receipts for goods. Atlantic Container Lines used dedicated lines between terminals at its offices in different ports to send messages between those offices. It generated a Data Freight Receipt which was given to the consignee or notify party. Such a receipt was not negotiable and gave buyers and banks little protection from further sale or rerouting of the goods by shipper in transit. The Cargo Key Receipt was similar, but also an advance over the prior approach, because it included a "no disposal" term in the shipper-carrier contract. Thus, this electronic message protected buyer from further sale or rerouting by seller in transit. It still could not be used to finance the transfer, however, because the electronic receipt, even if it named a bank as consignee, was not formally a negotiable document of title. The receipt was believed to give the bank only the right to prevent delivery to the buyer, not a positive right to take control of the goods for itself.

The Chase Manhattan Bank created the SEA-DOCS Registry which was intended to create a negotiable electronic bill of lading for oil shipments. The Registry acted as custodian for an actual paper negotiable bill of lading issued by a carrier, and maintained a registry of transfers of that bill from the original shipper to the ultimate "holder." The transfers were made by a series of electronic messages, each of which could be authenticated by "test keys", or identification numbers, generated by SEA-DOCS. SEADOCS would then, as agent, endorse the paper bill of lading in its custody. At the end, SEADOCS would electronically deliver a paper copy of the negotiable bill of lading to the last endorsee to enable it to obtain the goods from the carrier. While SEADOCS was a legal success, showing that such a program was technically feasible; it was not a commercial success, lasting less than a year.

The Comite Maritime International (CMI) has adopted Rules for Electronic Bills of Lading (1990). Under those rules, any carrier can issue an electronic bill of lading as long as it will act as a clearinghouse for subsequent transfers. Upon receiving goods, the carrier sends an electronic message to the shipper describing the goods, the contract terms and a "private key" which can be used to transfer shipper's rights to a third party. Under the CMI Rules, the shipper now has the "right of control and transfer" over the goods, and is called a "holder." Under Rules 4 and 7, an electronic message from shipper which includes the private key can be used to transfer the shipper's rights to a third party, who then becomes a new holder. The carrier then cancels the shipper's "private key" and issues a different private key to the new holder. Upon arrival, the carrier will deliver the goods to the then-current holder or a consignee designated by the holder

The original parties to the transaction agree that the CMI Rules will govern the "communications" aspects of the transaction. All parties also agree that electronic messages satisfy any national law requirements that a bill of lading be in writing. This is an attempt to create an "electronic" writing which is a negotiable document of title by contract and estoppel. Some commentators have observed that this is an attempt by private parties to create a negotiable document, a power usually reserved to legislatures.

The Commission of the European Committees has sponsored the BOLERO electronic bill of lading initiative, which is based on the CMI Rules. However, under the BOLERO system, neither a bank nor a carrier is the repository of the sensitive information of who has bought and sold the cargo covered by the electronic bills of lading. Instead BOLERO establishes a third party who is independent of the shipper, the carrier, the ultimate buyer and all intermediate parties as the operator of the central registry.

American bankers have been skeptical of the device created by the CMI Rules. The registries maintained by each carrier do not have the same level of security associated with SWIFT procedures. (See "Electronic Letters of Credit" in Chapter 3.) In addition to fraudulent transactions, there is a risk of misdirected messages. Thus, a bank could find itself relying on "non-existent rights based upon fraudulent information in a receipt message transmitted to it by someone pretending to be the carrier." The banks are concerned as to whether carriers will accept liability in their new role as electronic registrars for losses due to such fraudulent practices. See Winship, in Current Developments Concerning the Forms of Lading (A.N. Yiannaopolis ed. 1995). The banks are also concerned that the full terms and conditions of the contract of carriage are not available to subsequent "holders." Thus, use of the CMI Rules does not yet seem to be widely adopted, and bills of lading are still primarily paper-based in both the "payment against documents" and letter of credit transactions.

The experiments discussed above all attempted to substitute an electronic message for the paper-based bill of lading, but otherwise did not change the bill of lading system. A very different approach is proposed in an experiment called Trade Card, discussed in more detail in Chapter 3.

CHAPTER THREE

FINANCING THE INTERNATION-AL TRADING OF GOODS

THE INTERNATIONAL DOCUMENTARY SALE AND DOCUMENTARY LETTER OF CREDIT

THE PROBLEM

Unlike most domestic sales transactions, in a sale of goods across national borders the exporter-seller and importer-buyer may not have previously dealt with one another; or each may know nothing about the other, or the other's national legal system. The seller does not know: (1) whether buyer is credit-worthy or trustworthy; (2) whether information received on these subjects from buyer's associates is reliable; (3) whether exchange controls will hinder movement of the payment funds (especially if in "hard currency"); (4) how great is the exchange risk if payment in buyer's currency is permitted, and (5) what delays may be involved in receiving unencumbered funds from buyer.

On the other hand, buyer does not know: (1) whether seller can be trusted to ship the goods if buyer prepays; (2) whether the goods shipped will be of the quantity and quality contracted for; (3) whether the goods will be shipped by an appropriate carrier and properly insured; (4) whether the goods may be damaged in transit; (5) whether the seller will furnish to buyer sufficient ownership documentation covering the goods to allow buyer to claim them from the customs officials; (6) whether seller will provide the documentation necessary to satisfy export control regulations and import customs and valuation regulations (e.g., country of origin certificates, health and other inspection certificates); and (7) what delays may be involved in receiving unencumbered possession and use of the goods in the buyer-importer's location.

Where the parties are strangers, these risks are significant, possibly overwhelming. Since they operate at a distance from each other, seller and buyer cannot concurrently exchange the goods for the payment funds *without the help of third parties*. The documentary sale, involving the use of a letter of credit, illustrates how these potentially large risks can be distributed to third parties who have special knowledge, can properly evaluate each risk assumed, and thereby can reduce the transaction risks to insignificance.

THE DOCUMENTARY SALE TRANSACTION

The third party intermediaries enlisted are banks (at least one in buyer's nation and usually a second one in seller's nation) and at least one carrier. Thus, the parties involved are: (1) a buyer, who is also presumably a "customer" of (2) Buyer's Bank,

(3) a seller, (4) a bank with an office in seller's nation (hereafter "Seller's Bank"), and (5) at least one carrier. Among them, these parties are able to take a large risk which is not subject to any firm evaluation, and divide it into several small, calculable risks, each of which is easily borne by one party. Thus, the documentary sale is an example that not all risk allocation is a "zero sum game," but may in fact create a "win-win" situation.

These parties will be related by a series of contracts—but not all of the parties to the transaction will be parties to each contract. The contracts include (A) the sale of goods contract between buyer and seller; (B) the bill of lading, a receipt and contract issued by the carrier; and (C) the letter of credit, a promise by Buyer's Bank (and, if confirmed, also by Seller's Bank) to pay seller under certain conditions concerning proof that seller has shipped the goods.

(A) The contract underlying the entire series of transactions is the contract for the sale of goods from buyer to seller. Buyer and seller are parties to this contract, but the banks and the carrier are not parties. Seller is responsible to deliver the contracted quantity and quality of goods, and buyer is responsible for taking the goods and paying the stated price. (For conditions and further elaborations on this point, see the discussion of the Convention on Contracts for the International Sale of Goods in Chapter 2.)

(B) In documentary sales, buyers and sellers are usually distant from each other, and the goods must be moved. Thus, an international carrier of the goods is usually employed, and either seller or buyer will make a contract with the carrier to transport the goods. (For our illustration, seller will make that contract.) Seller (or, in the language of a contract of carriage, "shipper") makes a contract with carrier that the goods will be transported to buyer's ("consignee's") location.

This second contract in our transaction will be expressed in the "bill of lading" issued by the carrier. Under the terms of the bill of lading contract, in return for payment of the freight charge, carrier promises to deliver the goods to either (1) the named "consignee" in a "straight" (or non-negotiable) bill of lading, or (2) the person in possession ("holder") of an "order" (or negotiable) bill of lading. The order (negotiable) bill of lading should be used in the documentary sale (letter of credit transaction), so that the buyer is able to obtain delivery of goods *only if* buyer has physical possession of the bill of lading. Such a bill of lading controls access to and delivery of the goods, so that the bill of lading is also a "document of title."

(C) Before seller ("shipper") delivers the goods to the carrier, seller wants assurance that payment will be forthcoming. A promise from buyer may not be sufficient. Even a promise from a bank in buyer's nation may not be sufficient, because seller does not know them or know about them. Instead, seller wants a promise from a bank known to it, and preferably in seller's location.

What seller wants is the third contract in our transaction—a confirmed, irrevocable letter of credit. A letter of credit is a contract—a promise by a bank (usually Buyer's Bank) that it will pay to seller (or, "will honor drafts drawn on this bank by seller for") the amount of the contract price. The bank's promise is conditioned upon seller's presenting evidence that the goods have been shipped via carrier to arrive in buyer's port, along with any other documents required by the contract for the sale of goods. What would furnish such evidence? The bill of lading between seller and carrier, the second contract in our transaction, furnishes the evidence that seller has shipped the goods.

Further, if it is a negotiable bill of lading, it also controls the right to obtain the goods from carrier. Thus, a negotiable bill of lading delivered by seller to Seller's Bank will assure Bank that: (1) the goods have been delivered to carrier, (2) they are destined for buyer and not some third party, and (3) Bank can control carrier's delivery of the goods to buyer by simply retaining possession of the order bill of lading. In other words, when a bank pays seller, it receives from seller a "document of title" issued by carrier which gives the bank control of carrier's delivery of the goods. Buyer cannot obtain possession of the goods from a carrier without physical possession of the bill of lading, so after the banks have paid seller for that piece of paper, they can obtain payment (or assurances that buyer will pay them) before buyer receives the ability to obtain the goods from carrier.

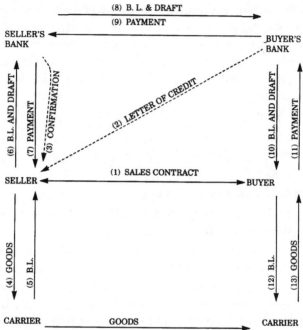

How does the international documentary sales transaction work? An international documentary sale is diagramed above. When buyer and seller are forming their contract for the sale of the goods, seller will insist that the contract have both a "Price" term and a "Payment" term. For maximum protection, seller will seek payment to be by "Confirmed, Irrevocable Letter of Credit," and should specify what documents are required with great detail. The reason for putting this payment term in the sales contract is that, since buyer is expected to establish a letter of credit and "to pay against the documents," rather than after delivery and inspection of the goods themselves, that payment term must be bargained for and expressed in the sales contract. It will not normally be implied.

What documents will be required? Usually, they include the:

(1) negotiable bill of lading (showing transportation company's receipt of the goods to be shipped and obligation to deliver them only to the holder of the document)

(2) commercial invoice (which sets out the terms of purchase such as grade and number of goods, price, etc.)

(3) policy of marine insurance (if goods are to go by sea)

(4) certificate of inspection (issued by a commercial inspecting firm and confirming that the required number and type of goods are being shipped)

(5) export license and/or health inspection certificate (showing that the goods are cleared for export)

(6) certificate of origin (relevant to the rules of origin used by customs personnel in importer's country for determining tariff assessments).

If buyer agrees to a letter of credit payment term, buyer (or, in the language of the letter of credit, the "account party" or "customer") will contract with

Buyer's Bank ("issuer" or "issuing bank") to issue a letter of credit ("credit") to seller ("beneficiary"). The letter of credit is a direct promise by the issuing bank that it will pay the contract price to seller ("beneficiary"), if seller presents to it the documents specified in the letter of credit (and previously in the sales contract). Buyer's Bank will be aware of buyer's creditworthiness, and will make appropriate arrangements to receive the funds from buyer (through either immediate payment or future repayment of a loan). These arrangements will be made before the letter of credit is issued, for Buyer's Bank is bound to the letter of credit terms after issuance if it is irrevocable.

If seller requires an obligation of a bank known to seller, the letter of credit must be confirmed by a Seller's Bank ("confirming bank"). Buyer's Bank will forward its letter of credit to seller through another bank, Seller's Bank. By merely indicating "We confirm this credit," Seller's Bank makes a direct promise to seller that it will pay the contract price to seller, if seller presents the required documents to it. If no confirmation of the credit is required by the sales contract, Buyer's Bank can forward the letter of credit through a "notifying bank" or an "advising bank" which is near seller. These banks will not be obligated to seller, but will take the documents and forward them to Buyer's Bank for collection purposes only.

Once the letter of credit is issued and confirmed, seller will pack the goods and prepare a commercial invoice, and procure an insurance certificate (another form of contract) covering the goods during transit. If an inspection certificate is required, the goods will be made available to the inspector designated in the sales contract, and the inspecting firm will issue a certificate (another contract) stating that the goods conform to the description in the sales contract. Seller will also prepare the necessary documents for the customs officials in its nation (e.g., export license) and in buyer's nation (certificate of origin). Seller then sends the goods to the carrier, which issues a negotiable bill of lading as a combination receipt and contract. This bill of lading will commonly require carrier to deliver the goods only "to seller or order"—i.e., only to seller or a person seller may designate by an appropriate endorsement.

Seller now has the complete set of documents needed, and takes these documents to Seller's Bank, which (as a confirming bank) is obligated to pay seller the contract price upon presentation of the documents. To obtain payment, seller attaches a "draft" to the documents; and in the letter of credit the banks have promised to honor such a draft. The draft (sometimes also called a "bill of exchange") resembles a check written by seller and drawn on Seller's Bank or on Buyer's Bank for the amount of the contract price. A draft can be payable on demand ("at sight") in a cash sale, or payable at a later time (e.g. "30 days after sight") in a credit sale. If a "demand draft" is used, the bank will pay the amount immediately, usually by crediting seller's bank account; if a time draft is used, the bank will "accept" it (write on it the bank's promise to pay it later). In the latter case, seller can still raise funds immediately by selling the paper on the strength of the bank's credit.

Seller's Bank never sees the goods, only the documents—so the bank inspects the documents rigorously to determine that they comply exactly with the requirements of the letter of credit, for the documents are its only protection. Substantial performance by seller is not acceptable. Thus, where a credit called for "100% acrylic yarn" and the invoice stated "imported acrylic yarn", the credit was not satisfied, even though the packing list stated "100% acrylic yarn". *Courtaulds North America, Inc. v. North Carolina Nat. Bank,* 528 F.2d 802 (4th Cir.1975).

In return for the bank's payment, seller will endorse both the draft and the negotiable bill of lading to Seller's Bank and transfer the other documents to it. Seller's Bank, in turn, will endorse and present the draft and its accompanying documents to Buyer's Bank, which is obligated under the letter of credit to "honor" (accept) the draft and reimburse Seller's Bank if the documents attached to the draft are conforming. Buyer's Bank then contacts buyer and presents the documents to buyer for payment. Buyer, like the banks, must pay "against the documents" and not the goods themselves, which is why it is necessary to specify the terms of the documents in the original contract for the sale of goods, and then repeat those specifications precisely in the letter of credit. Once buyer has paid, or arranged to pay, Buyer's Bank, it will obtain possession of the bill of lading and only then will it be entitled to obtain the goods from carrier.

Note the limited risks to each party. If seller ships conforming goods, it has independent promises of payment from both buyer and two banks. The banks' promises are enforceable despite assertions of non-conformity of the goods, so long as the documents conform. Thus, as a practical matter, seller is at risk only if Seller's Bank fails (and also Buyer's Bank and buyer), a risk it can probably evaluate. If Seller's Bank unjustifiably refuses to perform its obligation, seller has a cause of action in a local court against a "deep pocket defendant."

Even though Seller's Bank is obligated to pay seller on the documents, it is entitled to reimbursement from Buyer's Bank and from buyer, and practically is at risk only if Buyer's Bank (and buyer) fails or refuses to perform its obligation—risks which Seller's Bank should be able to evaluate accurately. Buyer's Bank is at risk only if buyer fails or refuses to perform, risks which Buyer's Bank had an opportunity to evaluate before issuing the letter of credit, and for which it could adjust its price (interest rate).

On the other hand, for its payment of the price, buyer has a document from carrier entitling it to delivery of the goods, an insurance certificate protecting buyer against casualty loss and perhaps an inspection certificate warranting that the goods conform to the sale contract. In other words, buyer should receive what it bargained for—delivery of conforming goods or insurance proceeds sufficient to cover any loss.

THE GOVERNING RULES

The law relating to letters of credit developed before World War I principally in England, and thereafter by courts in the United States. In the United States, the governing law is usually the applicable state's version of Article 5 of the Uniform Commercial Code. However, most of UCC Article 5 is not mandatory law, and therefore most Article 5 provisions defer to the contract terms of the parties as expressed in the contract. The International Chamber of Commerce (I.C.C.) has developed and published the Uniform Customs and Practices for Documentary Credits (the UCP), which is incorporated by reference in most international letters of credit. The UCP constitutes a rather detailed manual of operations for banks, but they are a restatement of "custom" in the industry, and they do not purport to be law. They are incorporated as an express statement of contract terms and banking trade usage, and the UCP contract terms furnish the rules which usually determine the actions of the parties. In New York, Alabama, Arizona and Missouri, a non-uniform amendment in UCC § 5–102(4) states that the UCP alone governs if it is incorporated into the credit. That provision should make such credits subject to 1940s caselaw, but the relevant courts have wisely ignored the provision or used UCC Article 5 by analogy, when necessary.

Both UCC Article 5 and the UCP have recently been revised. The Revised Article 5 was adopted by the Uniform Commissioners and the American Law Institute in 1995, and has been enacted by 40 state legislatures, although not yet by New York. The most recent version of the UCP is the 1993 Revision (I.C.C. Publ. No. 500). The rules set forth in each are relatively similar, but there are some differences. The UCP provisions will have more impact on the analysis of non-fraud issues, and the UCC Article 5 provisions will be used to resolve issues related to allegations of fraud. Therefore, this chapter will describe the UCP rules for all non-fraud issues, and the UCC provisions on fraud.

The UCP establishes four categories of banks in the letter of credit transaction: an issuing bank, an advising bank, a confirming bank, and a nominated bank. An issuing bank promises to honor drafts on itself, if the documents stated in the letter of credit (conforming documents) are presented to it. An advising bank advises the beneficiary (usually the Seller) of the documentary credit, but makes no promise to pay against documents. It is obligated to take "reasonable care" to check the authenticity of the credit before advising, but is not otherwise obligated. A confirming bank receives the credit from the issuing bank and adds its own promise to honor drafts presented to it if accompanied by conforming documents. A nominated bank is a bank in Seller's locality designated by the issuing bank to pay or negotiate the drafts which accompany the required documents. It may, or may not, be a confirming bank.

There are two basic principles of the letter of credit rules promulgated by the UCP (and also of UCC Article 5). One is that the banks' obligations under the letter of credit are independent of the buyer's and seller's obligations under the contract for the sale of goods. (UCP Article 3.) The second is that banks deal only with documents, and not with performance of the underlying sales contract. (UCP Article 4.) The promises of an issuing bank or a confirming bank are not subject to claims or defenses by the applicant (Buyer) that the beneficiary (Seller) has not performed its obligations under the sales contract. (UCP Article 3(a).) However, the bank's promises may still be subject to claims by the applicant (Buyer) of fraud by the beneficiary (Seller), as will be discussed below. The UCP has no provisions concerning fraud, and therefore such issues must be analyzed under UCC Article 5, where U.S. law is applicable.

Since the banks pay the beneficiary (Seller) against the documents, and never see the goods, banks insist on "perfect tender" and "strict compliance" with all documentary conditions. The primary document for describing the goods in a documentary sale transaction is the commercial invoice. The description in the commercial invoice must be specific and must "correspond with the description in the credit;" descriptions in all other documents can be general and need only be "consistent" with the description in the credit. English courts gained renown by determining that "machine shelled groundnut kernels" was not the same description as "Coromandel groundnuts," even though it was agreed that the same goods were described by either label. Bankers could not be expected to know that, or to find it out. *J.H. Rayner & Co. Ltd. v. Hambro's Bank, Ltd.* [1943] 1 K.B. 36 (Court of Appeal).

The more difficult litigated issues concerning the strict conformity of documents seem to arise in transportation terms. Express conditions in the credit that loading, presentment or other acts must be performed by a certain time will be strictly enforced. A credit calling for "Full Set Clean On board ocean bills of lading" is not satisfied by a tender of "truckers bills of lading," even though evidence was presented that the bills of lading were in customary Mexican form and that Mexican truckers did not specify on the bill of lading that the goods were "on board." *Marine Midland Grace Trust Co. of N.Y. v. Banco Del Pais, S.A.*, 261 F.Supp. 884 (S.D.N.Y.1966).

However, there are circumstances in which the courts may seem to use a different standard. Suppose the seller-shipper does not prepay the freight charges on a CIF contract, but instead credits the freight charges against the amount of the invoice price, and then submits the resulting documents to the issuing bank. Should the issuing bank reject the documents, and refuse to pay the draft accompanying the documents, as non-conforming? Such documents do not strictly comply with CIF terms. However, in *Dixon, Irmaos & Cia, Ltda v. Chase Nat.*

Bank, 144 F.2d 759 (2d Cir.1944), the court held
that the documents were conforming because of
"ancient usage" which permitted shippers to take
such action. Other types of discrepancies which
seem not to warrant rejection include technically
invalid clauses in bills of lading which limit the
carrier's liability. *British IMEX Indus., Ltd. v. Midland Bank, Ltd.*, [1958] 1 All Eng.Rep. 264. A line
of American cases which seemed to permit payment
upon substantial performance by the beneficiary
(*Banco Espanol de Credito v. State Street Bank &
Trust Co.*, 385 F.2d 230 (1st Cir.1967), cert. denied
390 U.S. 1013 (1968)), has now been rejected by the
Revised Article 5 (Revised § 5–108 and Comment).

Discrepancies in tendered documents are an everyday occurrence. Expert testimony in one case
stated that discrepancies are discovered in nearly
one half of all documentary transactions (*Banker's
Trust Co. v. State Bank of India*, [1991] 1 Lloyd's
Rep. 587, affirmed [1991] 2 Lloyd's Rep. 443 (C.A.)).
Other commentary and cases indicate between one
half and two thirds of all such presentations contain
at least one discrepancy. That rate of error should
not be surprising if one understands that the presentation in *Banker's Trust*, above, consisted of 967
pages of documents. However, it is clear that the
"strict compliance" standard itself causes problems.

Under UCP Article 13(a), "banks must examine
all documents . . . with reasonable care, to ascertain
whether or not they appear, on their face, to be in
compliance. . . . Compliance . . . shall be determined
by international standard banking practice as re-

flected in these Articles." According to the draftsmen, the reference to "international banking practice" is intended to prevent "sharp, dishonest or
negligent" use of strict compliance standards, and
therefore to add some flexibility to the previous
standards. But, since the "international ... practice" must be "as reflected in these Articles," it is
difficult to be certain whether any change is intended at all, since no other UCP provision deals with
the issue. Further, there may be no "international
standard banking practices," since practices in London are different from those in developing countries. Thus, the prior "strict compliance" standard,
with all its problems, is likely to continue.

When documents are tendered to an issuing or a
confirming bank (or a nominated bank acting for
them), it has two duties. One is to examine the
documents to determine whether they conform to
the terms of the letter of credit. The second is to act
upon any discrepancies found.

The examination must be, not only thorough, but
also quick. If the bank does discover discrepancies,
it may reject the documents without consulting its
customer, the applicant (Buyer). However, in many
situations, the discrepancies may be trivial or typo-
graphical, and the customer may want the payment
made, and the goods delivered, despite the discrepancy. Thus, UCP Article 14(c) allows, but does not
require, the bank to consult the applicant, its customer, for a waiver of the discrepancies it has
discovered. That provision does not permit the bank
to seek help from the applicant to find further

discrepancies. There was evidence in *Banker's Trust*, above, that about 90% of the times they are consulted by the issuing bank, applicants will in fact waive the discrepancies discovered by the bank. Thus, the system seems to work because the non-bank parties (Buyer and Seller) want the transaction to be completed despite the technical difficulties imposed by the banking system.

UCP Article 13(b) gives the bank a "reasonable time, not to exceed seven banking days ... to determine whether to take up or refuse the documents." If the bank discovers no discrepancies, there is no particular difficulty in meeting this deadline, and a "reasonable time" may be significantly shorter. The 967 pages of documents in *Banker's Trust*, above, were examined twice by the issuing bank in two and a half days. Once the bank has decided to accept the documents, it must notify the party from whom it received them.

If the bank discovers discrepancies, however, it may be subject to time pressures. The "seven banking days" deadline includes not only time to examine the documents presented, but also time to consult the bank's customer (Buyer) about waiving the discrepancies *and* notifying the party from whom the documents were received. It is the latter two requirements which can create difficulties. It is easier to deduce a "reasonable time" for clerks to examine documents than it is to determine such a time period for consulting with the customer, the applicant, and obtaining a response. The issuing bank may also delay notification of prior parties of discrepancies, because it must be very careful in making that notification.

UCP Article 14(d) requires any bank which rejects a presentation of documents to "state all discrepancies" that it will rely upon in its notice to the person who presented the documents. Under UCP Article 14(e), failure to state all the discrepancies "precludes" the bank from claiming non-compliance due to any unstated discrepancy, without the necessity of proving waiver or estoppel. Thus, banks which reject documents have only one chance to identify all the discrepancies on which they can ever rely. The rationale for this rule is to inform the beneficiary (Seller) of all the discrepancies at once, so that it can determine whether they all can be cured and whether such cure is cost-effective. But the rule can also lead the issuing bank to delay notification for additional re-examinations to ensure that all defects are discovered.

The seven-day deadline should not become a "reasonable time" in all transactions, especially in simple transactions where all the documents can be examined in an hour or two. If seven banking days did become the norm, a beneficiary would not know for three weeks whether the funds were firm or not in transactions involving a non-confirmed letter of credit with a local nominated bank. Current practice is much quicker than that.

Under the UCP, banks deal only in documents. (UCP Article 4.) The parties may provide conditions upon the credit, as long as compliance with those conditions can be satisfied through documentary evidence. Thus, letters of credit must state precisely the documents, and the terms of the documents, against which payment is to be made. (UCP Article 5(b).) It is the responsibility of the issuing bank and its customer, the applicant (Buyer), to ensure that satisfaction of each condition can be evidenced by documents. Otherwise, the condition need not be satisfied. UCP Article 13(c) provides that if a letter of credit contains any condition which is not satisfied by a document to be presented to evidence compliance with it, the bank can ignore that condition as though it were not written.

The most important of the documents required by a letter of credit is the transportation document. Under prior versions of the UCP, this had referred to ocean bills of lading, evidencing an assumption that the goods would be carried by sea. However, there are new developments in the transport industry and new technological applications. Thus the 1993 Revision of the UCP provides separate articles for negotiable ocean bills of lading, non-negotiable sea waybills, charter party bills of lading, multimodal transport documents, air transport documents, road, rail or inland waterway transport documents, and courier and post receipts.

Under UCP Article 23, an ocean bill of lading must name the port of loading, the port of discharge, the carrier and specify the parties which will be acceptable signatories. Banks have no duty, however, to check the signature or initials accompanying an "on board" notation, absent a special arrangement with the bank. The bill of lading may indicate an "intended vessel." In such cases, any "on board" notation must specify the vessel on which the goods have been loaded. The medieval custom of issuing "a set" of bills of lading, and hoping one of them would arrive and be honored, is now disapproved; and the UCP seeks to have only a single original bill of lading issued as the norm.

A charter party bill of lading does not identify the carrier, and is now a permissible transport document for use with a letter of credit. UCP Article 25(b) relieves the banks from any duty to examine the terms of the charter party, under the assumption that only sophisticated parties with considerable knowledge of the trade will use them.

In multimodal transportation arrangements, the bill of lading is likely to be issued by a freight forwarder and not by a carrier. Thus, it does not name a carrier and it does not contain a receipt by the bailee (who is the carrier), which is the norm for documents of title. However, if the letter of credit authorizes its use, such a bill of lading may be used under UCP Article 30, if the freight forwarder issues it as either a multi-modal transport operator or an agent for a carrier. Otherwise, such "house bills" of freight forwarders are not acceptable transport documents for letters of credit under the UCP.

If the original documents are lost or destroyed, a bank may accept copies of the documents as originals, if the copies have been signed. Under UCP

Article 20(b), allowable signatures include handwriting, facsimiles, perforated signatures, stamps, symbols, and other mechanical and electronic methods. However, many civil law countries (e.g., Germany) do not accept facsimile signatures and have ruled that *any* non-handwritten signature is invalid.

The liability of the confirming bank is separate and independent of the liability of the issuing bank. To establish the confirming bank's liability, documents may be presented by the beneficiary to the confirming bank or to any other nominated bank under UCP Article 9. This provision can create difficulties for the confirming bank by creating liability without providing it an opportunity to examine the documents. However, under UCP Article 42, the letter of credit must specify both a place for presentation of the documents and an expiration date for the presentation of the documents. Thus, the confirming bank would like to insist that it be the nominated bank, but that is not always possible. Instead, the confirming bank that is not the nominated bank can insist that its office is designated as the place for presentation of the documents.

ELECTRONIC LETTERS OF CREDIT

Electronic communication has taken over some aspects of letters of credit practice, but not others. They dominate the issuance process in bank-to-bank communications, and are sometimes used by applicants to stimulate the issuance process. However, at this time they have not been able to create an entirely paperless transaction pattern for many reasons. First, the beneficiary still wants a piece of paper committing the banks to pay upon specified conditions. Second, electronic bills of lading still are not accepted in most trades as transferable documents of title for the reasons discussed in the preceding chapter. Thus, in the collection of the letter of credit, physical documents will be forwarded, while funds settlement may be electronic.

About three quarters of letter of credit communication between banks, for other banks' issuance, advice, confirmation or negotiation of letters of credit is paperless; and the communication is electronic. While bank-to-bank communication is electronic, bank-to-beneficiary (Seller) communication is still paper-based. Letter of credit issuers can now communicate directly with beneficiaries' computers, however, and use of this practice should be expected to increase. The UCP rules are now written in terms of "teletransmissions," rather than paper-based terminology, which facilitates the use of electronic practices.

Most bank-to-bank communication concerning letters of credit are routed through the dedicated lines of SWIFT (the Society for Worldwide Interstate Financial Telecommunications). SWIFT is a Belgian not-for-profit organization owned by banks as a cooperative venture for the transmission of financial transaction messages. It requires all such messages to be structured in a uniform format, and uses standardized elements for allocating message space and for message text. Thus, messages can be communicated on a computer-to-computer basis without being re-keyed.

A bank issuing a letter of credit communicates that message to the nearest SWIFT access point. The message is then routed on a dedicated data transmission line to a regional processor, where it is validated (see below). From the regional processor, it is routed over a dedicated line to one of two main switches located in either the United States or Europe. From there it is routed through a regional processor to a SWIFT access point to the receiving bank. The message switching and sometimes necessary storage can be performed by computers, if the standardization of the format of the financial messages is sufficiently developed and comprehensive. SWIFT seems to have achieved this level of uniformity.

The bank which receives a SWIFT electronic letter of credit message does not have to send a reply stating that it accepts the request to advise or the authorization to negotiate or pay the letter of credit. It needs only to perform by advising, negotiating or paying, and it is entitled to reimbursement by the issuing bank. However, the SWIFT messages only transmit the letter of credit and their authorizations and requests. SWIFT messages do not effect the settlements of letters of credit or other transfers of funds between issuing banks and other banks. SWIFT is not a clearing house for bank settlements like, for example, CHIPS (Clearing House for Interbank Payment Systems). Under the SWIFT letter of credit system, participating banks must use other arrangements (such as CHIPS) to settle their accounts and accomplish a transfer of funds.

SWIFT relies upon both incryption of messages and authentication to provide security to its users. The authentication of SWIFT messages is accomplished by the use of algorithms, which are mathematical formulas that calculate the contents of a message from header to trailer. If a SWIFT message requires authentication, and all letter of credit messages do, the issuing bank computes the contents and compiles a result based on the number of characters and data fields. At the regional processor, SWIFT checks the authentication trailer for the number of characters in the authentication. However, a more rigorous authentication will be performed by the receiving bank, using an algorithm contained in an authentication key provided by the issuing bank. The computations involving these authentication procedures will indicate a mismatch if the message is fraudulent or has been altered. There are also "log in" procedures, application-selection procedures, message numbering and error checking capabilities, and control of access to the system hardware. SWIFT also retains records of each transaction. In all, the security devices are numerous and complex.

Most SWIFT messages are delivered within minutes of their issuance by a bank, although delays of up to two hours are possible. Thus, delays in the system are slight, but present. When is the issuer of an electronic letter of credit bound? The UCP provides no set rules on the issue, but Revised UCC

Article 5 establishes that such messages are effective and enforceable upon transmission by the issuer, not delivery to the receiving bank. Revised § 5–106(a) and SWIFT rules require no reply. This UCC rule conforms to the understanding of bankers involved in the trade.

Under SWIFT rules, Belgian law governs all relations between SWIFT and its users. SWIFT is liable for negligence or fraud of its own employees and agents and for those parts of the communication system that it controls, such as regional processors, main switches and the dedicated lines that connect them. But SWIFT disclaims liability for those parts of the communication system that it does not control, such as the bank computers that issue and receive messages and the dedicated lines from bank to a regional processor. Even where SWIFT is liable, its liability is limited to "direct" damages (loss of interest), and liability for indirect (consequential) damages is not available. Whether Belgian law also governs relations between SWIFT and the non-bank parties to the transaction (applicants and beneficiaries), or between banks and their customers, does not seem yet to have been tested in court.

It is now possible for an applicant (Buyer, in the documentary credit transaction) to draft a proposed electronic letter of credit. The electronic proposed credit can then be transmitted to the issuing bank for it to issue over the SWIFT system. This procedure is usually used where the applicant seeks multiple credits and there is a master agreement between the issuing bank and the applicant. The issuing bank will first check to see whether the proposed credit is authorized and contains the required security codes. Then it will determine whether it is within the previously authorized credit limits and is stated in the standardized elements and uniform format for electronic messages. Both SWIFT and UCP requirements must be analyzed, and changes in the proposed message may be necessary. Thus, the procedures are not yet fully automatic.

On the other end of the electronic communications, the beneficiary (Seller, in the documentary sale), who must be induced to part with value on the basis of the bank's promises, wants a "hard copy", a written letter of credit in the traditional form. The receiving bank therefore will convert the SWIFT electronic message into such a written, paper credit. However, the SWIFT message has been designed for bank-to-bank use, and not necessarily for use by beneficiaries, which creates some problems. First, it does not bear a signature in the traditional sense, even though it has been thoroughly authenticated within the computer-based transmission mechanisms. Thus, the beneficiary is entitled to doubt whether the sending bank is bound to the beneficiary to perform by the written credit derived from the SWIFT electronic message.

The issue if usually framed as: "Is the SWIFT message to be considered to be *the* operative credit instrument as far as the beneficiary is concerned?" The issue is of importance to beneficiaries not only in the original issuance of the credit, but also in the myriad of amendments to the credit which may follow. Under SWIFT rules, SWIFT users treat the electronic message as a binding obligation, and treat the authentication as the functional equivalent of a signature. However, the beneficiary is not a SWIFT user, and banking practice has been that a beneficiary can rely on an electronic message only after it has been issued in a paper-based format, properly signed or otherwise authenticated. Revised UCC § 5–104 states that a letter of credit "may be issued in any form," including an electronic format, but that provision does not necessarily answer the question as to whether the unsigned, paper-based transcription of a SWIFT message, generated by the recipient of that message, is the operative credit instrument and binds the issuing bank.

Under the UCP, whether an electronic message is the operative credit instrument or not depends upon the terminology in the message itself. UCP Article 11(a)(ii) provides that, if the electronic message states "full details to follow," or states that a mail confirmation will be the operative credit instrument, then the electronic message is not that instrument, and the subsequent message is. However, UCP Article 11(a)(i) states that other authenticated electronic messages to advise or amend credits *are* the operative credit instrument. In the latter transactions, mail confirmations should not be sent, and are to have no effect if sent.

However, there is some doubt as to whether SWIFT-generated transcriptions are subject to the UCP. SWIFT internal rules provide that credits issued through its system are subject to the UCP, but the transcription into a hard copy may bear no reference to the UCP. UCP Article 1 states that the UCP provisions govern "where they are incorporated into the text of the credit." That language is deemed, in some parts of the world, to require an express reference to the UCP in the message to the beneficiary.

The attempts to create an electronic bill of lading have been discussed earlier in Chapter 2. If successful, an electronic bill of lading could help facilitate the electronic letter of credit transaction. However, to date, while electronic bills of lading have been used successfully to replace the straight (non-negotiable) bill of lading, its use to replace the negotiable bill of lading has been met with skepticism. Although SEDOCS showed that an electronic approach was technically feasible, it was not a commercial success. American bankers have been skeptical of their rights to any actual goods under electronic bills of lading issued under CMI (Comite Maritime International) Rules. However, the Commission of the European Communities has just initiated the BOLERO program under the CMI Rules, and it may prove to be more successful. It is discussed in more detail in Chapter 2.

The experiments discussed above all attempted to substitute an electronic message for the paper-based bill of lading, but otherwise did not change traditional letter of credit system, based on the bill of lading. A very different approach is proposed in an experiment called Trade Card. This approach attempts to provide an electronic system, rather than just an electronic message in a paper-based system. It is loosely based on a credit card or debit card system used by banks. However, for this system to be feasible, all the parties must be members of the Trade Card system. This includes not only the shipper, the carrier and all of the banks involved, but also all of the potential buyers of the goods while they are in transit. Whether Trade Card will be a success remains to be seen, because only a pilot program has been initiated to date. Even if Trade Card should not be successful, one should expect that there will be other attempts to create an electronic letter of credit transaction which follows an electronic model, not the traditional model but with an electronic bill of lading.

STANDBY LETTERS OF CREDIT

Third world governments often require a financial assurance (by way of a financial guarantee) that foreign firms which undertake to supply goods or to perform a construction project will do so competently and in accordance with the terms of the contract covering the sale or project. Performance bonds can serve as an adequate assurance, but United States banks are barred from issuing insurance contracts, including performance bonds. They have, however, developed an alternative—the "standby" letter of credit, which is a second type of letter of credit transaction. It involves a letter of credit which is issued by the seller's bank and runs in favor of the buyer—truly a backwards arrangement—and payable against a writing which certifies that the seller has not performed its promises. Such a standby letter of credit is not for the purpose of ensuring payment to the seller for goods shipped. Instead, this standby letter of credit is used as a guarantee, or a performance bond, or as insurance of the seller's performance. Under current federal law, banks are not allowed to issue guarantees or performance bonds or insurance policies. 12 U.S.C.A. § 24 (Seventh). However, the use of stand-by letters of credit can accomplish the same results, and is not prohibited by bank regulatory agencies. The result has been the creation of a new commercial device, which is now commercially accepted for its own value, and which has supplanted the performance bond in many fields of endeavor.

Below is an example of a standby letter of credit issued by seller's bank from *Dynamics Corp. of America v. Citizens & Southern Nat. Bank*, 356 F.Supp. 991 (N.D.Ga.1973).

" ... TO: THE PRESIDENT OF INDIA

INDIA

BY ORDER OF: ELECTRONICS SYSTEMS DI-
VISION OF DYNAMICS CORPORATION OF
AMERICA

For account

of same

GENTLEMEN:

WE HEREBY ESTABLISH OUR IRREVO-
CABLE CREDIT IN YOUR FAVOR, FOR
THE ACCOUNT INDICATED ABOVE, FOR
A SUM OR SUMS NOT EXCEEDING IN
ALL FOUR HUNDRED TEN THOUSAND
FOUR HUNDRED SEVENTY TWO AND
60/100 US DOLLARS (US$410,472.60)—
AVAILABLE BY YOUR DRAFT(S) AT sight,

DRAWN ON: us

Which must be accompanied by:

1. Your signed certification as follows: "The
President of India being one of the parties to the
Agreement dated March 14, 1971 signed and exchanged between the President of India and the
Dynamics Corporation of America for the license
to manufacture, purchase and supply of radio
equipment as per Schedule I thereof for the total
contract value of $1,368,242.00, does hereby certi-

fy in the exercise of reasonable discretion and in good faith that the Dynamics Corporation of America has failed to carry out certain obligations of theirs under the said Order/Agreement.... "

In it, the seller (account party) has contracted to have the seller's bank (issuing bank) issue an irrevocable letter of credit in favor of the third world government (beneficiary) that payment will be made upon presentation of a document which is only a simple statement by the beneficiary that the account party has failed to carry out its obligations under a contract (called a "suicide credit"). Some require no document, but provide for payment to be made upon the beneficiary's demand. This transaction is almost a mirror image of the letter of credit in the documentary sale. In the standby credit, the account party is the seller or contractor, the beneficiary is the purchaser (not the seller), and the documents do not control the goods and have no independent value of their own. Often the required documentation is a mere certification by the beneficiary that the contractor has failed to perform under the contract or, perhaps, has failed to return an advance payment.

Standby letters of credit are governed by the UCP, and are governed by the same rules as those applicable to documentary credits "to the extent they may be applicable." UCP Art. 1. If the documents presented conform precisely to the terms of the letter of credit, the Confirming Bank and the Issuing Bank are obligated to pay the beneficiary or to honor its draft. The beneficiary is not subject to defenses arising out of the underlying sales transaction, so the conformity of the goods is, with exceptions noted below, irrelevant to the bank's decision. The decision is to be based upon the documents alone. Further, the documents need not conform to the underlying sales contract either, so long as they comply with the letter of credit. This is the "independence principle" which underlies the legal setting for letters of credit.

Some legal commentators question whether the traditional "independence principle" of letter of credit rules is being or should be applied to standby credits, in light of the facts that such letters do not assure an exporter about payment for goods to be shipped, but serve principally a non-payment function to assure an importer (beneficiary) about payment if an exporter (the account party) does not deliver on its contract (to supply goods, services or raw materials). However, the text of both the UCP and Revised UCC Article 5 make it clear that the drafters intended them to cover standby letters of credit, and to apply the "independence principle" to such bank obligations.

NEW INTERNATIONAL RULES
FOR STANDBY LETTERS
OF CREDIT

Even though both the UCP and Revised UCC Article 5 expressly include standby letters of credit within their coverage, it is clear that they were designed to cover the documentary letter of credit transaction and not the standby transaction. Thus, they impose many unnecessary document-related conditions on the use of standbys. The UCP, in particular, contains many provisions on the proper presentation of transportation documents and the requirements for drawing installment payments, both of which are irrelevant to the usual standby letter of credit transaction. The UCP also does not address several issues, such as fraud and choice of law, which are significant to standby transactions.

In response to these difficulties, the United Nations Commission on International Trade Law (UN-CITRAL) has developed the United Nations Convention on Independent Guarantees and Stand-by Letters of Credit (1995) which will enter into force on January 1, 2000. For the same reason, the International Chamber of Commerce (I.C.C.) has developed the Rules on International Standby Practices (ISP 98), which became effective on January 1, 1999. The Convention currently has five Contracting States (Ecuador, El Salvador, Kuwait, Panama and Tunisia). The ISP 98 was designed to replace the UCP and be its equivalent in international practice regarding standby letters of credit.

The U.N. Convention on standbys is limited to international undertakings by the issuing bank, so that the issuer and at least one other party must have their places of business in different nations. It also provides choice of law provisions, allowing the parties to choose the applicable law. If the parties do not specify a choice of law, the Convention provides a default rule that the law of the issuer's place of business shall govern the transaction. The Convention also provides rules for allegations of fraud and the seeking injunctive relief. Payment can be withheld from a beneficiary if a document is not genuine, or does not provide a basis for demanding payment. A court may issue an order blocking payment on freezing proceeds of a standby credit if it finds "strong evidence" of such a circumstance.

ISP 98 deletes all the provisions concerning transportation documents, but does require that any official documents be certified. It also places a floor on the amount of information a beneficiary must provide, and requires "magic words," in regard to the presentation of certificates of default under a standby. The ISP also provides rules to govern electronic demands for payment under standby letters of credit. However, since the ISP is not a statute, but merely trade terms incorporated into the contract by reference, it does not attempt to include provisions on fraud and injunctive relief. Perhaps surprisingly, it also does not include any choice of law provisions.

THE FRAUD DEFENSE

Where the documents are forged or fraudulent, or there is fraud in the transaction, however, a different analysis is applied. The "independence principle" promotes the utility of the letter of credit transaction, by offering certainty of payment to the beneficiary who complies with a credit's requirements. But, where there is fraud or forgery, rather than a "mere" breach of the underlying sales contract, a counter principle comes into play. "There is as much public interest in discouraging fraud as in encouraging the use of letters of credit." *Dynamics Corp.*, supra. Where the seller's fraud has been called to the bank's attention before the drafts and documents have been presented for payment, the principle of "the independence of the bank's obligation under the letter of credit" should not be extended to protect the unscrupulous seller. *Sztejn v. J. Henry Schroder Banking Corp.*, 177 Misc. 719, 31 N.Y.S.2d 631 (1941).

Thus, there are two competing principles, and the courts have created compromises which limit the impact of the independence principle when there are forged or fraudulent documents, or fraud in the transaction. Vexing problems are raised by claims of fraud and, more particularly, of "fraud in the transaction", but the doctrine that there is a "fraud exception" to the "independence principle" seems to be generally recognized. However, there is still a significant debate about how broad and extensive the fraud exception should be.

This "fraud exception" is available where the credit is expressly subject to the UCP, even though the UCP has no specific provisions on the subject. Since the UCP is silent, the courts have generally held that the UCC provisions govern as a "gap-filling provision." The principle underlying this approach is that the courts will not allow their process to be used by a dishonest person to carry out a fraud. Most of the cases have arisen in New York courts, where there is a non-uniform amendment to the UCC, discussed above, making it inapplicable to credits expressly subject to the UCP. New York's highest court has permitted the account party to seek to maintain an injunction against payment of a credit subject to the UCP. In so doing, the court used pre-UCC caselaw as its precedent, but used all the concepts expressed in the UCC. This approach has been followed in both the state and federal courts in cases arising out of New York.

While the concept of enjoining payment due to fraud has not been widely used in the documentary letter of credit transaction, it has been widely sought in the stand-by letter of credit transaction. Some limiting concepts in the documentary letter of credit transaction, such as "strict compliance" of the documents, become somewhat meaningless when the "document" becomes a mere allegation by one party that the other party failed to perform properly under the contract. When the limitations which give structure to the transaction become meaningless, the transaction can become a breeding ground for fraud.

Under Revised UCC § 5–109, there is a series of limitations on the availability of the fraud exception for use by the beneficiary. The first limitation is that "the issuer shall honor presentation, if honor is demanded by a nominated person who has given value in good faith without notice of material injury or fraud." Thus, confirming banks who have paid against the documents in good faith and without notice of any defense to, or defect in, the documents are entitled to reimbursement, despite fraud on the beneficiary. So also is an advising bank which has been authorized to pay against the documents, rather than merely to accept the documents for collection. Under the UCC, if the documents are presented by such a confirming bank, or authorized advising bank, and the documents appear on their face to comply with the credit, the issuing bank *must* pay the confirming bank, even though the documents are forged or fraudulent or there is fraud in the transaction.

A second limitation is that, if the documents are presented by anyone else (beneficiary, advising bank authorized to take for collection only, confirming bank which took with notice of defects or defenses, etc.), the issuing bank *may* still pay, even though it has been notified that the documents are forged or fraudulent, or that there is fraud in the transaction, as long as it acts in good faith. In the latter case, the issuing bank *may* also refuse to pay, but that is not very likely. Reasons for the issuing bank not refusing to pay range from its reluctance to be known as an unreliable source of funds in letter of credit transactions to its inability to evaluate the available evidence of fraud, especially on an *ex parte* basis. Banks are paid to handle documents, not to become judge and jury.

The account party is, however, given the power to obtain a court order against payment, so long as it can prove forgery, fraud or fraud in the transaction. Thus, under the UCC, if the account party obtains a court injunction against payment from a court having proper jurisdiction, the issuing bank is permitted to dishonor the presentment. But the Revised UCC Article 5 leaves only a very narrow avenue for the account party to seek and obtain judicial intervention through injunctive relief in the letter of credit transaction. To beneficiaries, the concept creates great uncertainty about prompt payment, because they know nothing about the judicial system and fear the worst. To account parties, the concept has created a theoretical argument, but there have been very few reported cases in which they were successful.

The Revised Article 5 provision limits itself in several ways:

First, the fraud must be "material," but material is not defined. The Comments to Revised § 5–109 cite some prior decisions favorably, but its meaning will be decided on a case by case basis. Second, the account party must present sufficient evidence of fraud or forgery, not merely allegations of it. Third, all the procedural requirements for injunctive or other relief must be met. Fourth, the relief can be denied if third parties are not "adequately protected," and no relief will be granted if a confirming or advising bank has paid funds to the beneficiary. However, this concept has been expanded in the Comments to include protection against incidental damages, such as legal fees, by *bond* or otherwise. All of these are limitations which have been found in the prior cases and which would be expected in an action for injunctive relief.

The principal new limitation is one stated in Revised § 5–109. A forgery or a fraud in the document may permit an injunction of payment if perpetrated by anyone, but a fraud in the underlying transaction is cognizable only if it is "committed by the beneficiary," and not by some third party, such as a carrier. The difference between the two concepts is illustrated by the approach of English and Canadian courts to the fraud exception.

The English and Canadian courts have each recognized the "fraud exception," based upon the persuasive precedent of the American cases. However, each of them, in addition to the requirements of the pre-Revision UCC, place great stress on the *scienter* requirements of common law fraud and require the account party to establish that the beneficiary itself made, or was responsible for, the misrepresentation that was the foundation for the fraud claim. A misrepresentation made by any other party to the transaction would not permit an injunction against payment of the beneficiary. Thus, the House of Lords, while recognizing the basic fraud concept, refused to extend it to protect the buyer when the fraud was committed by a third party (a loading broker) without seller's knowledge. *United City Merchants (Investments) Ltd. v. Royal Bank of Canada (The American Accord)*, 1983 A.C. 168 (H.L. 1982). Under the English–Canadian formulation: (1) Where the credit requires loading by May 15 and the bill of lading shows loading on the 16th, the bank must dishonor. (2) Where the credit requires loading on May 15, and bank knows that the beneficiary has altered a document in a non-apparent manner, the bank must dishonor. (3) But, where the credit requires loading by May 15, and bank knows that a freight forwarder has altered a document in a non-apparent manner, the bank must *honor* the credit.

Under Revised § 5–109, American courts would reach such a result if the misrepresentation was considered a fraud in the underlying transaction. However, such a misrepresentation is more likely to be considered arising out of the document itself. If so, the identity of the perpetrator would be irrelevant. Revised § 5–109 does not attempt to define fraud, which is a product of caselaw and varies widely from state to state.

The traditional difference between fraud doctrines and breach of contract concepts was that the former consider the state of mind of the seller, while breach of contract concerns only whether the goods lived up to particular objective standard set by their description. Fraud concepts have expanded enormously since 1952, and conduct which would not have been actionable during the first half of the 20th Century is now routinely within current caselaw concepts. The modern fraud doctrines often do not require any evil intent, but only that seller know that a particular fact is not true—or, that he does not know whether a particular fact is true or not when he states it—or, that he believes that a fact is true when it is not, and a court decides that he should have made a more thorough investigation before speaking.

As an outgrowth of the 1979 change of government in Iran, increased attention was given to the potential that a standby letter's beneficiary could require payment for what was characterized as "bad faith" or "arbitrary" reasons, or at least for reasons not related to the contractor's intentional failure to perform on the contract (e.g., perhaps because of conditions surrounding a civil insurrection).

Many courts have declined to enjoin payment because of insufficient evidence of fraud, or because an account party sought to expand the definition of fraud. Other courts have been willing to issue a "notice injunction" requiring issuers to give some prior notice (usually three to ten days) to the account party before transferring money to the beneficiary of a standby credit after demand for payment, while a few courts have granted preliminary injunctions of indefinite duration.

The United Nations Commission on International Trade Law (UNCITRAL) has drafted a U.N. Convention on Independent Guarantees and Stand-by Letters of Credit. Article 19 of that Convention permits a court to issue a "provisional order" that the beneficiary not receive payment, or that the funds are blocked if paid, if the applicant can show that a document is not genuine, that the document shows that no payment is due, or that "the demand has no conceivable basis." The Convention also describes five illustrations of the latter principle. The Convention expressly prohibits a court from enjoining payment on any other basis. There is some doubt as to whether "fraud in the transaction" is covered by the criteria of Article 19.

OTHER LETTERS OF CREDIT: BACK TO BACK AND REVOLVING CREDITS

Although the irrevocable documentary letter of credit is used most often in international commercial transactions, documentary letters may also be "revocable," giving the beneficiary a right to payment "unless previously canceled" by the account party. Under the UCP, a letter of credit is presumed to be irrevocable unless it states that it is revocable. UCP Article 6.

Letters of credit may be "sight" (payable on demand) or "time" (such as, six months following presentation of documents). A time draft will grant credit to the account party, (buyer) and give the beneficiary (seller) an instrument (an accepted draft) which can be negotiated to banks to raise cash now. The confirming or issuing bank will "accept" the draft which accompanies the documents, thus making the bank primarily liable on the draft. A "general" letter of credit does not restrict the beneficiary's right to transfer its rights thereunder, while a "special" letter of credit limits permissible transferees, usually to one or more banks. A letter of credit is "fixed" if it can become "exhausted" either when drafts for payment have been drawn by beneficiary for the full amount of the letter or when the time period for drawing upon the letter has expired.

Brokers of goods have a problem because they often have two transactions in the same goods. They will sell the goods to a buyer in one transaction and then buy them from a supplier in a separate transaction. If both sales transactions involve payment by letters of credit, the broker will be the beneficiary (seller) of the letter of credit in the first transaction and the account party (buyer) in the second. If the documents required by each letter of credit are *identical,* the broker can assign its rights in the first credit to the issuing bank of the second credit. Such arrangements are facilitated if the credits specify the use of time drafts (e.g. "pay 30 days after sight"). This arrangement is a "back to back credit" and allows broker to finance its purchase of the goods from supplier with the credit of its buyer. Such arrangements work more easily using general letters of credit, although special credits can be used by giving an issuing bank a security interest in its proceeds.

However, back to back credits can also become unworkable if one of the credits is amended, and no similar amendment is made to the other credit. Thus, most banks prefer not to use the back to back letter of credit transaction. Instead, they recommend that sellers and brokers obtain financing through a "transferable letter of credit" or an "assignment of proceeds" from a letter of credit.

A transferable letter of credit is one that expressly states that it can be transferred by the original
beneficiary to third parties, who become new and
substitute beneficiaries. UCP Article 48(b). Thus, a
broker who is the beneficiary of a transferable letter
of credit can use its rights under that credit to
finance the purchase of the goods from suppliers by
transferring part of the broker's rights under the
credit to the suppliers. Partial transfers are allowed,
so the broker can use this device to finance purchases from several suppliers. However, although
substitute commercial invoices and drafts may be
used, all other necessary documents must be presented to the original account party, which will
reveal the identity of the substitute beneficiary.
That may compromise commercially sensitive information, and so brokers tend to avoid use of such
credits.

The beneficiary of a letter of credit may irrevocably assign a portion of the credit's proceeds to a
third party. If the proceeds are assigned, the advising bank notifies the assignee of the assignment.
Thus, a broker who is the beneficiary of a letter of
credit that permits assignment of proceeds can use
its rights under that credit to finance the purchase
of the goods from a supplier by assigning a part of
the broker's rights under the credit to the supplier.
The assignment of proceeds does not change the
parties to the letter of credit. The original account
party is obligated to pay only if it receives documents which conform to the credit, so the assignee
will not be paid unless it ships the goods using

conforming documents. The assignee is not a party
to the original credit, it may not know what the
terms of the credit are, and must trust the broker
(the original beneficiary) to fulfill those terms. The
assignment is not governed by the UCP, but by the
applicable law of contract. UCP Article 49.

Rapid expansion of turn-key construction contracts (e.g. for building a complete steel mill or
cement plant needing someone only to "turn a key"
to begin plant operation) has expanded use of "revolving" letters of credit as a vehicle for ensuring
that contractors are given progress payments
promptly as initial construction phases are completed and to permit further construction phases to
occur. Revolving letters of credit are usually clean
(no documents required), sight letters which work
in the same way and are subject to the same legal
rules for fixed letters of credit. But there are differences—first, the importer (often a third world host
government) pays, by way of a letter of credit, to
import services (building skills) and raw materials
rather than finished goods, and second the importer
(account party) restores the amount of the letter
(by payment to issuer) to an agreed level of further
payment to beneficiary (the foreign construction
company) following each time that beneficiary has
drawn upon the letter for payment. Revolving letters may be documentary (requiring presentation of
a certificate of construction phase completion), but
"red tape" in obtaining such interim certifications
prompts many contractors to seek less formal ar-

rangements, requiring the account party to trust
the contractor not to draw upon the letter before
such action is appropriate. As a result, the payment
ceiling (amount) of the revolving letter will usually
be a modest fraction of the total value of the construction contract.

CHAPTER FOUR

MONEY AND INTERNATIONAL BUSINESS TRANSACTIONS

A business which wishes to move money across national borders should have some overview of the international financial system. The first part of this Chapter is intended to provide such an overview. The second part of this Chapter surveys national financial systems and then focuses on those parts of national banking systems which furnish special services for international transactions. The final parts of this Chapter discuss the mechanics of the operation of such systems in three types of transactions: the payment transaction, Eurodollars, and transfer pricing. The letter of credit transaction is discussed in Chapter 3.

THE INTERNATIONAL MONETARY SYSTEM AND THE IMF

Most nations have a national currency and pursue an internal monetary policy to meet its own political and economic goals. Eleven EU nations have joined in a common currency, the Euro, managed by the European Central Bank. No central authority controls a world monetary system; world monetary policy is decentralized. Since 1944, nations have coordinated national monetary policies through several international ad hoc arrangements about relationships among national currencies and also through international monetary institutions, such as the International Monetary Fund (IMF).

Both the IMF and the International Bank for Reconstruction and Development (the "World Bank") arose out of the Bretton Woods Conference in 1944. The World Bank was to facilitate loans by capital surplus countries (e.g., then the United States) to countries needing foreign investment for economic redevelopment after World War II. The IMF was to stabilize currency exchange rates, assist countries in their balance of payments, and repair other war damage to the international monetary system. Twenty-nine countries became party to the IMF Articles of Agreement in 1945, and United States participation in the IMF was authorized in 22 U.S.C.A. § 286 et seq. Today, over 150 countries are members of the IMF.

The IMF goals are to "facilitate the expansion and balanced growth of international trade", to assist in "the elimination of foreign exchange restrictions which hamper the growth of international trade", and to "shorten the duration and lessen the disequilibrium in the international balances of payments of members." Article I. The mitigation of wide currency fluctuations is achieved through a complex lending system which permits a country to borrow money from other Fund members or from the Fund (by way of "Special Drawing Rights" or "SDRs") for the purpose of stabilizing the relationship of its currency to other world currencies. These monetary drawing arrangements permit a member country to support its national currency's relative value when compared with national currencies of other countries, especially the "hard" ("reserve") currencies such as the British pound, the Euro, Japanese yen, and United States dollar.

In recent years, IMF loans have normally been "conditioned" upon adoption of specific economic reforms by the debtor states, especially in Asia and Latin America. This has led to the perception that the IMF is the world's "sheriff", setting the terms for refinancing national debts and protecting the interests of commercial bank creditors. The IMF does function as the first line of negotiation in an international "debt crisis," and commercial and national banks often conform their loans to IMF conditions. These IMF conditions can have dramatic political and social repercussions in debtor nations.

An American business person who incurs expenses and pays bills in U.S. dollars wishes to be paid in U.S. dollars—even for goods or services which are sold outside of the United States. Similarly, a French business person wishes to have Euros. Both have a need for, and must rely upon, the convertibility of currencies (e.g., dollars for Euros and vice versa) so that payments can be made abroad or foreign income can be used to pay bills at home. Convertibility in the international setting has been achieved at different times by using, as a common reference point or standard, different forms of "international money". Gold has been an international money for centuries. The U.S. dollar is both a national currency and a primary form of international money. The Europeans hope to challenge the dollar's supremacy with the Euro.

The International Monetary Fund has established a form of international money which is not a national currency and is called a Special Drawing Right (SDR). Certificates of deposit are denominated in SDRs; short-term SDR loans may be obtained commercially; and some OPEC nations have begun to value their national currencies in SDRs. Mechanically, an SDR is an international medium of exchange having a 1991 composite value based 39 percent on the U.S. dollar, 32 percent on the Euro, 18 percent on the Japanese yen, and 11 percent on the British pound. Each exchange rate fluctuation in any one of the five "basket currencies" produces commensurately only a smaller, fractional fluctuation in the value of an SDR. On September 1, 1999, an SDR was worth $1.37 (U.S.).

Although the SDR has been talked about as if it is a supranational currency, the SD "Right" is more technically a "unit of account" created by an IMF process. When an IMF member country, having a negative balance of payments position, runs short of its currency "reserves" (which may be its stocks of "hard" "reserve" currencies or gold), the member country may exercise its "Right" to make a "Special Drawing" from the IMF Special Drawing Account (e.g., the country may exercise its Special Drawing Right to ask the IMF to arrange for that country to receive $40 million (U.S.) worth of currency other than gold). Upon receipt of the Drawing "request", the IMF approaches another member country, having a fuller stock of "reserves" (which "back up" its national currency), and requests that country to provide currency to the requesting country (e.g. to provide $40 million worth of currency other than gold). In return for having supplied the currency, the supplying country acquires additional Special Drawing Rights (e.g. worth $40 million) which it may revoke if ever its currency "reserves" get too low. Each IMF Member Country participating in the SDR scheme has a finite allocation of SDRs available for its possible use. A net result of the SDR scheme is that countries "swap" currencies to help other countries from time to time in maintaining existing, relative values between their national currency and other currencies of the world.

There have also been regional efforts to use the "unit of account" to stabilize relationships among currencies within a region and thereby to promote regularity of currency settlements. Of these regional efforts the "Ecu" of the European Monetary System (EMS) was the most successful. The Ecu was used by EU countries to establish relative values of Member Country currencies. The Ecu, however, has been succeeded by the Euro, which is a "regional," rather than a national, currency. The Euro is issued by the European Central Bank. On January 1, 1999 the Euro became the currency of the 11 Member States of the EMS, replacing the German mark, the French franc and the national currencies of Austria, Belgium, Finland, Ireland,

Italy, Luxembourg, the Netherlands, Portugal and Spain. Those national currencies are now subdivisions of the Euro. Euro banknotes and coins will be issued on January 1, 2002; and the national coins and banknotes must be withdrawn by July 1, 2002.

REGIONAL AND OTHER DEVELOPMENT BANKS

Groups of countries have joined in international agreements to establish several, multi-nation development banks (multilateral development banks). The World Bank Group (capitalized at over $125 billion) has three principal institutions: the International Bank for Reconstruction and Development (IBRD), the International Development Association (IDA), and the International Finance Corporation (IFC). IFC activity includes direct investment (purchase of shares) in the promotion of productive enterprises on a mixed loan and equity basis; standby and underwriting arrangements; work with development finance companies; and provision of technical assistance to further a country's economic goals. In 1994, the IFC provided $2.5 billion for investments and loans in 231 projects in 65 countries, which had total costs of $15.8 billion.

Regional development banks include the African Development Bank, the Asian Development Bank, the European Bank for Reconstruction and Development, and the InterAmerican Development Bank. Capitalized by governments and functioning as non-profit lending institutions, the development banks offer loan guarantees and extend loans through both "hard loan windows" at close to market rates and through "soft loan windows" for long term at low rates.

For example, the Asian Development Bank (ADB) has both "developing" and "developed" countries in its membership; the "developing" members are in the Asian region, and "developed" members include the United States, Canada and twelve Western European countries. Paid-in capital of the ADB is provided by member subscriptions both of local currency and of hard currency. Loans are made to governments and to private entities for the purposes of promoting investment, fostering economic growth and increasing cooperation among member countries in the region. The ADB provides also technical assistance in preparation, evaluation and execution of development plans; additionally, the Bank finances technical assistance programs. In 1982, the ADB started equity financing of (and share participation in) certain private investment ventures and initiated co-financing arrangements with private commercial banks.

Similar to the ADB, the InterAmerican Development Bank (IADB) is a regional financing institution established in 1959 to aid high priority and social development projects in member developing countries within Latin America. The Bank makes loans at near market rates to national governments, to smaller political subdivisions and to private enterprises located in public and private sectors within eligible countries. Loans have been used to develop the economic infrastructure of such countries through the construction of highways, irrigation projects, ports, power plants, and telecommunication facilities. Forty-two countries are members of the Islamic Development Bank which acts in ways similar to the ADB and AIDB.

The aggregate of such international ad hoc arrangements and international institutions is frequently called the International Monetary System. Its usual importance in an international business transaction stems primarily from its stabilizing influence upon money value and upon money movement worldwide.

NATIONAL MONETARY SYSTEMS

In most nations, there is a hierarchy of organizations which implement internal monetary policy and facilitate private transactions. At the highest political level a government entity (such as a ministry of finance, or in the United States, the Treasury Department) sets national fiscal policy and handles financial functions of the government. The government entity makes regulations and policy about international financial transactions which begin or end in the country and sets broad monetary policy.

At a next lower political level is the central bank, which in the United States is the Federal Reserve System. The central bank is usually owned and controlled by the national government. It functions between the private and governmental sectors and between the domestic and international sectors, and it carries out the day-to-day implementation of monetary policy. Among other things, it usually issues bank notes and other currency and as the lender of last resort, providing liquidity to the economy when money supply is too tight (limited).

At a different level are the commercial banks which maintain deposit accounts, accepting deposits and paying out proceeds. In the United States, deposit accounts are available through various types of financial institutions—"full service" commercial banks, savings banks, savings and loan associations, and credit unions—but the deposit accounts most likely to be involved in an international transaction are available through commercial banks. The most familiar deposit account is the checking account, but there are now a bewildering array of other deposit accounts with special features. Commercial banks lend money, accept time deposits, issue certificates of deposit, offer trust services, act as consultants and carry out other financial functions. Commercial banks may be owned by governments or by private persons.

Specialized financial functions may be performed by other kinds of financial institutions, such as investment banks, merchant banks, factors, and some kinds of finance companies. For example, commercial banks may not finance some export-import transactions because of high risk terms or because central bank regulations will not permit certain types of financing by commercial banks. A number of finance companies have grown, both in the United States and abroad, which fill this gap in financing services. These companies typically offer medium and short term financing for export-import transactions at comparatively higher rates and perform a role similar to that of the factoring company in domestic U.S. trade. Such companies often offer two to five year loans for working capital for specific types of operations such as vessel charters and equipment leases.

Banks often open branches and subsidiaries in foreign countries, and a number of large banks have substantial international networks despite differing bank regulatory rules in various countries. For example, foreign bankers recognized that many areas within the United States (outside of New York) were "underbanked" by international standards, and foreign bank branches in the United States grew rapidly in the 1970s. Such branches of foreign banks were not under the supervision or regulation of any federal banking agency, but only under the supervision of state authorities. To provide federal supervision, in 1978 Congress enacted the International Banking Act which established nationwide rules for U.S. branches of foreign banks. In the United States, a Federal authorization for U.S. commercial banks to participate in international banking or international financing through a subsidiary company is provided by the Federal Reserve Act (12 U.S.C.A. §§ 611–631)(the "Edge Act"), as supplemented by Regulation K (see 12 C.F.R. Part 211). Under certain conditions, such Edge Act corporations may acquire an equity position in corporations not doing business in the United States as well as providing information to investors about methods of financing overseas investment projects. Additionally, "Agreement Corporations" may be established by national banking associations that desire to enter the international banking field (see 12 U.S.C.A. §§ 601–604).

EXPORT FINANCING PROGRAMS

National governments engage in lending and in loan guaranty programs to encourage world trade patterns which help domestic economic priorities. Supporters of United States efforts, made through the Export–Import Bank (Eximbank), claim that each $1 billion in export creates 40,000 jobs within the United States. Countries such as Canada, France, Germany, Italy, Japan, the United Kingdom, and the United States as well as regional groups like the European Union assist persons in financing the purchase of export products. Such assistance may include the extension, to overseas buyers, of loans ("buyer credits") at interest rates substantially below prevailing rates in private capital markets. Loan guarantees and insurance are also given by governments to lenders who finance exports. Moreover, some foreign buyers may be offered lines of credit to purchase exported goods. Export credit wars, particularly involving agricultural goods, sometimes break out among major industrial countries despite OECD attempts at regulating export financing rates and programs. Such wars are a frequent focus of the international law of subsidies and countervailing duties. A credit war broke out in the early 1980s over the award of New York City Metropolitan Transit Authority contracts for subway cars. A Canadian company eventually won the war, obtaining export subsidies later held subject to U.S. countervailing duty law.

The Eximbank, created by Congress, makes direct loans and gives loan guarantees to foreign purchasers of goods exported from the United States. The Eximbank regularly supports U.S. exports of heavy capital equipment, airplanes and large scale installations which are normally financed for a term beyond five years. Eximbank also supports borrowers who (in theory) cannot obtain private market financing and whose exports penetrate new markets. Pursuant to the 1982 Export Trading Company Act, Eximbank offers loan guarantees and revolving lines of credit to meet pre-export, short term loan needs. In 1980, Eximbank approved its first guaranty of a foreign currency loan, involving Dutch and U.S. banks, in order to help a Dutch company buy two Boeing 737 jetliners. Eximbank cooperates closely with private commercial banks in the United States and U.S. foreign aid programs.

On a more modest scale, the United States Small Business Administration offers an export loan guaranty program. The Commodity Credit Corporation (CCC) and Agency for International Development (Bureau for Private Enterprise) assist with the financing of exports, especially agricultural goods. In 1985, a special CCC fund (the Export Enhancement

Program) was created to target potential buyers of U.S. agricultural goods in markets thought to have been "unfairly" lost to EU export subsidies. Commercial banks offer limited export financing. Some states within the United States have created counterparts of Eximbank to promote their exports.

OFFSHORE BANKING (AND TAX HAVENS)

Bank regulation varies substantially from country to country. For example, the United States and England regulate banking closely. Some countries (and other independent banking jurisdictions such as the Cayman Islands or the Isle of Man) have few or virtually no banking regulations. Typically, such places also have strict business confidentiality (secrecy) laws which encourage banks to locate there. License and other revenues accrue to the country (or tax jurisdiction), and businesses are shielded by local law from inquiries about their structure, activities, financial worth, and sometimes even their business name. They are especially shielded from inquiries by taxing authorities from another country. Moreover, such havens typically have no treaty obligations or government information exchange programs, are usually "currency free" (free of any exchange controls), and have reduced taxation. Although Hong Kong, Singapore and Switzerland are labeled as "tax havens", principal offshore banking centers include also the Netherlands Antilles (Islands), the Cayman Islands, and nearly twenty-five other small, island states such as Nauru. There are also "tax treaty havens," which combine nominal local taxation with tax treaty benefits for foreign banks and investors. All tax havens have increasingly come under I.R.S. attack, particularly in the Caribbean where tariff and tax deductibility incentives created in the Caribbean Basin Economic Recovery Act of 1983 are offset by tax information exchange requirements.

Movement of money from the United States to "offshore" banking jurisdictions has increased as the government has tried to maximize the extent to which it taxes money earned abroad which is owned or controlled by U.S. taxpayers and to restrain capital outflow from the country. Restrictions governing loans and reserve assets have also prompted lenders to seek or to establish "shell banks" outside of the United States to serve foreign borrowers. Beginning in 1981, the United States has tried to encourage the return of overseas money by establishing International Banking Facilities (IBFs) in "free zones" (zones free from usual United States banking regulations). Such zones (and IBFs) are located in many cities, including New York City, Chicago, Miami, New Orleans, and San Francisco. IBFs may participate in the huge lending business involving Eurodollars; such dollars may now be deposited in the United States but remain owned by persons overseas. IBFs are also "tax havens", free from state and local taxation. For MNE borrowers present within the United States (but "domiciled" outside of the U.S.), IBFs have also lower "political risk" (unexpected currency blockage or seizure by a host country), are closer to corporate decision makers, and are freer of time zone complications.

INTERNATIONAL MOVEMENT OF MONEY

A few cities have developed international financial markets which serve primarily international needs. Because of geographic location, political stability, relatively few restrictions upon international economic transactions, well developed institutions, and well trained workers, these cities are able to provide markets and transfer facilities for the implementation of international financial transactions. Two international finance centers for the entire world are London and New York. Other important financial centers are found in Hong Kong and Singapore.

Money is found typically in the form of currency or interbank deposits. It is issued and regulated almost invariably by a government or a government controlled financial institution. Money exchanged within the nation issuing the currency is easily recognizable and reasonably predictable in its value. "International" money is less recognizable and less predictable.

Commercial banks which engage in international banking have correspondent banks or branches in other countries. Banks are called correspondents when they open accounts with each other. For example, Bank A in the United States will open an account in pounds sterling in Bank B in the United

Kingdom; similarly Bank B will open an account with Bank A in the United States by depositing U.S. dollars with Bank A. This arrangement, multiplied by many banks and many countries, is the fundamental means by which money is transferred internationally.

When one of Bank A's customers in the United States wishes to pay a bill in sterling to an obligee in England, he may accomplish this in several ways. One method is for Bank A to draw a bank check, payable in sterling, on its account with Bank B, then send it to the obligee in England. This is slow, but flexible, because the obligee can negotiate the bank check to third parties and get its money from them. A second method is for the customer to ask Bank A to "wire transfer" the funds to the obligee. Bank A can then instruct Bank B to pay the necessary amount to the obligee in sterling.

As to the first method, the United Nations has adopted a proposed Convention on International Bills of Exchange and Promissory Notes, and opened it for signature and ratification. See U.N. General Assembly Doc. A/42/17, Annex 1, and 28 Int. Legal Mat. 170 (1989). This Convention was drafted by the U.N. Commission on International Trade Law (UNCITRAL). The United States has signed but has not yet ratified the Convention. UNCITRAL has also drafted a Model Rules for International Credit Transfers, which applies primarily to international "wire transfers." 32 Int. Legal Mat. 587 (1993).

As to wire transfers, Fedwire is available within the United States to both "member banks" of the Federal Reserve System and to nonmember banks. Thus, it can be used by branches of foreign banks physically located in the U.S., as well as U.S. banks. It allows "virtually instantaneous" movement of funds between these banks. Fedwire has funds settlement capability through the debiting and crediting of reciprocal accounts, usually held at the Federal Reserve Bank, and settlement between the banks is on the same basis. In 1993, Fedwire moved more than $800 million each day, and the average amount of each transfer was over $3 million. Fedwire rules are set forth in Regulation J, Subpart B (12 C.F.R. §§ 210.25–210.38) and accompanying circulars.

The Clearing House Interbank Payment System (CHIPS) is operated by the New York Clearing House Association. It is estimated to handle 90% of both national and international interbank transfers of U.S. funds. CHIPS also moves over $1 trillion each day, and the average amount of each transfer is approximately $3 million. Like Fedwire, CHIPS is capable of funds settlement, usually on a same day basis, so funds are considered available on the day the transfer order is received. Losses of funds and losses from errors are allocated by internal rules, and usually protect the system from obligation.

The Society for Worldwide International Financial Telecommunications (SWIFT) is a communications system organized under Belgian law, which provides banks with a message concerning a transaction—but (unlike Fedwire and CHIPS) has no fund settlement capability. The message usually either advises a bank that a payment is being made or requests that a payment be made, or it can be used to issue a letter of credit. (See Chapter 3, above.) But the funds supporting the transfer do not accompany the message; that must be accomplished by other means. Thus, in the example above, Bank B would pay the obligee and then reimburse itself by taking an appropriate amount of sterling out of Bank A's account in Bank B.

FOREIGN EXCHANGE AND EXCHANGE CONTROLS

Entering the realm of international business transactions brings one face to face with new currencies. Goods sold to a French buyer may be paid for in French francs; those sold to a Guatemalan buyer may be paid in Guatemalan quetzals. The U.S. seller may have little difficulty in converting the francs to dollars, but the seller's U.S. bank may not be willing to accept the Guatemalan quetzals. The reason is that when the bank (or another U.S. bank in the chain of converting the currency to dollars) attempts to exchange the quetzals for dollars with the Guatemalan central bank, the Guatemalan bank may say that there are no dollars available, or that there are Guatemalan exchange controls which may limit or prohibit an exchange for this form of transaction. Developing nations often have very limited supplies of *hard* currencies.

Hard currencies are those freely exchangeable; those which are not freely exchangeable are usually called *soft* currencies.

It is not only the sale of goods across borders which brings one into the world of currency exchanges and exchange controls. A U.S. company planning an investment abroad will need other currencies. If IBM expands its plant in Mexico, it will need pesos to pay local costs for the construction of the building. It may use peso accounts in Mexico from past profits, or borrow pesos in a host nation bank, or convert dollars to pesos. It may wish to avoid doing the last, exchanging dollars for pesos, when it knows that later exchanging pesos for dollars may be difficult or impossible. One possible alternative would be to take advantage of the Mexican debt and participate in a debt-equity swap, discussed below.

Exchange rates and the convertibility of many currencies are often regulated by the governments of the countries issuing those currencies. But exchange rates of the major industrial nations' currencies are determined by a largely free market in these currencies. The exchange rates fluctuate daily according to how those who deal in currencies feel about the comparative value of the currencies. The going rate, and the predicted rate in the future, may be included in financial news, such as the Wall Street Journal or Financial Times. Governments and central banks may intervene to protect their own or other currencies, in an attempt to stabilize foreign exchange rates. That control may be in the form of buying weaker currencies. For example, in the late 1980s Germany and Japan helped support the dollar by purchasing dollars when the U.S. currency was falling. Other controls may include mandating obtaining licenses for the purchase of foreign currency, and the imposition of withholding taxes on interest paid on foreign deposits.

Some nations have established an official rate of exchange of their currency in relation to the U.S. dollar. The Mexican peso was long linked to the dollar at fixed amounts. Now it floats against the dollar, but with significant government attempts at regulation of the rate of change. The dollar is so important to Mexico, and used so regularly in transactions even within Mexico, that Mexico is sometimes said to be "dollarized." That means that a second currency is in a sense a de facto national currency. In Argentina the dollarization has been taken a step further, it is an officially acceptable currency. That has been done to support the Argentine peso, which is not only linked in value to the dollar, but which may be freely exchanged for dollars at any time. The Argentine government has even restricted the central bank from printing more pesos, and from increasing private bank money supplies for additional lending. To some degree, Argentina has delegated monetary policy to the U.S. Federal Reserve Bank. A further step would be to adopt the dollar. Panama uses the dollar as the official currency, there are no Panamanian bills in circulation. Panama has clearly deferred to the U.S. for monetary policy. Mexico and Canada have both debated adopting the dollar, and rejected such possibility. More acceptable might be adoption of a NAFTA currency, much like the Euro in the European Union, discussed below.

License requirements and mandatory exchanges through a central bank can be used to guarantee observance of the fixed rate, but can mean also that the value of that currency, relative to all other national currencies, will fluctuate as the relative value of the U.S. dollar fluctuates. As long as the United States is a significant trading partner for these countries, this method affords a measure of currency stability. Thus the discussion among trading partners of a separate currency (i.e., the Euro), or close formal linkage such as Argentina and the U.S. dollar.

Foreign exchanges are normally handled by foreign exchange traders in commercial banks. Often, foreign exchange "brokers" match up exchange traders (also known as "dealers") who have currencies to buy or sell. Most currency bought and sold in the exchange market is in the form of demand deposits. The following is a simple example of the operation of a foreign exchange transaction. An American businessman wishes to purchase a large quantity of woolen goods from England. The London seller insists on payment in sterling. The American goes to his bank in Atlanta to obtain the English pounds. The trader in the bank telephones other traders to see if any have pounds to sell. A trader with pounds quotes a price based on a certain rate of exchange for the two currencies. The

Atlanta bank trader buys the pounds and sells them to the American customer at cost plus a certain increase. The selling trader (possibly a large U.S. bank) arranges delivery of the pounds to the Atlanta bank's overseas account by sending payment instruction to a British bank, where the trader has pounds on deposit. It instructs the British bank to debit the trader's account for the amount of pounds and to transfer that amount to the overseas account of the Atlanta bank in London. The Atlanta bank will pay for the pounds by placing a correct amount of dollars in a demand deposit account maintained by the trader either in the Atlanta or another bank. This is a simplified transaction but reflects the basic elements of the system for exchanging currencies. Traders maintain balances in their foreign accounts, or may allow those accounts to go into overdraft according to their anticipation of market changes. Traders buy and sell among each other in large, round lots, e.g., $1 million or more at a time.

The foreign exchange market in the United States is one of the world's largest financial markets. Billions of dollars worth of many different currencies are exchanged every day in the United States alone. But there is no foreign exchange building or organization comparable to the New York Stock Exchange. Foreign exchange market activities are very decentralized, involving contact by individual bank foreign trading departments with brokers and with many other banks outside of the United States. The market is largely unregulated. Deals are normally made over the telephone or by unauthenticated telex messages which are followed later by written confirmations.

Oral exchange contracts are nearly always over $5,000 in value. Traders who deal orally over the telephone avoid statute of frauds problems without the aid of lawyers and courts, because a dealer's word must be believed or no other dealer will trade with him. The rules of the market are thus self-enforcing; a trader who doesn't play by the rules does not play at all. The pace of the foreign exchange market demands that a dealer make a deal by accepting an offer immediately. These contracts must be performed. If traders disagree subsequently about the terms, they usually split the difference.

There is nearly always a delay between the time when the contract for foreign exchange is made and the time when it is "settled," i.e., when funds are transferred into the accounts of the trading banks. Foreign exchange contracts are described usually as being either "spot" contracts or "future" contracts. Spot contracts are settled within a short period of time, usually within three days. Future, or forward, contracts are settled sometime after the spot. The date for settlement is always specified for a future contract.

Rates of exchange for spot delivery are different than rates for future delivery. The difference reflects a premium or discount based on what the experienced foreign exchange traders expect to happen in the market for the two currencies between the day of the trade and the day delivery will be made. The cost of borrowing in the respective currencies, expected changes in the balance of payments between the two nations of the exchanged currencies, and many other factors determine how traders set forward rates. Future contracts permit a business to balance its payments and receipts in each currency according to when it is needed.

EXCHANGE RISK

Lessening exchange risk is important when the exchange market is volatile. As an example, assume an American company agreed to buy goods from both Japan and Mexico, the contracts being signed on August 1, 1994. The goods were to be delivered December 31st. Payment was to be made on the latter date in yen to the Japanese seller, and in pesos to the Mexican seller. The Japanese contract price was 10,190,000 yen, that with Mexico 336,000 pesos. Each amount on August 1st was equal to $100,000 U.S. Between the contract date and the delivery and payment date the yen was strengthening. But the Mexican peso nearly collapsed in December. When the American buyer went to its bank in late December to obtain the needed yen and pesos it discovered that the August rates had significantly changed. The dollar was worth 96.4 yen on December 31st, in contrast to 101.9 yen on August 1st. To pay the contract price of 10,190,000 yen, the company had to exchange $105,705, an addition of some 5.7 percent to the price. It was not pleased that it had not covered the risk. But it discovered the situation with Mexico was very different. The dollar was worth 6.21 pesos on December 31st, in contrast to 3.36 pesos on August 1st. To pay the 336,000 pesos due required payment of only $54,-106, rather than $100,000. It more than covered the loss on the yen-dollar rate.

Companies buying and selling products across borders usually are not in the business of playing currency fluctuations. But the risk can be lessened by anticipating when foreign currencies should be purchased or sold and making advance provision for such purchases or sales through futures contracts with a foreign exchange dealer. The American purchaser from Japan and Mexico above could ask a foreign exchange dealer in the United States for a quote on the rate for delivery of the needed yen and pesos on December 1st. If the rate is consistent with the profit the American purchaser seeks when it resells the goods in the United States, he may buy a forward contract and sign the purchase agreement with the Japanese and Mexican sellers. Having thus made provision for the currency exchange risk, the profit will not be lessened by exchange risk; the buyer has shifted the risk to the currency trader which is better equipped to accept that risk by delivering yen and pesos from its own stock or by borrowing or purchasing yen and pesos in the market. The American buyer might have decided only to cover the yen transaction, because the yen in 1994 was generally strengthening against the dollar. But the buyer might have forgone covering the peso, which was suspected to be weak and over-valued.

Financial managers at some MNEs, which need to acquire certain foreign currency, sometimes initiate inquiries (directly or through a broker) to find another MNE which has similar but reverse needs for currency. The two MNEs then arrange a currency "swap". The technique works well in situations where an overseas MNE, holding much local currency within that country, is prevented by currency control laws from removing its local currency from that country. Currency clauses are an increasingly common part of international contracts; such clauses may provide that one party has the obligation to pay an amount in a named currency on a specific date, thus placing exchange risk on that party.

Because of the size of the American economy, and the widespread use of the U.S. dollar as a trading currency, most imports to and exports from the United States are paid for in U.S. dollars. This will change when and if the dollar becomes less dominant in the world market. More Americans involved in international business will then have to become more familiar with aspects of foreign exchange.

INTERNATIONAL DEPOSITS AND LOANS: EURODOLLARS

International deposits and loans occur in several ways. An American exporter may leave the proceeds of foreign sales to Great Britain deposited in Barclay's Bank in London in English pounds. Assuming free convertibility of currency, American investors may exchange dollars in the United States for currency of a foreign country, for example German Deutschmark, and then invest those funds in Germany. Other types of money market activities use an international (overseas) pool of money, called commonly the Eurodollar market or "Euro" market. The eurodollar should not be confused with the Euro, the latter being the increasingly accepted name for the new currency of the European Union, replacing the earlier used "ecu" (for European currency unit).

While Eurodollars are by definition dollars, any currency for which there is a ready market outside of that currency's home country can be treated as an "international deposit." Hence, there are Eurofrancs, Euromarks, etc. West Germany and Japan objected vigorously in 1982 to the issuance of (German) mark and (Japanese) yen certificates of deposit within the United States.

London is the center of the Eurodollar Market. But a parallel to Eurodollars exists, for example in Singapore, where they are called Asian Dollars and in Panama, where they are Latin Dollars. They are traded by dealers in financial centers throughout the world.

Eurodollars are created when holders of dollars who are not U.S. residents deposit the dollars with a bank in London, or another financial center, for a fixed period at an interest rate set by the dealer at the bank of deposit. That bank lends the money in turn for fixed periods at an interest rate slightly higher than the rate paid out on deposits.

The foregoing is a simple description of any money market where fixed time deposits offset fixed loans (which may, in fact, be time deposits placed with yet another bank). The Euromarket differs from domestic money markets in several important ways. The Bank of England and the central banks of Panama and Singapore impose very few controls upon the movement and use of foreign currency deposits. Interest rate ceilings which might be imposed for dollar deposits in the United States are not imposed upon the Euromarkets. Nor are any reserve requirements imposed upon Eurodollar deposits because, in part, the Bank of England does not have primary responsibility for the stability of the United States dollar or the integrity of the United States banking system. Therefore, it does not regulate those dollars which have found their way into British banks. Bankers who accept Eurodollar deposits may lend every penny taken in deposit. The pool of Eurodollars is substantial because of long running U.S. balance of payment deficits and because of fluidity afforded by the efficient Eurodollar market. Over one trillion "overseas" United States dollars are estimated to be in banks outside of the United States. Normally, a borrower of United States dollars can obtain them easily and at a free market rate in the Euromarket. There has been very little litigation over international deposits.

The Eurodollar pool has become a major source of funds in international finance. Long term loans are usually offered at a percent over the best London interest rate for Eurodollars. The long term loans may be refinanced at shorter intervals (e.g., 90 to 180 days), and a new interest rate is calculated based upon the cost of funds in the market place. The Eurodollar market is a truly international market both for obtaining and for placing funds. It is a market characterized by high liquidity and fast turnover. It is also relatively unregulated. There is no lender of last resort to stabilize this market when needed.

When money is borrowed in one country and is invested in another, the latter country may tax interest earned or profits made in that country by foreign residents, and an investor's projection of income from a foreign investment should take such taxes into account in calculating the overall cost of borrowing.

Other possible costs may appear if the law of the country where the investment is made is not entirely favorable to the investor should a local borrower default on payment. The possibility of experiencing an expropriation and potential difficulty in getting money out of a country where invested (e.g., currency controls) may move an investor to require that an international business transaction be financed locally within a host country. Local financing may be helped if an investor gives a guarantee to act as a surety for loans taken out by partners or affiliates in that country.

Where an international business transaction consists of the export of goods from one country and import of those goods into another, there are a number of ways that a transaction can be structured so that it is financed by an importer. For example, an importer may be required to pay on placing an order, or an irrevocable letter of credit (see Chapter 3, above) may be issued by the importer's bank. The transaction may be financed also by banker's acceptances, and perhaps by government programs either in the importer's country or by the exporter's government. It may be that an exporter rather than an importer may wish to finance the transaction. For example, the exporter may ship the goods on an open book account receivable (i.e., goods are shipped before payment is made and the importer pays upon their receipt). The exporter can ship goods on documents consigned to the order of his bank which, in turn, can endorse the documents to a bank in the importer's country, with instructions to release the title documents to the goods only upon payment by the importer. The exporter can ship on consignment with payment to be made after the importer has sold the goods. Goods may be shipped with documents against acceptance. (This arrangement is similar to an arrangement with documents against payment, except that the bank will release title documents to the importer upon the importer's "accepting" a draft on him payable a number of days after acceptance.)

The exporter may refinance his international sales by selling his accounts receivable to a factor in his own country. Because both the debt discount and collection activity may cross national boundaries, choice of law and place of enforceability (forum selection) are two clauses which should be included in the international sales contract (see Chapter 8 on Dispute Settlement, below).

FINANCIAL PRACTICES OF MULTI-NATIONAL ENTERPRISES: TRANSFER PRICING

Affiliated parts of a multinational enterprise often lend to each other across national borders. Since the enterprise as a whole has goals which each part seeks to assist in achieving, dealing with certain parts of the whole may be structured to advance corporate goals while achieving favorable tax or dividend consequences. The MNE effectively reallocates costs and revenues within its worldwide structure so that profits are increased where tax and exchange controls are considered favorable, and decreased where those controls are considered most severe. This is transfer pricing.

Host nations sometimes impose limits on profits that may be remitted abroad by foreign investor's local operations. The MNE may seek to offset the effect of these limits on profit remittances. The foreign parent may attempt to charge more for technology transferred to the affiliate, or for raw materials or components sold to the foreign affiliate. The host nation may respond by limiting amounts which may be paid for technology, and by demanding that the raw materials or components be obtained locally. Developing nations have strongly objected to MNEs' transfer pricing practices when the result appears to be very low or no profits in the developing nation because the parent has charged the local subsidiary very high prices for technology, raw materials and components transferred to the subsidiary, but the MNE parent appears to be profitable. Why has the MNE done this? Because the developing nation has high taxes on profits. Or because there are limits on profit remittances due to exchange controls, which are more lenient or do not exist for technology transfers, or for permitted imports of raw materials or components. What may anger the nation even more, and also local shareholders when the MNE has agreed to a joint venture with local equity, is when the same transfer pricing practices lead to few profits to distribute as dividends to the local shareholders.

It is not only the developing nations which object to artificial transfer pricing practices. Australia, Canada, Japan and the United States formed the Pacific Association of Tax Administrators to combat transfer pricing's possible interrelationship with tax evasion. Developing country monitoring of transfer pricing has not been very effective, partly because of a reluctance of the developed nations to participate in joint efforts which might transfer tax revenue away from the United States, and partly because much intracorporate transfer information is regarded as confidential.

The Organization for Economic Cooperation and Development (OECD) released in mid–1995 a discussion draft for the second part of a three part report on transfer pricing guidelines for multinational companies. The expected three part report will replace the OECD 1979 report on transfer pricing. Part II focuses on penalties and excessive documentation requirements. The draft is fairly consistent with the final IRS regulations, noted below, but suggests a more pragmatic approach towards required documentation and establishing clarity in the guidelines.

Transfer pricing has been addressed by several individual countries, not only international organizations. Within the United States, the Internal Revenue Service issued regulations under Section 482 in July, 1994. The regulations impose penalties for intercompany pricing not conducted under the regulation's arm's-length standards, which adopt a "best method" rule. The IRS practices have been criticized as arbitrary and unreasonable. But the IRS claims companies do not properly calculate transfer pricing. The Tax Court has had to resolve these conflicts, and is likely to be a frequent player as the IRS steps up its attack on improper transfer pricing.

Mexico has transfer pricing rules affecting the border industries or maquiladoras. The government has not strictly enforced provisions of the Mexican Tax Code which would require that the maquiladora recognize some level of profit for its services. The reason has been to protect jobs and the entire program itself, but the government could demand taxes on an arm's length basis for the services performed by the maquiladoras, and many foreign companies have adopted practices establishing a fee for services even though the parent has considered the maquiladora a contract assembler. The experience of the United States and Mexico illustrate how different nations may pursue problems of transfer pricing, from a vigorous attack on the practice to inaction to promote social goals, such as job creation.

CHAPTER FIVE

TECHNOLOGY TRANSFERS

Issues surrounding the transfer of knowledge across national borders have provoked intense discussions during the last decade. The discussions promise to continue unabated. At the core is the desire of third world countries (often advanced developing countries like Brazil, South Korea, Taiwan and Singapore) to obtain protected information quickly and affordably irrespective of the proprietary rights and profit motives of current holders (usually persons from the most developed countries). Developing countries want production processes which maximize uses of abundant, inexpensive labor but which result in products that are competitive in the international marketplace. Capital intensive production processes (e.g., robot production of automobiles) may be of less interest. MNEs may be willing to share (by way of license or sale) a good deal of proprietary information, but are reluctant to part with their "core technology."

Among the industrialized countries, efforts often occur to acquire (even by way of stealing) "leading edge" technology. One example involved attempted theft of IBM computer technology by Japanese companies ultimately caught by the F.B.I. In the United States, the Office of Export Administration uses the

export license procedure to control strategic technological "diversions." But in 1984 falsification of
licensing documents by prominent Norwegian and
Japanese companies allowed the Soviets to obtain
the technology for making vastly quieter submarine
propellers. In the ensuing scandal, "anti-Toshiba"
legislation was adopted in the U.S. Congress. See
Section 2443 of the 1988 Omnibus Trade and Competitiveness Act. Leading Japanese executives re-
signed their positions, which is considered the highest form of apology in Japanese business circles.

The predominant vehicle for controlling technology transfers across national borders is the "license"
or "franchise" contract. The holder of information
in one country first acquires the legally protected
right to own the information in another country.
The holder then licenses the right, usually for a fee,
to a person in that other country. The very sharing
of information raises a risk that proprietary control
of the technology may be lost or, at a minimum,
that a competitor will be created. Absent authorized
transfers, piracy of intellectual property is increasingly commonplace. Indeed, in some countries such
theft has risen to the height of development strategy.

The developing nations (as a "Group of 77"), the
industrialized nations and the nonmarket economy
nations have tried to agree in UNCTAD upon an
international "Code of Conduct" for the transfer of
technology. Wide disparities in attitudes toward
such a Code have been reflected by the developing
nations' insistence that it be an "internationally

legally binding Code," and the industrialized nations' position that it consist of "guidelines for the international transfer of technology." Some economics of the debate are illustrated by the fact that persons in the United States pay about one-tenth in royalties for use of imported technology than they receive in royalty payments from technology sent abroad. Many considered development of an international technology transfer Code the most important feature of the North–South dialogue. But it was not to be. Instead, to some degree the TRIPS Agreement from the Uruguay Round of GATT negotiations functions as such a code.

THE URUGUAY ROUND TRIPS AGREEMENT

The Uruguay Round accords of late 1993 include an agreement on trade-related intellectual property rights (TRIPs). This agreement is binding upon the over 130 nations that are members of the World Trade Organization. In the United States, the TRIPs agreement was ratified and implemented by Congress in December of 1994 under the Uruguay Round Agreements Act. There is a general requirement of national and most-favored-nation treatment among the parties.

The TRIPs Code covers the gamut of intellectual property. On copyrights, there is protection for computer programs and databases, rental authorization controls for owners of computer software and sound recordings, a 50–year motion picture and sound recording copyright term, and a general obligation to comply with the Berne Convention (except for its provisions on moral rights).

On patents, the Paris Convention (1967) prevails, product and process patents are to be available for pharmaceuticals and agricultural chemicals, limits are placed on compulsory licensing, and a general 20–year patent term from the date of application is created. United States law, which previously granted 17 year patents from the date of issuance, has been amended to conform. For trademarks, internationally prominent marks receive enhanced protection, the linking of local marks with foreign trademarks is prohibited, service marks become registrable, and compulsory licensing is banned. In addition, trade secret protection is assisted by TRIPs rules enabling owners to prevent unauthorized use or disclosure. Integrated circuits are covered by rules intended to improve upon the Washington Treaty. Lastly, industrial designs and geographic indicators of alcoholic beverages (e.g., Canadian Whiskey) are also part of the TRIPS regime.

Infringement and anticounterfeiting remedies are included in the TRIPs, for both domestic and international trade protection. There are specific provisions governing injunctions, damages, customs seizures, and discovery of evidence.

PATENT PROTECTION

For the most part, patents are granted to inventors according to national law. Thus, patents represent *territorial* grants of exclusive rights. The inventor receives Canadian patents, United States patents, Mexican patents, and so on. Since over one hundred countries have laws regulating patents, there are relatively few jurisdictions without some form of patent protection. However, legally protected intellectual property in one country may not be protected similarly in another country. For example, many third world nations *refuse* to grant patents on pharmaceuticals. These countries often assert that their public health needs require such a policy. Thailand has traditionally been one such country and unlicensed "generics" have been a growth industry there.

Nominal patent protection in some developing nations may lack effective forms of relief—giving the appearance but not the reality of legal rights. Since international patent protection is expensive to obtain, some holders take a chance and limit their applications to those markets where they foresee demand or competition for their product. Nevertheless, U.S. nationals continue to receive tens of thousands of patents in other countries. But the reverse is also increasingly true. Residents of foreign countries now receive over 50 percent of the patents issued under United States law. In many countries, persons who deal with the issuance and protection of patents are called patent agents. In the United

States, patent practice is a specialized branch of the legal profession. Obtaining international patent protection often involves retaining the services of specialists in each country.

What constitutes a "patent" and how it is protected in any country depends upon domestic law. In the United States, a patent issued by the U.S. Patent Office grants the right for 20 years to exclude everyone from making, using or selling the patented invention without the permission of the patentee. The United States grants patents to the "first to invent," not (as in many other countries) the "first to file." Patent infringement can result in injunctive and damages relief in the U.S. courts. "Exclusion orders" against foreign-made patent infringing goods are also available. Such orders are frequently issued by the International Trade Commission under Section 337 of the Tariff Act of 1930, and are enforced by the U.S. Customs Service. A U.S. patent thus provides a short-term legal, but not necessarily economic, monopoly. For example, the exclusive legal rights conveyed by the patents held by Xerox on its photocopying machines have not given it a monopoly in the marketplace. There are many other producers of non-infringing photocopy machines with whom Xerox competes.

There are basically two types of patent systems in the world community, registration and examination. Some countries (e.g., France) grant a patent upon "registration" accompanied by appropriate documents and fees, without making an inquiry about the patentability of the invention. The validity of such a patent grant is most difficult to gauge until a time comes to defend the patent against alleged infringement in an appropriate tribunal. In other countries, the patent grant is made following a careful "examination" of the prior art and statutory criteria on patentability or a "deferred examination" is made following public notice given to permit an "opposition." The odds are increased that the validity of such a patent will be sustained in the face of an alleged infringement. The United States and Germany have examination systems. To obtain U.S. patents, applicants must demonstrate to the satisfaction of the U.S. Patent Office that their inventions are novel, useful and nonobvious. Nevertheless, a significant number of U.S. patents have been subsequently held invalid in the courts and the Patent Office has frequently been criticized for a lax approach to issuance of patents. In 1998, over 150,000 U.S. patents were issued, an increase of 33 percent above 1997. Much of this growth is centered in high-tech industries, including computer software patents.

The terms of a patent grant vary from country to country. For example, local law may provide for "confirmation," "importation," "introduction" or "revalidation" patents (which serve to extend limited protection to patents already existing in another country). "Inventor's certificates" and rewards are granted in some socialist countries where private ownership of the means of production is discouraged. The state owns the invention. This was the case in China, for example, but inventors now may obtain patents and exclusive private rights under the 1984 Patent Law. Some countries, such as Britain, require that a patent be "worked" (commercially applied) within a designated period of time. This requirement is so important that the British mandate a "compulsory license" to local persons if a patent is deemed unworked. Many developing nations have similar provisions in their patent laws . . . the owner must use it or lose it.

INTERNATIONAL RECOGNITION OF PATENTS

The principal treaties regarding patents are the 1970 Patent Cooperation Treaty and the 1883 Convention of the Union of Paris, frequently revised and amended. To some extent, the Paris Convention also deals with trademarks, servicemarks, trade names, industrial designs, and unfair competition. Other recent treaties dealing with patents are the European Patent Convention (designed to permit a single office at Munich and The Hague to issue patents of all countries party to the treaty), and the European Union Patent Convention (designed to create a single patent valid throughout the EU).

The Paris Convention, to which over 100 countries including the U.S. are parties, remains the basic international agreement dealing with treatment of foreigners under national patent laws. It is administered by the International Bureau of the World Intellectual Property Organization (WIPO) at Geneva. The "right of national treatment" (Article

2) prohibits discrimination against foreign holders of local patents and trademarks. Thus, for example, a foreigner granted a Canadian patent must receive the same legal rights and remedies accorded Canadian nationals. Furthermore, important "rights of priority" are granted to patent holders provided they file in foreign jurisdictions within twelve months of their home country patent applications. But such rights may not overcome prior filings by others in "first to file" jurisdictions. Patent applications in foreign jurisdictions are not dependent upon success in the home country. Patentability criteria vary from country to country. Nevertheless, the Paris Convention obviates the need to file simultaneously in every country where intellectual property protection is sought. If an inventor elects not to obtain patent protection in other countries, anyone may make, use or sell the invention in that territory. The Paris Convention does not attempt to reduce the need for individual patent applications in all jurisdictions where patent protection is sought. Nor does it alter the various domestic criteria on patentability.

The Patent Cooperation Treaty (PCT), to which about 40 countries including the U.S. are parties, is designed to achieve greater uniformity and less cost in the international patent filing process, and in the examination of prior art. Instead of filing patent applications individually in each nation, filings under the PCT are done in selected countries. The national patent offices of Japan, Sweden, Russia and the United States have been designated International Searching Authorities (ISA), as has the European Patent Office at Munich and The Hague. The international application, together with the international search report, is communicated by an ISA to each national patent office where protection is sought. Nothing in this Treaty limits the freedom of each nation to establish substantive conditions of patentability and determine infringement remedies. However, the Patent Cooperation Treaty also provides that the applicant may arrange for an international preliminary examination in order to formulate a non-binding opinion on whether the claimed invention is novel, involves an inventive step (non-obvious) and is industrially applicable. In a country without sophisticated search facilities, the report of the international preliminary examination may largely determine whether a patent will be granted. For this reason alone, the Patent Cooperation Treaty may generate considerable uniformity in world patent law. In 1986 the United States ratified the PCT provisions on preliminary examination reports, thereby supporting such uniformity.

KNOWHOW

Knowhow is commercially valuable knowledge. It may or may not be a trade secret, and may or may not be patentable. Though often technical or scientific, e.g. engineering services, knowhow can also be more general in character. Marketing and management skills as well as simply business advice can constitute knowhow. If someone is willing to pay for the information, it can be sold or licensed internationally.

Legal protection for knowhow varies from country to country and is, at best, limited. Unlike patents, copyrights and trademarks, you cannot by registration obtain exclusive legal rights to knowhow. Knowledge, like the air we breathe, is a public good. Once released in the community, knowhow can generally be used by anyone and is almost impossible to retrieve. In the absence of exclusive legal rights, preserving the confidentiality of knowhow becomes an important business strategy. If everyone knows it, who will pay for it? If your competitors have access to the knowledge, your market position is at risk. It is for these reasons that only a few people on earth ever know the Coca Cola formula, which is perhaps the world's best kept knowhow.

Protecting knowhow is mostly a function of contract, tort and trade secrets law. Employers will surround their critical knowhow with employees bound by contract to confidentiality. But some valuable knowledge leaks from or moves with these employees, e.g. when a disgruntled retired or ex-employee sells or goes public with the knowhow. The remedies at law or in equity for breach of contract are unlikely to render the employer whole. Neither is torts relief likely to be sufficient since most employees are essentially judgment proof, though they may be of more use if a competitor induced the breach of contract. Likewise, even though genuine trade secrets are protected by criminal statutes in a few jurisdictions, persuading the prosecutor to take up your business problem is not easy and criminal penalties will not recoup the trade secrets (though they may make the revelation of others less likely in the future).

Despite all of these legal hazards, even when certain knowhow is patentable, a desire to prolong the commercial exploitation of that knowledge may result in no patent registrations. The international chemicals industry, for example, is said to prefer trade secrets to public disclosure and patent rights with time limitations. Licensing or selling such knowhow around the globe is risky, but lucrative.

The Economic Espionage Act of 1996 creates *criminal* penalties for misappropriation of trade secrets for the benefit of foreign governments or anyone. For these purposes, a "trade secret" is defined as "financial, business, scientific, technical, economic or engineering information" that the owner has taken reasonable measures to keep secret and whose "independent economic value derives from being closely held." In addition to criminal fines, forfeitures and jail terms, the Act authorizes seizure of all proceeds from the theft of trade secrets as well as property used or intended for use in the misappropriation (e.g., buildings and capital equipment).

TRADEMARK PROTECTION

Virtually all countries offer some legal protection to trademarks, even when they do not have trademark registration systems. Trademark rights derived from the use of marks on goods in commerce have long been recognized at common law and remain so today in countries as diverse as the United States and the United Arab Emirates. The latter nation, for example, had no trademark registration law in 1986, but this did not prevent McDonald's from obtaining an injunction against a local business using its famous name and golden arches without authorization. However, obtaining international trademark protection requires separate registration under the law of each nation.

Roughly 50,000 trademark applications are filed each year by United States citizens with the appropriate authorities in other countries. In the United States, trademarks are protected at common law and by state and federal registrations. Federal registration is permitted by the U.S. Trademark Office for all marks capable of distinguishing the goods on which they appear from other goods. Unless the mark falls within a category of forbidden registrations (e.g. those that offend socialist morality in the People's Republic of China), a mark becomes valid for a term of years following registration.

In some countries (like the U.S. prior to 1989), marks must be used on goods before registration. In others, like France, use is not required and speculative registration of marks can occur. It is said that ESSO was obliged to purchase French trademark rights from such a speculator when it switched to EXXON in its search for the perfect global trademark. Since 1989, United States law has allowed applications when there is a bona fide intent to use a trademark within 12 months and, if there is good cause for the delay in actual usage, up to 24 additional months. Such filings in effect reserve the mark for the applicant. The emphasis on bona fide intent and good cause represent an attempt to control any speculative use of U.S. trademark law.

The scope of trademark protection may differ substantially from country to country. Under U.S. federal trademark law, injunctions, damages and seizures of goods by customs officials may follow infringement. Other jurisdictions may provide similar remedies on their law books, but offer little practical enforcement. Thus, trademark registration is no guarantee against trademark piracy. A pair of blue jeans labeled "Levi Strauss made in San Francisco" may have been counterfeited in Israel or Paraguay without the knowledge or consent of Levi Strauss and in spite of its trademark registrations in those countries. Trademark counterfeiting is not just a third world problem, as any visitor to a United States "flea market" can tell. Congress created criminal offenses and private treble damages remedies for the first time in the Trademark Counterfeiting Act of 1984.

In many countries trademarks (appearing on goods) may be distinguished from "service marks" used by providers of services (e.g., The Law Store), "trade names" (business names), "collective marks" (marks used by a group or organization), and "certification marks" (marks which certify a certain quality, origin, or other fact). Although national trademark schemes differ, it can be said generally that a valid trademark (e.g., a mark not "canceled," "renounced," "abandoned," "waived" or "generic") will be protected against infringing use. A trademark can be valid in one country (ASPIRIN brand tablets in Canada), but invalid because generic in another (BAYER brand aspirin in the United States). A trademark can be valid, e.g., CHEVROLET NOVA brand automobiles in the U.S. and Mexico, but diminished in value for reasons of language. If you were Mexican, would you buy a CHEVROLET promising to "no va"?

Unlike patents and copyrights, trademarks may be renewed continuously. A valid mark may be licensed, perhaps to a "registered user" or it may be assigned, in some cases only with the sale of the goodwill of a business. A growing example of international licensing of trademarks can be found in franchise agreements taken abroad. And national trademark law sometimes accompanies international licensing. The principal U.S. trademark law, the Lanham Act of 1946, has been construed to apply extraterritorially (much like the Sherman Antitrust Act) to foreign licensees engaging in deceptive practices. See especially *Scotch Whiskey Association v. Barton Distilling Co.,* 489 F.2d 809 (7th Cir.1973).

Foreigners who seek a registration may be required to prove a prior and valid "home registration," and a new registration in another country may not have an existence "independent" of the continuing validity of the home country registration. Foreigners are often assisted in their registration efforts by international and regional trademark treaties.

INTERNATIONAL RECOGNITION OF TRADEMARKS

The premium placed on priority of use of a trademark is reflected in several international trademark treaties. These include the Paris Convention, the 1957 Arrangement of Nice Concerning the International Classification of Goods and Services, and the 1973 Trademark Registration Treaty done at Vienna. The treaties of widest international application are the Paris Convention and the Arrangement of Nice, as revised to 1967, to which the United States is signatory. The International Bureau of WIPO plays a central role in the administration of arrangements contemplated by these agreements.

The Paris Convention reflects an effort to internationalize some trademark rules. In addition to extending the principle of national treatment in Article 2 and providing for a right of priority of six months for trademarks (see patent discussion ante), the Convention mitigates the frequent national requirement that foreigners seeking trademark registration prove a pre-existing, valid and continuing home registration. This makes it easier to obtain foreign trademark registrations, avoids the possibility that a lapse in registration at home will cause all foreign registrations to become invalid, and allows registration abroad of entirely different (and perhaps culturally adapted) marks. Article 6 bis of the

Paris Convention gives owners of "well known" trademarks the right to block or cancel the unauthorized registration of their marks. One issue that frequently arises under this provision is whether the mark needs to be well known locally or just internationally to obtain protection.

The Nice Agreement addresses the question of registration by "class" or "classification" of goods. In order to simplify internal administrative procedures relating to marks, many countries classify and thereby identify goods (and sometimes services) which have the same or similar attributes. An applicant seeking registration of a mark often is required to specify the class or classes to which the product mark belongs. However, not all countries have the same classification system and some lack any such system. Article 1 of the Nice Agreement adopts, for the purposes of the registration of marks, a single classification system for goods and services. This has brought order out of chaos in the field.

The 1973 Vienna Trademark Registration Treaty (to which the United States is a signatory) contemplates an international filing and examination scheme like that in force for patents under the Patent Cooperation Treaty. This treaty has not yet been fully implemented, but holds out the promise of reduced costs and greater uniformity when obtaining international trademark protection. At least twenty-nine European and Mediterranean countries are parties to the Madrid Agreement for International Registration of Marks (1891, as amended). This agreement already permits international filings to obtain national trademark rights and is administered by WIPO. A Common Market trademark has been developed by the European Community.

COPYRIGHT PROTECTION

Nearly one hundred nations recognize some form of copyright protection for "authors' works." The scope of this coverage and available remedies varies from country to country, with some uniformity established in the roughly 80 nations participating in the Berne and Universal Copyright Conventions, *infra*. In the United States, for example, the Copyright Act of 1976 protects all original expressions fixed in a tangible medium (now known or later developed), including literary works, musical works, dramatic works, choreographic works, graphic works, audiovisual works, sound recordings and computer programs. It is not necessary to publish a work to obtain a U.S. copyright. It is sufficient that the work is original and fixed in a tangible medium of expression. Prior to 1989, to retain a U.S. copyright, the author had to give formal notice of a reservation of rights when publishing the work. Publication of the work without such notice no longer dedicates it to free public usage.

U.S. copyright protection now extends from creation of the work to 70 years after the death of the author. The author also controls "derivative works," such as movies made from books. Only the author (or her assignees or employer in appropriate cases) may make copies, display, perform, and first sell the work. Registration with the U.S. Copyright Office is not required to obtain copyright rights, but is important to federal copyright infringement remedies. Infringers are subject to criminal penalties, injunctive relief and civil damages. Infringing works are impounded pending trial and ultimately destroyed. But educators, critics and news reporters are allowed "fair use" of the work, a traditional common law doctrine now codified in the 1976 Copyright Act.

The marketing of copyrights is sometimes accomplished through agency "clearinghouses." This is especially true of musical compositions because the many authors and potential users are dispersed. In the United States, the American Society of Composers, Authors and Publishers (ASCAP) and Broadcast Music, Inc. (BMI) are the principal clearinghouses for such rights. Thousands of these rights are sold under "blanket licenses" for fees established by the clearinghouses and later distributed to their members. Similar organizations exist in most European states. Their activities have repeatedly been scrutinized under United States and EU antitrust law. See *Broadcast Music, Inc. v. Columbia Broadcasting System, Inc.,* 441 U.S. 1 (1979); *Re GEMA,* 10 Common Mkt.L.Rep. D34 (1971), 11 Common Mkt.L.Rep. 694 (1972). A Joint International Copyright Information Service run since 1981 by WIPO and UNESCO is designed to promote licensing of copyrights in the third world. This Service does not act as an agency clearinghouse for authors' rights, a deficiency sometimes said to promote copyright piracy.

Copyright protection in other countries may be more or less comprehensive or capable of adaptation to modern technologies. The copyrightability of computer programs, for example, is less certain in many jurisdictions. In some developing countries, "fair use" is a theme which is expansively construed to undermine copyright protection. But these differences seem less significant when contrasted with the worldwide problem of copyright piracy, ranging from satellite signal poaching to unlicensed tapes and books.

In the United States, the Copyright Felony Act of 1992 criminalized all copyright infringements. The No Electronic Theft Act of 1997 (NET) removed the need to prove financial gain as element of copyright infringement law, thus ensuring coverage of copying done with intent to harm copyright owners or copying simply for personal use. The Digital Millenium Copyright Act of 1998 (DMCA) brought the United States into compliance with WIPO treaties and created two new copyright offenses; one for circumventing technological measures used by copyright owners to protect their works ("hacking") and a second for tampering with copyright management information (encryption). The DMCA also made it clear that "webmasters" digitally broadcasting music on the internet must pay performance royalties.

INTERNATIONAL RECOGNITION
OF COPYRIGHTS

Absent an appropriate convention, copyright registrations must be tediously acquired in each country recognizing such rights. However, copyright holders receive national treatment, translation rights and other benefits under the Universal Copyright Convention (UCC) of 1952 (U.S. adheres). Most importantly, the UCC *excuses* foreigners from registration requirements provided notice of a claim of copyright is adequately given (e.g., © Folsom, Gordon and Spanogle, 1995). Some countries like the U.S. took advantage of an option *not* to excuse registration requirements. The exercise of this option had the effect at that time of reinforcing the U.S. "manufacturing clause" requiring local printing of U.S. copyrighted books and prohibiting importation of foreign copies. This protectionist clause finally expired under U.S. copyright law in 1986. The UCC establishes a minimum term for copyright protection: 25 years after publication, prior registration or death of the author. It also authorizes compulsory license schemes for translation rights in all states and compulsory reprint rights and instructional usage in developing countries.

National treatment and a release from registration formalities (subject to copyright notice requirements) can be obtained in Pan–American countries under the Mexico City Convention of 1902 and the Buenos Aires Convention of 1911, the U.S. adhering to both. Various benefits can be had in many other countries through the Berne Convention of 1886 (as revised). Like the UCC, the Berne Convention suspends registration requirements for copyright holders from participating states. Unlike the UCC, it allows for local copyright protection independent of protection granted in the country of origin and does not require copyright notice. The Berne Convention establishes a minimum copyright term of the life of the author plus 50 years, a more generous minimum copyright than that of the UCC. It also recognizes the exclusive translation rights of authors. The Berne Convention does not contemplate compulsory licensing of translation rights. Most U.S. copyright holders previously acquired Berne Convention benefits by simultaneously publishing their works in Canada, a member country.

In 1989, the United States ratified the Berne Convention. U.S. ratification of the Berne Convention creates copyright relations with an additional 25 nations. Ratification has eliminated U.S. registration requirements (reserved under the UCC) for foreign copyright holders and required protection of the "moral rights" of authors, i.e. the rights of integrity and paternity. The right of paternity insures acknowledgement of authorship. The right of integrity conveys the ability to object to distortion, alteration or other derogation of the work. It is generally thought that unfair competition law at the federal and state levels will provide the legal basis in U.S. law for these moral rights. A limited class of visual artists explicitly receive these rights under the Visual Artists Rights Act of 1990.

FRANCHISING IN THE
UNITED STATES

Franchising is an important sector in the United States economy. Thousands of franchisors have created and administer franchise systems throughout the nation. United States franchisees number in the hundreds of thousands. These franchisees are typically independent business persons, and their local franchise outlets employ millions of people. It has been estimated that approximately one-third of all retail sales in the United States take place through franchised outlets. Just as United States franchisors have found franchising particularly effective for market penetration abroad, Canadian, European and Japanese companies are increasingly penetrating the United States market through franchising.

Franchising is a business technique that permits rapid and flexible penetration of markets, growth and capital development. In the United States, there are traditional distinctions between product franchises and business format franchises. Product franchises involve manufacturers who actually produce the goods that are distributed through franchise agreements. For example, ice cream stores, soft drink bottling companies and gasoline retailers are often the subject of product franchises. Business format franchises are more common. These do not involve the manufacture by the franchisor of the product being sold by the franchisee. More typically, the franchisor licenses intellectual property rights in conjunction with a particular "formula for success" of the business. Fast food establishments, hotels, and a variety of service franchises are examples of business format franchising.

United States regulation of franchise relationships occurs at both the federal and state levels of government. Such regulation can be as specific as the Federal Trade Commission Franchising Rule and state franchise disclosure duties or as amorphous as the ever present dangers of state and federal antitrust law.

INTERNATIONAL FRANCHISING

International franchising raises a host of legal issues under intellectual property, antitrust, tax, licensing and other laws. The significance of these issues is magnified by the rapid growth of international franchising. Many U.S. franchisors start in Canada, with Japan and Britain following. Some U.S. investors have found franchising the least risky and most popular way to enter Central and Eastern Europe. Franchising is not just a U.S. export. Many foreign franchisors have entered the United States market. Most franchisors have standard contracts which are used in their home markets and receive counsel on the myriad of laws relevant to their business operations. Such contracts need to be revised and adapted to international franchising without significantly altering the franchisor's successful business formula. Franchise fees and royalties must be specified, the provision of services, training, and control by the franchisor detailed, the term and area of the franchise negotiated ("master franchises" conveying rights in an entire country or region are common in international franchise agreements), accounting procedures agreed upon, business standards and advertising selected, insurance obtained, taxes and other liabilities allocated, and default and dispute settlement procedures decided. At the heart of all franchise agreements lies a trademark licensing clause conveying local trademark rights of the franchisor to the franchisee in return for royalty payments.

Were franchising unaffected by regulation, the attorney's role would be limited to negotiation and drafting of the agreement. But international franchising is increasingly regulated by home and host jurisdictions, including regional groups like the EU. In third world countries, especially Latin America, technology transfer laws, aimed principally at international patent and knowhow licensing, also regulate franchise agreements. These laws benefit franchisees and further development policies, e.g., conservation of hard currencies by control of royalty levels. In 1986, the European Court of Justice issued its first major opinion on the legality of franchise agreements under competition law. *Pronuptia de Paris GmbH v. Pronuptia de Paris Irmgard Schillgallis,* 45 Common Mkt.L.Rep. 414 (1986). This decision indicates that European law can depart significantly from leading American antitrust law on market division arrangements for distributors. The Europeans have since implemented a comprehensive regulation on franchise agreements. Commission Regulation No. 4087/88. Compare *Con-*

tinental T.V., Inc. v. GTE Sylvania Inc., 433 U.S. 36 (1977)(location clauses not per se illegal).

There is often a perception of being invaded culturally that follows franchising. Local laws sometimes respond to the cultural impact of foreign franchises, as when McDonald's wishes to introduce its large golden arch into the traditional architecture of Europe. But this did not stop McDonald's from opening in Moscow with great success. In India and Mexico, nationalist feelings hostile to the appearance of foreign trademarks on franchised products have produced laws intended to remove such usage. For example, the Mexican Law of Inventions and Tradenames (1976)(repealed 1987) anticipated requiring use of culturally Mexican marks in addition to marks of foreign origin. Other nations require local materials (olive oil in the Mediterranean) to be substituted. This could, for example, alter the formula for success (and value) of fast food franchises. Still others (e.g., Alberta, Canada) mandate extensive disclosures by franchisors in a registered prospectus before agreements may be completed. Disclosure violations can trigger a range of franchisee remedies: rescission, injunction, and damages. Such laws are also found in many of the American states.

Franchise advertising must conform to local law. For example, regulations in the People's Republic of China prohibit ads which "have reactionary ... content." Antitrust and tax law are important in international franchising. Double taxation treaties, for example, will affect the level of taxation of royalties. Antitrust law will temper purchasing requirements of the franchisor, lest unlawful "tying arrangements" be undertaken. Tying arrangements involve coercion of franchisees to take supplies from the franchisor or designated sources in return for the franchise. Such arrangements must, by definition, involve two products: the tying and tied products. They are subject to a complex, not entirely consistent, body of case law under the U.S. Sherman Antitrust Act, Articles 81 and 82 of the Rome Treaty and other laws.

One leading United States case treats the trademark license as a separate tying product and the requirement of the purchase by franchisees of nonessential cooking equipment and paper products unlawful. *Siegel v. Chicken Delight, Inc.,* 448 F.2d 43 (9th Cir.1971). Another case permits franchisors to require franchisees to purchase "core products" (e.g., chicken) subject to detailed specifications, or from a designated list of approved sources. *Kentucky Fried Chicken Corp. v. Diversified Packaging Corp.,* 549 F.2d 368 (5th Cir.1977). Sometimes, the "core product" and the trademark license are treated as a single product incapable of being tied in violation of the law. *Krehl v. Baskin–Robbins Ice Cream Co.,* 664 F.2d 1348 (9th Cir.1982)(franchisees must buy Baskin–Robbins ice cream). Still another leading case suggests that anything comprising the franchisor's "formula for success" may possibly be tied in the franchise contract. *Principe v. McDonald's Corp.,* 631 F.2d 303 (4th Cir.1980). (franchisees

required to lease land and buildings from Mc-
Donald's).

INTERNATIONAL PATENT AND
KNOWHOW LICENSING

This section concerns the most common form of
lawful international technology transfer—patent
and knowhow licensing. Before any patent licensing
can take place, patents must be acquired in all
countries in which the owner hopes there will be
persons interested in purchasing the technology.
Even in countries where the owner has no such
hope, patent rights may still be obtained so as to
foreclose future unlicensed competitors. Licensing is
a middle ground alternative to exporting from the
owner's home country and direct investment in host
markets. It can often produce, with relatively little
cost, immediate positive cash flows.

International patent and knowhow licensing is
the most critical form of technology transfer to
third world development. From the owner's standpoint, it presents an alternative to and sometimes
a first step towards foreign investment. Such licensing involves a transfer of patent rights or
knowhow (commercially valuable knowledge, often
falling short of a patentable invention) in return
for payments, usually termed royalties. Unlike foreign investment, licensing does not have to involve
a capital investment in a host jurisdiction. However, licensing of patents and knowhow is not without legal risks.

From the licensee's standpoint, and the perspective of its government, there is the risk that the licensed technology may be old or obsolete, not "state of the art." Goods produced under old technology will be hard to export and convey a certain "second class" status. On the other hand, older more labor intensive technologies may actually be sought (as sometimes done by the PRC) in the early stages of development. Excessive royalties may threaten the economic viability of the licensee and drain hard currencies from the country. The licensee typically is not in a sufficiently powerful position to bargain away restrictive features of standard international licenses. For all these reasons, and more, third world countries frequently regulate patent and knowhow licensing agreements. Such law is found in the Brazilian Normative Act No. 17 (1976) and the Mexican Technology Transfer Law (1982)(repealed 1991), among others. Royalty levels will be limited, certain clauses prohibited (e.g., export restraints, resale price maintenance, mandatory grantbacks to the licensor of improvements), and the desirability of the technology evaluated.

Regulation of patent and knowhow licensing agreements is hardly limited to the third world. The Common Market, for example, after several test cases before the European Court of Justice, issued a "block exemption" controlling patent licensing agreements. Many of the licensing agreement clauses controlled by this 1984 Regulation were the same as those covered by third world technology transfer legislation. Its successor, Regulation 240 of 1996, broadly regulates technology transfer agreements. Regulation 240/96 prohibits production restraints, forbids the fixing of retail prices for the licensed product by the licensor, does not permit the licensor to select to whom the licensee may sell, limits the power of the licensor to require the licensee to "grant back" product improvements, and preserves the licensee's right to challenge the validity of the patent. It also governs exclusive licensing arrangements, the allocation of geographic territories among licensees, trademark usage, tying arrangements, fields of use of the patent, the duration of the license, protection of related knowhow, quality controls, and discrimination between licensees by the licensor. Regulation of patent and knowhow licensing in the United States is less direct and predominantly the concern of patent and antitrust law (e.g., tying practices).

The licensor also faces legal risks. The flow of royalty payments may be stopped, suspended or reduced by currency exchange regulations. The taxation of the royalties, if not governed by double taxation treaties, may be confiscatory. The licensee may produce "gray market" goods (*infra*) which eventually compete for sales in markets exclusively intended for the licensor. In the end, patents expire and become part of the world domain. At that point, the licensee has effectively purchased the technology and becomes an independent competitor (though not necessarily an effective competitor if the licensor has made new technological advances).

Licensing is a kind of partnership. If the licensee succeeds, the licensor's royalties (often based on sales volumes) will increase and a continuing partnership through succeeding generations of technology may evolve. If not, the dispute settlement provisions of the agreement may be called upon as either party withdraws from the partnership. Licensing of patents and knowhow often is combined with, indeed essential to, foreign investments. A foreign subsidiary or joint venture will need technical assistance and knowhow to commence operations. When this occurs, the licensing terms are usually a part of the basic joint venture or investment agreement. Licensing may also be combined with a trade agreement, as where the licensor ships necessary supplies to the licensee, joint venturer, or subsidiary. Such supply agreements have sometimes been used to overcome royalty limitations through a form of "transfer pricing," the practice of marking up or down the price of goods so as to allocate revenues to preferred parties and jurisdictions (e.g., tax havens).

PROTECTION FROM PIRACY

Theft of intellectual property and use of counterfeit goods are rapidly increasing in developing and developed countries. Such theft is not limited to consumer goods (Pierre Cardin clothing, Rolex watches). Industrial products and parts (e.g. automotive brake pads) are now being counterfeited. Some developing countries see illegal technology transfers as part of their economic development.

They encourage piracy or choose not to oppose it. Since unlicensed producers pay no royalties, they often have lower production costs than the original source. This practice fuels the fires of intellectual property piracy. Unlicensed low cost reproduction of entire copyrighted books (may it not happen to this book) is said to be rampant in such diverse areas as Nigeria, Saudi Arabia, and South Korea. Apple computers have been inexpensively counterfeited in Hong Kong. General Motors estimates that about 40 percent of its auto parts are counterfeited in the Middle East. Recordings and tapes are duplicated almost everywhere without license or fee. And the list goes on.

Legal protection against intellectual property theft and counterfeit goods is not very effective. In the United States, trademark and copyright holders may register with the Customs Service and seek the blockade of pirated items made abroad. Such exclusions are authorized in the Lanham Trademark Act of 1946 and the Copyright Act of 1976. Patent piracy is most often challenged in proceedings against unfair import practices under Section 337 of the Tariff Act of 1930. Section 337 proceedings traditionally involve some rather complicated provisions in Section 1337 of the Tariff Act of 1930. Prior to 1988, the basic prohibition was against: (1) unfair methods of competition and unfair acts in the importation of goods, (2) the effect or tendency of which is to destroy or substantially injure (3) an industry efficiently and economically operated in the U.S. Such importation was also prohibited when it prevented the establishment of an industry, or restrained or monopolized trade and commerce in the U.S.

The Omnibus Trade and Competitiveness Act of 1988 revised Section 337. The requirement that the U.S. industry be efficiently and economically operated was dropped. The importation of articles infringing U.S. patents, copyrights, trademarks or semiconductor chip mask works is specifically prohibited provided a U.S. industry relating to such articles exists or is in the process of being established. Proof of injury to a domestic industry is not required in intellectual property infringement cases. Such an industry exists if there is significant plant and equipment investment, significant employment of labor or capital, or substantial investment in exploitation (including research and development or licensing).

Determination of violations and the recommendation of remedies to the President under Section 337 are the exclusive province of the International Trade Commission (ITC). Most of the case law under Section 337 concerns the infringement of patents. While not quite a per se rule, it is nearly axiomatic that any infringement of United States patent rights amounts to an unfair import practice for purposes of Section 337. Section 337 proceedings result in general exclusion orders permitting seizure of patent counterfeits at any U.S. point of entry. However, the Customs Service finds it extremely difficult when inspecting invoices and occasionally opening boxes to ascertain which goods are counterfeit or infringing. Many counterfeits do look like "the real thing."

For most seizure remedies to work, the holder must notify the customs service of an incoming shipment of offending goods. Use of private detectives can help and is increasing, but such advance notice is hard to obtain. Nevertheless, the Customs Service seized $7.6 million worth of counterfeit goods in the first six months of fiscal 1987. More than one-third of the goods seized were toys and the three major sources were Taiwan, Korea and Hong Kong.

Infringement and treble damages actions may be commenced in United States courts against importers and distributors of counterfeit goods, but service of process and jurisdictional barriers often preclude effective relief against foreign pirates. Even if such relief is obtained, counterfeiters and the sellers of counterfeit goods have proven adept at the "shell game," moving across the road or to another country to resume operations. Moreover, the mobility and economic incentives of counterfeiters have rendered the criminal sanctions of the Trademark Counterfeiting Act of 1984 largely a Pyrrhic victory. Ex parte seizure orders are also available under the 1984 Act and the Lanham Trademark Act when counterfeit goods can be located in the United States. Goods so seized can be destroyed upon court order.

International solutions have been no less elusive. The GATT agreement on TRIPS addresses these problems, but its effectiveness remains to be tested. Various United States statutes authorize the President to withhold trade benefits from or apply trade sanctions to nations inadequately protecting the intellectual property rights of U.S. citizens. This is true of the Caribbean Basin Economic Recovery Act of 1983, the Generalized System of Preferences Renewal Act of 1984, the Trade and Tariff Act of 1984 (amending Section 301 of the 1974 Trade Act), and Title IV of the 1974 Trade Act as it applies to most favored nation tariffs. Slowly this carrot and stick approach has borne fruit. Under these pressures for example, Singapore drafted a new copyright law, Korea new patent and copyright laws, and Taiwan a new copyright, patent, fair trade and an amended trademark law. Brazil introduced legislation intended to allow copyrights on computer programs. Though these changes have been made, there is some doubt as to the rigor with which the new laws will be enforced when local jobs and national revenues are lost.

GRAY MARKET GOODS

One of the most controversial areas of customs law concerns "gray market goods," goods produced abroad *with authorization* and payment but which are imported into *unauthorized* markets. Trade in gray market goods has dramatically increased in recent years, in part because fluctuating currency exchange rates create opportunities to import and sell such goods at a discount from local price levels.

Licensors and their distributors suddenly find themselves competing in their home or other "reserved" markets with products made abroad by their own licensees. Or, in the reverse, startled licensees find their licensor's products intruding on their local market shares. In either case, third party importers and exporters are often the immediate source of the gray market goods, and they have little respect for who agreed to what in the licensing agreement. When pressed, such third parties will undoubtedly argue that any attempt through licensing at allocating markets or customers is an antitrust or competition law violation.

In the early part of the century, gray market litigation provoked a Supreme Court decision blocking French cosmetics from entering the United States. *A. Bourjois & Co. v. Katzel,* 260 U.S. 689 (1923). A United States firm was assigned the U.S. trademark rights for French cosmetics as part of the sale of the American business interests of the French producer. The assignee successfully obtained infringement relief against Katzel, an importer of the French product benefitting from exchange rate fluctuations. The Supreme Court reversed a Second Circuit holding which followed a line of cases allowing "genuine goods" to enter the American market in competition with established sources. The Supreme Court emphasized the trademark ownership (not license) and independent public good will of the assignee as reasons for its reversal.

Congress, before the Supreme Court reversal, passed the Genuine Goods Exclusion Act, now appearing as Section 526 of the Tariff Act of 1930. This Act bars *unauthorized importation* of goods bearing trademarks of U.S. citizens. Registration of such marks with the Customs Service can result in the seizure of unauthorized imports. Persons dealing in such imports may be enjoined, required to export the goods, destroy them or obliterate the offending mark, as well as pay damages. The Act has had a checkered history in the courts and Customs Service. The Customs Service view (influenced by antitrust policy) was that genuine (gray market) goods may be excluded only when the foreign and U.S. trademark rights are not under common ownership, or those rights have been used without authorization. The practical effect of this position was to admit most gray market goods into the U.S., thereby providing substantial price competition, but uncertain coverage under manufacturers' warranty, service and rebate programs. Some firms, like K Mart, excel at gray market importing and may provide independent warranty and repair service contracts. Since 1986, New York and California require disclosure by sellers of gray market goods that manufacturers' programs may not apply.

An attempt in 1985 by Duracell to exclude gray market batteries under Section 337 of the Tariff Act of 1930 as an unfair import practice was upheld by the U.S. International Trade Commission, but denied relief by President Reagan in deference to the Customs Service position. See *Duracell, Inc. v. U.S.*

International Trade Commission, 778 F.2d 1578 (Fed.Cir.1985).

Injunctive relief under trademark or copyright law is sometimes available against gray market importers and distributors. But see *Quality King Distributors, Inc. v. L'anza Research International, Inc.* 523 U.S. 135 (1998) (first sale doctrine bars injunctive relief under copyright act). Injunctive relief, however, applies only to the parties and does not prohibit gray market imports or sales by others. This remedy is thus useful, but normally insufficient.

A split in the federal courts of appeal as to the legitimacy in light of the Genuine Goods Exclusion Act of the Customs Service position on gray market imports resulted in a U.S. Supreme Court ruling. *K Mart Corp. v. Cartier, Inc.,* 486 U.S. 281 (1988). In an extremely technical, not very policy oriented decision, the Supreme Court arrived at a compromise. The Customs Service can continue to permit entry of genuine goods when common ownership of the trademarks exists. The Service must seize such goods only when they were authorized (licensed), but the marks are not subject to common ownership. Many believe that the bulk of U.S. imports of gray market goods have continued under this ruling.

Most foreign jurisdictions permit entry of gray market goods. See Takamatsu, "Parallel Importation of Trademarked Goods: A Comparative Analysis," 57 *Wash.L.Rev.* 433 (1982). The use of intellectual property rights to block trade in gray market ("parallel") goods within the Common Market has been repeatedly denied by the European Court of Justice in its competition and customs law rulings. Once authorized goods reach the market and title has passed to others, intellectual property rights in them are said as a matter of European law to be "exhausted." But European intellectual property rights can be used to block the importation of gray market goods from outside the Common Market. In other words, the exhaustion doctrine does not apply externally. Levi Strauss, for example, has seized upon this distinction to actively pursue EU importers of blue jeans from non-EU sources.

TRANSBORDER DATA FLOWS

Because information transfers are linked with employment and trade patterns, many countries have taken a keen interest in regulating transborder data flows (TBDFs). Technical strides in satellite communications and in microelectronics make regulation a physical and legal challenge. On one level, some countries (e.g., Austria, Denmark, France, Germany, Sweden) have a longstanding concern with protecting personal data of local MNE employees from being spread internationally by machine. To the extent that such national laws address protecting "persons," the laws may embrace clients, subscribers and suppliers as well. At another level, developing countries see opportunities for closer control of MNE foreign subsidiaries by having access to TBDFs, and for greater control of the basic, communications aspect of national life. Scenarios for control include the establishment of government "data control centers," through which all TBDFs must pass, required government "licenses" for TBDFs, and governmental "national compliance commissioners" who have legal authority to "listen in" on telephone conversations and to inspect corporate office files. At a third level, many countries recognize the lead MNEs from the United States have in data technology (using data bases in the United States) and wish to narrow that lead. At still another level is cultural sensitivity and national pride about keeping information "home" and about taxing information exports as other exports are taxed.

In 1981, the OECD approved fourteen principles as Guidelines on the Protection of Privacy and TransBorder Flow of Personal Data. The Council of Europe has drafted a Data Protection Convention. The United Nations Center on Transnational Corporations has taken up the TBDF. In 1998, Europe finalized a data privacy directive that has U.S. companies worried. It is noticeably more protective of individual privacy than U.S. law. More regulation of TBDFs seems an assured part of international business transactions in the age of information.

SPECIAL 301 PROCEDURES

Extensive negotiations were conducted within the GATT under the Uruguay Round on trade-related intellectual property rights (TRIPS). The developed nations sought an Anti–Counterfeiting Code and greater patent, copyright and trademark protection in the third world. The developing nations within GATT have resisted on nearly all fronts. The TRIPS negotiations failed to reach a conclusion as scheduled in December of 1990. Meanwhile, faced with massive technology transfer losses, "Special 301" procedures were established unilaterally by the United States in the 1988 Omnibus Trade and Competitiveness Act. These procedures are located in Section 182 of the Trade Act of 1974. They can lead to initiation of Section 301 proceedings under that Act. Section 301 proceedings are generally used to obtain market access for U.S. exporters of goods and services, but are also capable of being used to pressure and perhaps sanction other nations whose intellectual property policies diverge from U.S. standards.

Special 301 requires the U.S. Trade Representative (USTR) to identify those countries that deny "adequate and effective protection of intellectual property rights" or deny "fair and equitable market access to United States persons who rely upon intellectual property protection." The USTR must also identify "priority foreign countries" whose practices are the most "onerous or egregious" and have the greatest adverse impact on the United States, and who are not entering into good faith negotiations or making significant progress in negotiations towards provision of adequate and effective protection of intellectual property rights.

The USTR has developed "watch lists" and "priority watch lists" under Special 301 while pursuing negotiations with the many nations on those lists. These negotiations have had some success. Argentina agreed, as a result of Special 301 negotiations, to modify registration procedures for and improve protection of pharmaceuticals under its patent law. Mexico was removed from priority status on the Special 301 watch list after it announced new patent legislation. This legislation increased the term of Mexican patents to 20 years, offered protection for chemical and pharmaceutical products as well as biotechnology processes, restricted use of compulsory licenses and made improvements to the Mexican law of trademarks and trade secrets. Intellectual property reforms in Korea, Taiwan and Saudi Arabia have also removed them from the USTR's priority watch list.

India, Thailand and the People's Republic of China were formally named the first priority Special 301 countries. Naming any country under Special 301 triggers the possibility of unilateral U.S. trade sanctions under Section 301 of the Trade Act of 1974. The European Union, Brazil and Australia were placed on the Special 301 priority watch list at that time. Some 23 other countries remained on the secondary watch list. Early in 1992, the United States and the PRC reached a last minute agreement on intellectual reforms in the PRC. This agreement avoided the first Special 301 trade sanctions.

To some degree, the potential for Special 301 trade sanctions has been diluted by U.S. participation in TRIPS. Since 1995, nearly all U.S. intellectual property complaints have gone to WTO dispute settlement. The Special 301 "naming" and "watching" process continues in full force.

CHAPTER SIX

TRANSACTIONS IN MARKET ECONOMY NATIONS

Since this and the following chapter discuss issues of international business transactions in *market* economy nations and *nonmarket* economy nations, respectively, there must be some labeling of groups of nations. Even within one group there may be additional groups, such as *developed* and *developing* nations.

DEVELOPED OR DEVELOPING/MARKET OR NONMARKET: CLASSIFYING NATIONS

There is always a danger in labeling groups of nations. While some nations may clearly fit the intended definition, there will be others that tend to possess characteristics of more than one label, or that do not really have sufficient characteristics of any chosen label to be so classified. The usefulness in labeling is to be able to identify characteristics of the group which may help in dealing with members of that group. For example, if a developed nation is to grant import preferences to the export goods of *developing* nations, it must define the beneficiaries—the developing nations. But what constitutes a developing nation has no generally accepted definition. All nations, even the most *developed*, hope that their economies will further grow, and are in that sense developing nations. Thus, to be distinguished from truly developed nations, developing nations are sometimes referred to as *less developed* nations. Less developed than what nation? Is Australia less developed than France? Or Italy less developed than Germany? Or Canada less developed than the United States? Adjectives like *less* or *more* or *mere* tend to modify a word already unclear, and thus add more mist to the fog of classification.

The United States must define developing nations for the purpose of its generalized system of preferences (GSP), which differs in important ways from the definition of developing nations used by other nations for their equivalent or similar programs, such as the nations of the European Union and their ACP–Lomé Conventions. Even within the concept of a developing nation used by the United States government, developing nations for the purpose of receiving GSP benefits may differ from developing nations for OPIC insurance, or various AID programs. Sometimes, programs benefitting developing nations attempt to give even greater preferences to the *least* developed nations, often distinguished from developing nations by the term *dependent*. Thus, the label developing has no generic meaning common to all purposes, and accepted by all nations. The same is true of the label *developed* nation, and the label sometimes used to describe nations which may be somewhere in the middle between developed and developing, the *advanced developing countries* (ADCs) or *newly industrializing countries* (NICs).

The United States, Japan, England, France, Italy and Germany are probably on most lists of developed nations. Likely also to be included are Canada, Australia, New Zealand, the Netherlands, Belgium, Switzerland, Austria, Sweden, Norway, Denmark, Luxembourg, Spain and Portugal. What about Greece, Turkey, South Africa? Have any of the "Four Tigers" of Asia moved to developed status? Perhaps Korea. Taiwan is quite developed, but is claimed to be a part of a developing (and nonmarket) nation, China. If some of the latter Asian nations are advanced developing or newly industrializing countries, so are Mexico, India, and Brazil. Should we add to that list Venezuela, Argentina, Chile, Nigeria or China? We are now close to the vast number of truly just plain developing nations, which would include Indonesia, Thailand, Uganda, Kenya, Egypt, Ecuador, Costa Rica and Guatemala, and so many others. Not included are Bangladesh, or Bolivia, or Honduras or Haiti, or a number of African nations which may better be labeled dependent nations. They are the world's poorest.

Some readers will disagree with this classification, and move nations to other levels. Noticeably absent from the list, with the exception of the reference to China, are nations which have, or are moving away from, a highly planned economy where the means of production and distribution are in the hands of the state. These are the *nonmarket*

economy nations (NMEs), the subject of the following chapter.

Omitted above is any mention of the *Third
World*. It is a synonym for developing, as the *First
World* is for developed. But where is the *Second
World*? Is that the advanced developing or newly
industrializing countries? Is there a *Fourth World*
consisting of the dependent nations? Perhaps we
tend to feel comfortable with the use of either
"developing" or "Third World" for many nations
which are clearly so. The authors of this volume
tend to believe that there is a single "world", and
that the "dependent, developing, advanced developing and developed" terminology is preferable to the
various levels of "worlds". Perhaps the former classification views single nations as moving through
the various stages of development while the latter
identifies a more static class.

Defining nations in their stages of development
has troubled and challenged economists for decades.
The most noteworthy and well accepted economic
classification is that of W.W. Rostow in his classic
1960 book *Stages of Economic Growth*. Rostow used
a five stage classification: the traditional society,
the pre-conditions for take-off, the take-off, the
drive to maturity, and the age of high mass-consumption. The *traditional society* usually has many
of the nation's resources devoted to agricultural,
the clan and family are important social structures
and there is little vertical mobility. These are essentially pre-Newtonian societies such as early civiliza-
tions in the Middle East and dynasties in China.

The *pre-conditions for take-off* describe countries in a transition where industry begins but remains low in productivity. There are old social structures, but a centralized national political system is developing. Some nations are probably still in this state, overlapping with what we have described above as the *dependent* nations, the poorest of the poor. It may even include some of the *developing* nations, which may not be the poorest, but are clearly not yet in an advanced developing country stage. The third stage, the *take-off*, occurs when growth becomes a normal condition, traditional resistance to growth having been conquered. Stimulating this growth stage are technological development, investment and savings. New industries are expanding, profits are reinvested, and service industries develop. The agricultural sector undergoes changes, more technology is introduced. Rostow suggested that this stage describes Britain for two decades after 1783, France and the United States to several decades preceding 1860, Germany in the third quarter and Japan in the fourth quarter of the 19th century, Russia and Canada in about 1890–1914, and India and China in the mid 20th century. India and China are probably still in this stage, and others have entered, such as Argentina, Brazil and Mexico. These would include what we describe above as the least poor of the *developing* nations, and certainly the *advanced developing countries*. The fourth level of Rostow is the *drive to maturity*. This is thought to arise approximately a half-century after take-off (take-off is assumed to be an approximately 20 year period, but seems considerably longer with many nations). This is the transition which Britain, the United States, Germany and France passed through at the end of the 19th century. There is a shift from basic production of such commodities as steel or coal to machine tools, chemicals and electrical equipment. It is doubtful that any of the advanced developing countries have entered this stage. Certainly none have entered the final, fifth stage, the *age of high mass-consumption*. The United States qualifies, as do some of the European nations, and Japan, and such others as Canada and Australia. Rostow suggested a further stage, *beyond consumption*. This is where Thomas Mann's final generation arrives: the first sought money, the second was born to money and sought social and civil prestige, and the third, born to comfort and prestige, looked to a life of music. It is also reflective of John Adams comment that he must study war and politics so that his sons could study mathematics and his grandsons could study painting and music. Are there any nations of artists or musicians? Rostow's classification is helpful but perhaps no more useful than that described above, using the dependent, developing, advanced developing and developed nation levels. However nations are to be described, they will be described for the various purposes noted above such as granting special tariffs to the less economically developed, or allowing exemptions in the WTO from adopting certain trade opening measures.

Another division of nations which attracts equal suspicion as to its accuracy is the distinction between *market* and *nonmarket* economy nations. Market economy nations, both developed and developing, tend to share characteristics affecting international business transactions which are often absent in nonmarket economy nations. Differences which exist are usually elements of government policy rather than ways in which individuals do business. There are of course common elements in doing business in developing and nonmarket nations. Both may use countertrade, although it is more pronounced in the nonmarket economies. Both may engage in the process of privatization of state owned enterprises, but the process is more complex in nonmarket economies where much more of the means of production and distribution is or was in the hands of the state, and little infrastructure for a market economy exists. The following chapter will discuss international business transactions in nonmarket economy nations.

COMMERCIAL TRANSACTIONS AND TRANSFERS OF TECHNOLOGY

International commercial transactions between parties in a developed and a developing nation tend to take place in much the same manner as similar commercial transactions between parties in two developed nations. A United States seller of goods to a Brazilian purchaser may have no greater or less fear of the purchaser's likelihood of breaching the contract than when the sale is to a French or English purchaser. The same is true when the United States party is the purchaser and the seller is the foreign party. There may be some differences in how other nations view certain aspects of the documentary sale, such as whether it is customary for trucker's bills of lading to specify that goods are "on board". *Marine Midland Grace Trust Co. of N.Y. v. Banco Del Pais, S.A.*, 261 F.Supp. 884 (S.D.N.Y.1966) [not so customary in Mexico]. But such differences are often not based on characteristics inherent to developing nations, but are simply different customs in different nations.

Although the developed nation seller or buyer may not fear the developing nation *purchaser* or *seller*, it may fear the developing nation *government*. Governments in developing nations are more likely to create roadblocks for a transaction. The motivation for such obstacles vary. Developing nations often resort to strict import permit schemes, usually to reduce the demand for hard currency. But imports are also blocked where domestic business is fearful of foreign competition and is able to persuade the government to close domestic markets by the adoption of difficult to obtain import permits. Even *export* permits are imposed at times, usually together with export taxes intended to raise revenue. But most governments realize that such practices usually diminish needed export earnings more than they raise taxes. Whatever the motivation, import or export permits add to the transactional costs, and must be absorbed by one of the parties.

The shortage of hard currency reserves which affects many developing nations is most often the reason behind import controls. In such case the products do not enter until the import duty is paid in hard currency. But some developing nations allow the foreign produced products to be imported and sold, only to later halt the export of currency for their payment. In other words, the goods may reach the consumer, who pays in local currency, but that soft currency cannot then be exchanged at the bank for hard currency to send to the foreign seller. The use of letters of credit by the foreign seller becomes very important. A letter of credit allows the foreign seller to receive payment from a *bank* (usually in the exporting seller's nation) upon turning the goods over to the carrier and receiving the bill of lading, and presenting all the required documents to the bank, rather than receiving payment from the *purchaser* in the developing nation after receipt and perhaps inspection of the goods. However, this shifts a risk of loss to the bank and banks are not inclined to confirm (or issue) letters of credit when the bank must collect from an issuing bank (or the purchaser) in a developing nation which has imposed currency controls.

The next stage after the occasional sale of goods across borders to a developing nation may be to establish some form of distribution of the goods in that developing nation. That raises the choice of an agency or distributorship. An agent will take the goods without assuming title, and sell them on behalf of the foreign producer. A distributor will take title to the goods and resell them. In the former case, the foreign producer assumes the risk noted above, that when the goods are ultimately sold, there may be some problem obtaining foreign hard currency to pay for the goods. But the agent may not have goods other than samples, and any sales the agent makes will vary likely be completed with the use of the above recommended letter of credit. Goods sold to a distributor will follow the same procedure, using a letter of credit. One of the differences in using an agent or distributor in a developing nation may involves restrictions imposed by the developing nation. These restrictions may include a distributorship law which regulates such sales, imposes limitations on the choice of form of distribution, and establishes procedures and rights of the parties upon termination of the distributorship.

The transaction may go beyond the sale of goods across borders to a developing nation, whether by means of occasional sales or frequent sales through a distributor. The transaction may constitute a transfer of technology to allow production in the developing nation. In such case, the characterization of the nation of the transferee as a developing nation may also cause the transfer to differ from where the transferee is in a developed nation. The transfer of technology to a party in a developing nation is more likely to be regulated by the developing nation than a similar transfer to a party in a developed nation. As in the case of currency controls, it is the developing nation government which imposes technology transfer restrictions. Many developing nations have established complex regulatory processes which include registration, review and approval or rejection of all proposed technology transfers from abroad. Additional controls may exist where the process of doing business is carried an additional step to include establishing a foreign direct investment in the developing nation. The most common investment control involves mandatory joint ventures, but sometimes extends to an absolute prohibition of foreign investment in certain areas. A review of proposed foreign investment is not limited to developing nations (and nonmarket economies), however, many developed nations review some foreign investment. The United States, under the Exon–Florio Act provisions of the 1988 Omnibus Trade & Competitiveness Act, reviews some foreign investment [foreign investment is discussed in the International Trade and Investment Nutshell].

Whether the transaction is an occasional sale to a buyer in a developing nation, or occasional purchase from a seller in a developing nation, or a sale through some form of distributorship, or even the more extensive involvement by licensing technology to a producer within the developing nation, there may be a perception that such transactions are more likely to lead to conflicts than when trading with other developed nations. This perception may be because business persons in developing nations, whether sellers, buyers, agents, distributors or licensees, may be more likely to view elements of the agreement differently, or because of the frequent presence of a third party in the form of the government. The developed nation party may therefore give greater thought to the possibility of a dispute arising, and the methods of settlement of that dispute. The developed nation party is therefore more likely to demand contract provisions which choose the developed nation's courts as the forum of any dispute, and the developed nation's law as the choice of law. Choice of forum and choice of law provisions are common in international business agreements. They are more common where the foreign party is in a developing nation. But some developing nations have laws prohibiting the use of foreign forums or laws, although such prohibitions are more commonly applied to transfer of technology and direct investment disputes, than to disputes involving the commercial sale of goods. Inability to stipulate the applicable forum or law has made developed nation parties select mandatory arbitration as a means of resolving disputes. Arbitration in the developed nation, or in a third neutral nation, i.e., French, Swedish or Swiss arbitration, has generally proven satisfactory to both parties, and usually to the developing nation government as well. But some developing nations insist that the arbitration be conducted in the developing nation.

Before returning in more detail to some of the issues involving commercial transactions and technology transfers with parties in developing nations, it ought to be noted that none of the characteristics of various restrictions found in some developing nations are common to *all* developing nations. Restrictions tended to be quite severe during the late 1960s and 1970s, when the North–South dialogue was at its most tense level of animosity. The cause was largely newly independent developing nations, joined by many nonmarket economy nations, claiming that they were poor *because* the developed nations were rich. These tensions have fortunately abated during the past two decades, due to a number of reasons. They include the acknowledged failures in most nonmarket economy nations; the debt crises of the early 1980s; the examples of success with relatively open, market economies, as illustrated by such Asian nations as Korea, Singapore and Taiwan (and by Hong Kong); the entry into bilateral and multilateral trade agreements such as the NAFTA; and perhaps even a change in attitude by developing nation leadership to recognize that it is possible to work a nation's way out of underdevelopment, and that such is more likely by joining the First World than leading the Third World. Whatever the reason, the 1990s may be remembered as a decade during which many developing nations reduced or eliminated the most severe restrictions on doing business in their nations. Certainly the GATT/WTO accomplishments have been a contributing factor to these lessened restrictions on international business transactions.

SALES AGENT AND DISTRIBUTOR-
SHIP AGREEMENTS IN
DEVELOPING NATIONS

The two most frequently used forms to distribute products abroad are (1) an *independent foreign agent*, or (2) an *independent foreign distributor*. Usually the decision is made by the United States exporter. But in doing business abroad, especially in developing nations, the choice of the form of distribution may not be the prerogative of the foreign company—the choice may be mandated by local law.

An independent foreign agent, who may be called a sales representative or commission agent, is a foreign person who does not take title to the goods and who usually is paid in the form of salary and commissions. This person does not bear the risk that the buyer might not pay. That risk remains the burden of the United States seller. The foreign agent usually does not have the power to bind the United States seller, but may be considered to have implied power to do so, and certainly may be given express authority to do so. The independent agent obtains orders for sales abroad and sends those orders to the United States seller. Thus, there is usually no need for the agent to store the goods in its nation.

The use of an independent foreign agent tends to create more legal problems for the company selling abroad than the use of an independent foreign distributor. Agency law may differ substantially in a foreign nation, especially nations with civil law tradition systems. Furthermore, the laws of some nations seem to blur the distinction between the two forms of distribution, and thus use of an independent foreign distributor may not always achieve the protection sought.

One important factor to understand is that the law of a developing nation may regulate the nature of the agency relationship substantially more than is the case in the United States. Civil law nation commercial codes may provide extensive detail regarding the agency relationship. Additionally, these rules may be mandatory and not be subject to alteration by contract. Foreign law may outline different forms of agents whose powers are quite carefully delineated. The powers may or may not be in conflict with what the United States party might wish to arrange by contract. It is essential to understand the forms of agents which exist, and their role, in any nation where the use of an agent is contemplated.

An independent foreign distributor, in contrast to the usual form of agent, buys the company's products and resells them through the foreign distributor's network. The foreign distributor, in taking title to the goods, consequently assumes such risks as not being able to resell them. The distributor is the one whom the purchaser must pay, and therefore the distributor is at risk for nonpayment. Because the distributor is essentially buying the goods for resale, it must find storage for the goods prior to final sale and distribution.

Unlike the uncertainty existing in the case of the independent agent, the independent distributor does not have power to bind the United States seller. This is because the distributor buys the goods for resale, rather than entering into contracts on behalf of the principal, as in the case of an agent. Of course the distributor might additionally have power to act as an agent for goods it does not obtain as a distributor, and in such case the issue of the power to bind the principal arises.

If an independent foreign distributor is used, the language in the distribution agreement should be as clear as possible in noting the principal-distributor rather than principal-agent relationship. Language used with establishing an independent contractor is most appropriate.

Developing nations often have special laws which govern the distribution agreement between their nationals *as agents* and foreign businesses. This is in addition to the domestic agency laws which apply to any agency relationship. There are far fewer countries which have laws governing agreements between foreign business and local independent distributors. Even though the distinction between the two is sometimes blurred, the distinction nevertheless remains important. For example, antitrust laws in some nations are enforced against distributorships, but not against agencies. This may affect assigning a distributor exclusive selling rights. Of course, when the agency form is that of an *employee* agent rather than an *independent* agent, the agency may clearly be exclusive. Some developing nations do not even recognize the distinction between their nationals as agents and their nationals as distributors, and govern both. But to be fair, what the United States supplier calls its foreign distributor is less important than being able to determine and formalize the characteristics of the relationship. If the characteristics suggest an agent, then the host nation is likely to consider the person an agent. The same is true for distributors.

Where foreign laws applicable to distribution agreements have been enacted, they are likely to be designed to (1) benefit local agents/distributors, especially in the area of termination; (2) restrict (or prohibit) the use of agents/distributors, essentially to protect the public from unfair agents/distributors; or (3) apply domestic labor law to the distribution agreement, in addition to any special laws applicable to the distribution agreement.

Civil law tradition nations tend to be more likely to restrict freedom to contract than common law tradition nations. Laws regulating agency and distributorship agreements in civil law countries may be separate and specific, or may be found in the civil or commercial codes. Developing nations are most likely to have special laws affecting the agency/distributor relationships.

Even where local law mandates use of local agents or distributors, it may be possible to use a local business entity as the agent which has majority foreign ownership. But many countries which mandate the use of local distributors additionally require that the ownership of artificial entities (i.e., local corporations) be at least majority domestic.

There are many areas of control which ought to be considered, such as setting prices and hiring sub-agents. Where control exists, the agent/distributor may be limited in many actions, including the ability to incur expenses on behalf of the principal, or to carry competing lines of products. Such actions as making foreign corrupt payments may be closely monitored where control exists. There is an obvious benefit to having control. But with control may come responsibility for actions of the agent which appear to a third party to be within the agent's authority. Such responsibility may be avoided by using a distributor who is fully independent of the company. But where the host foreign nation does not recognize this independence, the worst of both worlds may exist. The company has no control over the agent/distributor, but may be held responsible for much of the conduct of the agent/distributor. The best course is to know the law of the foreign host nation *before* deciding on the form of relationship.

The usual rule is to retain a business entity rather than an individual. The contract should very clearly state the identities of the parties to the distribution agreement. If the agent is an individual, local labor laws may apply even if the company attempts to define the local agent as an independent contractor. Labor laws in some developing nations are very protective and often prohibit termination at will, or require significant termination pay when termination is allowed. Using independent contractor language is useful, such as specifying that the compensation is to be in the form of commissions or discounts rather than a salary.

Termination is often the most common occasion for confronting different rules in a developing nation. It is very important to know what the termination laws are in any nation where a distributorship agreement is proposed. One may confront a rule that effectively means that the distributorship agreement may not be terminated, or may not be renewed, without the payment of what may be a substantial amount of compensation to the local agent/distributor. The potential costs of a termination, which at first may seem quite reasonable and justified under the laws of the principal's nation, may be very extensive under the laws of the host nation. Because termination often follows a realization that the agent/distributor relationship did not function as expected, it is essential to choose the agent/distributor with great care. Since termination problems are the most significant and potentially most costly matters regarding distribution agreements, contracting with the kind of agent/distributor one really needs will minimize the occurrence of unhappy times.

In addition to being aware of local termination laws, the issue of termination ought to be discussed thoroughly with the agent/distributor. An agent/distributor who is terminated and who believes that the termination was fair and reasonable, may not attempt to seek additional protection under domestic laws. Termination laws are more likely to be present in civil law tradition nations than common law tradition nations, and the causes for termination are likely to be limited by statute. Some developing nations have rather detailed termination rules, which provide different rights depending upon the classification of the relationship.

Some nations involve the government as a place of registration of all distributorship agreements. This may be merely a notification formality, or it may bring the government in as a third party, to *review*, and *approve* or *reject,* distributorship agreements which are filed with a government agency. Registration may further involve public disclosure, and create problems regarding information which the foreign company would prefer to remain confidential.

THE USE OF TRANSFER OF TECHNOLOGY AND FOREIGN INVESTMENT LAWS AS PART OF THE PROCESS OF DEVELOPMENT

In the 1960s and 1970s, a number of developing countries began to question the economic, political and social impact of foreign technology and investment in their nations. The United Nations became a major forum for their discussions, and their proposals. Studies by regional and international organizations outlined purported abuses from decisions made in the board rooms of parent corporations in developed nations ("foreign centers of decision making"), which allegedly adversely affected the economic development and sovereignty of the developing nations. The use of the term "Third World" assumed popularity, suggesting a solidarity in dealing with the allegedly evil "First World." At the root of some of the developing nation criticism was "dependency theory", the idea that "they are rich because we are poor." But there were other reasons for adopting new restrictions on the receipt of foreign technology and investment. Most of the developing nations had persistent balance of payments problems and were searching for alternatives to reduce the outflow of payments for technology and repatriated profits. These developing nations, furthermore, were determined to increase rates of development, believing that closer government control of decisions regarding accepting foreign technology and investment would assist that goal.

The first responses were national laws in a number of the more advanced developing countries or newly industrializing countries (ADCs or NICs), including Argentina, Brazil, India, Mexico and Nigeria. Regional groups responded as well. The Andean Common Market (ANCOM) enacted the famous (and later replaced) Decision 24, which severely restricted foreign investors who wished to introduce direct investment to any member nation of this integrated area, and even planned for the "fading out" of existing foreign equity. Limitations on profit repatriation resulted either directly from a specific maximum allowable profit repatriation, as in the ANCOM, or indirectly from either exchange controls or the shortage of hard currency. The former was usually the consequence of the latter. The form of these restrictive laws illustrated the diversity among developing nations regarding the approach to controlling foreign investment. Brazil regulated technology and maintained strict currency controls, but for the most part allowed total foreign ownership of investment. Mexico assiduously avoided exchange controls (except for four months subsequent to the August, 1982, debt troubles), but placed strict regulations on technology transfers, mandated joint ventures and passed an ill-fated attempt to require the linking of new Mexican origin trademarks with those familiar but foreign in origin.

By the early 1980s, while the restrictions on technology transfers and foreign investment had not been formally removed in many developing nations, the governments were relaxing requirements to encourage investment and technology transfers needed to generate exports and help pay the rapidly increasing foreign debts. When the foreign debt issue exploded in 1982, debt repayment became the dominant issue of the decade. One method to assist lowering the debt was to encourage investment in order to generate increased national income.

In the late 1980s some nations began to dismantle their restrictive transfer of technology and investment laws. Mexico adopted regulations which nullified much of the restrictiveness of the transfer of technology and investment laws. In 1991 Mexico replaced the strict 1982 transfer of technology law with an investment encouraging industrial property law, finally acknowledging that the earlier law discouraged the transfer of state-of-the-art technology. Some developing nations, such as India and Nigeria, have been much slower to open their economies to investment by adopting modifications to the old restrictive laws or replacing them with new investment encouraging laws, or if not laws, less restrictive policies.

This less restrictive attitude in developing nations often was generated by several changes in distant lands. One was the opening of trade, technology transfer and investment opportunities in Eastern European nations, which were adopting laws and policies far less restrictive than in the developing nations; and the second was the rapid rate of economic growth taking place in the "Four Tigers" (or "Four Dragons") of Asia—Hong Kong, Korea, Singapore and Taiwan. Succeeding in the competition to encourage foreign technology transfers and investment was likely to occur only with the adoption of laws which protected rather than restricted technology, and encouraged rather than restricted direct investment.

As the 1990s began, it was clear that the decade would be identified as the decade of the adoption of new legislation by many developing nations which removed much of the earlier registration and regulation, and which offered incentives to the transfer of foreign technology and to foreign investment. The incentives would assume the form of providing protection to intellectual property such as patents, copyrights and trademarks and allowing wholly foreign owned investment. The earlier decades of "nationalization" were being replaced by a decade of "privatization", changing state ownership to both foreign and domestic private ownership. But transfer of technology and investment laws persist in some developing nations, and an understanding of their typical characteristics is useful.

TRANSFER OF TECHNOLOGY LAWS OF DEVELOPING NATIONS

Transfer of technology laws effectively add the government of the host country as a third party to the agreement which transfers the technology from the foreign licensor to the host nation licensee. In many cases the foreign licensor and the developing nation licensee (whether a locally owned company or subsidiary of licensor) agree to the negotiated contract terms, but the developing nation government of the licensee disapproves the agreement. The government may require registration, review and approval/rejection under the theory that such intrusive participation of the government is necessary to avoid actual or alleged restrictive practices thought to be detrimental to the nation's economic development.

What technology is required to be registered varies from country-to-country, but is likely to include licensing patents, trademarks, copyrights, know how, commercial names, management or technical assistance, miscellaneous services, and of considerable contemporary importance, computer software.

Registration of an agreement may be denied for many reasons, among the most frequent have been:

1. the technology is thought to be obsolete or available locally,

2. the payment for the technology is considered excessive,

3. limitations are imposed on the licensee's research,

4. exclusive sales or territory restrictions apply,

5. grant back requirements exist for any new developments by the licensee,

6. the contract is for an excessive duration, or

7. a foreign forum and/or choice of law applies to disputes.

Failure to register and receive approval of a proposed transfer of technology is considered to invalidate the agreement. It may result in denial of the transfer of funds as royalty payments as well as severe penal sanctions.

The transfer of technology laws of the 1970s and 1980s of a number of developing nations were routinely moderated by liberal interpretation, by an implementation of regulations less restrictive than the laws, and even by the replacement of the restrictive laws with investment encouraging laws, as is true of Mexico. Some of the above examples of reasons for rejecting an agreement have been eliminated in many countries, and even the requirement of registration seems on the brink of extinction in those nations most determined to create an investment encouraging legal framework. Some nations retain a registration requirement, but eliminate any process of approval or rejection.

The transfer of technology issue has been addressed on a multilateral level, as well as by individual nations and regionally integrated areas. The proposed International Trade Organization (ITO), which ended with the demise of the Havana Charter in 1950 because of objections in the United States Senate, might have governed technology transfers as part of the governance of foreign investment. While the organizing nations formed the World Bank, the IMF and the GATT, the inability to create the ITO left no organization to deal with investment issues. The United Nations became the most likely organization to address such issues. In later years, the United Nations Conference on Trade and Development (UNCTAD) undertook the adoption of a Transfer of Technology Code (TOT Code), but disagreements regarding the applicable law in the event of a dispute and several other issues, resulted in the proposal being removed from active consideration. Developing nations insisted that technology disputes be settled in their domestic courts using their domestic (and usually very restrictive) law, while developed nations preferred that the contracting parties have a free choice to decide both the choice of forum and choice of law. Because the latter alternative usually meant the party with the greater leverage, i.e., the owner of the technology, was able to have its nation's courts and its nation's law apply, the law of the developing nation would infrequently be chosen in the negotiation of any transfer of technology agreement.

UNCTAD also drafted a Restrictive Business Practices Code (RBP Code), which was to govern technology transfers. This Code was approved by the General Assembly in 1980. But General Assembly actions do not create law, the Code merely provided a framework for adoption by individual nations. With the movement away from restrictive investment laws, governments showed little interest in adopting the provisions of the RBP Code, and it is a dead issue. While UNCTAD was working on the above codes, the UN's Commission on Transnational Corporations was drafting a Code of Conduct on Transnational Corporations (CTC Code). Only one of 73 provisions addressed the issue of technology transfers, and in very general terms. But like the UNCTAD proposed TOT Code, this Code draft was placed in a dormant status, so far on the back burner of ideas to develop that it fell behind the stove. These two proposed Codes are unlikely to again be raised for further consideration and debate, but they may influence domestic law enactments of developing nations. The shift towards less restrictive investment laws in the world has diminished the usefulness of these draft UN codes, even as persuasive models for domestic legislation.

In the late 1980s the discussion of the transfer of technology shifted from the UN to the GATT Uruguay Round, in the form of rules relating to the protection of intellectual property. Negotiation of Trade Related Aspects of Intellectual Property

(TRIPS) was promoted by developed nations, with developing nations concerned that shifting standards from domestic law to international law might be harmful to development. The developing nations argued that intellectual property negotiations should take place in the UN's World Intellectual Property Organization (WIPO), where the developing nations dominate, rather than the GATT, where the power tends to remain in the developed nations. The GATT as the proper forum won out, and the GATT/WTO includes a TRIPS agreement that is protective of foreign intellectual property, not restrictive in its transfer.

CHAPTER SEVEN

TRANSACTIONS IN NONMARKET AND TRANSITION ECONOMY NATIONS

As in the case of developed versus developing, there must be some was to distinguish *market* from *nonmarket* economy nations (NMEs). At least for the present, there are no such further distinctions with the market/nonmarket labels which are parallel to the least developing nations being called dependent, and the most developing nations being called advanced developing countries (ADCs) or newly industrializing countries (NICs). But because many NMEs are in a state of transition from a nonmarket economy to an intended market economy, there are some nations which are neither NMEs nor market economies. They are perhaps neomarket economy nations. We refer to them, however, as nations in transition. The transition is exclusively from NME to market economy status, not the reverse (although in the process of transition there are often brief reversals).

DEFINING NONMARKET AND
TRANSITION ECONOMY NATIONS

NMEs have generally been considered to be those nations in which the principal political and economy theory of business and trade asserts that the means of production and distribution ought to be largely or exclusively state owned and managed. The consequence of being an NME is that market economies may treat the NME very differently than they would treat other market economies in their trading relations, not because of how the NME may act in international business transactions, but solely because it *is* an NME. That different treatment may be reflected in such decisions as granting most favored nation (MFN) status to imports from an NME, or restricting exports to an NME, particularly of products capable of military use.

NMEs are often referred to as nations which are "socialist" or "communist", but these labels both have unclear definitions, and tend to emphasize the political structures more than may be justified by the label "nonmarket." Use of the political label may suggest that a nation which has a socialist or communist government, therefore cannot have a market economy. Such has been the argument with China and Cuba. China has progressed considerably along the path towards a market economy, while retaining a very socialist or communist government. Cuba continues to assert its devotion to socialism, while increasingly adopting characteristics of market economies. Trade with Cuba is prohibited by the United States because it is a socialist/communist nation, while trade is permitted with China and Vietnam notwithstanding that they are social-ist/communist nations. The reasons for the different policies are not always clear, but serve to illustrate that trade with some NMEs is prohibited because they are NMEs. In contrast, trade with developing nations is never prohibited because they are devel-oping nations. There is sometimes a prohibition of trade with another market economy when it has adopted social policies generally considered repre-hensible, and those policies conflict with basic con-cepts of international human rights. Trade boycotts imposed against South Africa by many nations dur-ing the period of apartheid are as example.

The identity of a nation as an NME is important because it creates the possibility of trade restric-tions which are not present when the trade is with market economy nations. The animosity towards an NME may be so great that it leads to prohibitions of trade with friendly market economy nations which do trade with that NME. The United States prohib-ited trade with several European nations of goods destined for use in the construction of a gas pipeline from the USSR to Western Europe, after the USSR invaded Poland. The animosity towards the Cuban leadership has led to restrictive laws regarding trade with companies in friendly market economy nations which do certain business in Cuba. This should emphasize the need for persons engaged in international business transactions to identify na-tions which are NMEs, as well as to be familiar with the nature of United States foreign relations with that nation. The latter may range from extremely hostile, meaning trade is likely to be prohibited, to quite cordial, meaning trade is permitted if not encouraged. Political risk analysis is necessary for every person in international business. While it usually means evaluating the risks to one's business because of the political instability of *another* nation (which could be developing as well as a NME), it may mean the risks to one's business because of one's *own* government's changing foreign policy towards the NME.

In this era of transition from NME to market economies, and often concurrently towards more democratic political systems, how do we view nations which in the past few decades seemed clearly to merit the label NME? We probably agree that North Korea and Cuba remain rather strongly committed to classical socialist tradition, however one may identify minor examples of domestic changes which merit the market economy label. China remains committed to a socialist government while making significant progress towards establishing a very sizable market sector in the economy. Vietnam may mirror the Chinese practice on a much smaller scale. The Commonwealth of Independent States (most of former USSR) and Eastern European nations (including nations carved out of the former Yugoslavia) are each entrenched in their own concepts of a process of political and economic transition. Some have succeeded to a degree that there is doubt about calling them NMEs. The label "transition" provides a safe haven from giving the nation its coveted label of "market economy," or continuing to relegate it to the status it may be sincerely trying to reject, that of an NME. As each successive edition of this book has been written, the list of NMEs has changed. As new editions are written in the future, the list will surely change again.

NMEs are identified by their domestic characteristics, such as state ownership of the means of production and distribution, and also by rules *other* market economy nations establish, either individually or as a group, to deal with them. Such rules are attributable to the perceived threat of NMEs as political and economic variants. For example, a number of developed nations formed the COCOM, or Coordinating Committee of the Consultative Group on Export Controls, to regulate the sale to NMEs of goods or technology which might be applied to military use. But it did not always work effectively. In the 1980s Japanese and Norwegian companies allegedly combined to divert U.S. technology to the USSR which allowed the manufacture of propellers permitting Soviet submarines to run more quietly and consequently with less chance of detection. Subsequent to the disintegration of the USSR, the COCOM was abolished in 1994, and was replaced by the initially 28 nation member Wassenaar Arrangement on Export Controls for Conventional Arms and Dual–Use Goods and Technologies. The purpose remains much the same as COCOM, but the Wassenaar Arrangement is criticized for lack of (1) a prior notification requirement, and (2) transparency in exchanging information on exports of dual use goods and conventional arms.

NONMARKET ECONOMY NATIONS IN TRANSITION

Prior to the mid–1980s, most commercial trading and investment activity with NMEs was confined to the smaller members of the NME group, particularly several of the nations of Eastern Europe. China and the USSR were often so committed to defending their respective socialist theologies that they would tolerate no deviation from the view that there could be no foreign investment, and only as little trading of goods as was absolutely necessary to relieve occasional shortages. Some of the most challenging and interesting opportunities for parties in the West arose because of two important changes in China and the USSR. First, the end of the Chinese Cultural Revolution in 1976 marked that nation's apogee of nonparticipation in trade with market economies. In the 1980s trade with and joint venture investment in China expanded with Malthusian dimensions, but with occasional brief periods when China retrenched to take stock of the domestic impact of this new activity. The size of China makes even a modest opening to trading with the West an important event. To improve its position as a world trader, especially as an exporter, China is determined to become a member of the WTO. It was a charter member of the GATT in 1947, but withdrew during the 1949 Revolution. Even without formal WTO membership, China has obtained favorable MFN treatment from its most important trading customer, the United States. The United States President annually reviews a grant of MFN treatment to China, notwithstanding the opposition of many in Congress because of (1) the events of Tiananmen Square, when the PRC leadership brought to an abrupt end much of the developing political freedom, (2) the use of prison labor to produce goods for export, and (3) inadequate protection of intellectual property. The United States and other developed nations are concerned about the impact of such a huge potential exporter of goods, but pleased with the prospect of a very large domestic market, *if* the market actually opens *and* China uses the hard currency earned from its exports to pay for imports. If the United States finds it difficult to deal with the trade deficit with Japan, it must be prepared to deal with a deficit with China which may dwarf that of Japan. As well as increasing foreign trade, China has also opened to limited foreign investment. But limited as it is, Chinese joint ventures, in number and value of investment, exceed similar investment in all other NMEs combined.

The second important change in dealing with NMEs is because of the changes in the USSR and Eastern Europe. Political *glasnost* began to establish some confidence by market economy business persons that trade and investment would be more welcome than before, but the actual process of dismantling the USSR (and Yugoslavia) created many new uncertainties about the stability of the region. The desire of these nations to trade and receive investment appears to be well established, evidenced partly by the extensive privatization in most of these nations. But the infrastructure to carry out the transition to market economies and increase trade is not well developed. Not only is the physical infrastructure inadequate (roads, railways, ports, communications, etc.), but the legal structure needed to accommodate trade and investment often is archaic and demands modernization, including laws regulating commercial transactions, business organizations, bankruptcy, banking and securities regulation.

At the time of the dismantling of the socialist world, the USSR was in the process of becoming a member of GATT. Its overtures for membership were first rebuffed in 1986, but later accepted in 1990. But the negotiations for the WTO delayed admission. The Commonwealth of Independent States (CIS) nations must continue to alter legal rules if they expect to be compatible with the market economy foundations of the WTO. WTO membership for the Commonwealth of Independent States (or for China) has far more serious implications than for such smaller transitional NMEs as Hungary or Poland. The failure to offer (or fulfill promises of) reciprocal trade benefits by a group as large as the new CIS (or China) could have serious trade balance implications for some WTO members. If the member states of the CIS negotiate trade relations individually, however, the formidability of the CIS as a trade entity lessens. Each new nation in the old USSR thus may be considered separately for MFN treatment by other nations, and for WTO membership.

Member nations of the GATT struggled with accepting NMEs into the GATT collection of mostly market economy nations. The smaller nations of Eastern Europe (Czechoslovakia [now divided], Hungary, Poland, and Romania) slowly gained acceptance into the GATT. While such membership was not assurance that MFN treatment would be automatically accorded, i.e., the U.S. suspended MFN status to Poland from 1982–1987, for the most part these nations in transition have been accepted with full benefits. Nevertheless, domestic trade laws may impose some restrictions. The United States trade laws include several provisions which restrict trade to NMEs. See Trade Act of 1974, 19 U.S.C.A. §§ 2431–2440 [they are discussed in the authors' Nutshell on International Trade and Investment]. Because these provisions grant the President considerable discretion in determining the degree to which the United States will trade with NMEs, trade policies with NMEs sometimes seem quite unclear and contradictory.

EXPORTING GOODS TO A NONMARKET ECONOMY NATION—FTOS AND STOS

International business transactions assume three major stages, (1) the trading of goods or services across borders, (2) the transfer of technology, and

(3) direct foreign investment. This Nutshell considers the first two stages and explores some of the major differences which arise when the other nation is a nonmarket economy.

Exporters to NMEs confront various choices in seeking buyers of their products or services. Before the significant changes in the 1980s, when many Eastern European NMEs began to open their markets, foreign traders were usually required to deal with a state agency, usually called either a foreign trade organization (FTO) or state trading organization (STO). A United States (or other foreign) exporter was unable to deal directly with the end user of the product or services. The FTOs usually were supervised by a Ministry of Trade, which was in charge of regulating foreign trade so as to achieve the goals of a national economic plan, often a five year plan. Extensive and detailed central planning was a quintessential characteristic of a NME. It was usually totally ineffective in adequately providing for the needs of the economy, thus placing pressure on opening the markets to the tainted economies of the market economy world. In the 1980s, NMEs began to allow increasing degrees of decentralization in an attempt to rectify the failures of central planning. The rate of decentralization in different Eastern European NME nations depended upon a combination of the belief that the market focus would succeed and that the USSR would not intervene, as it had so often and so damagingly in the past. Usually the new adoptions were quite modest. But they established a pattern which proved unlikely to be reversed. These decisions allowed supply and demand to play a small role in the process that government planners previously had exclusively co-opted. Ultimately, the trend affected the USSR. The 1987 USSR Law on State Enterprises was an important move toward decentralization in a nation which had resisted the process, not only for itself, but in other Eastern European nations by threats and coercion.

By the end of the 1980s, the monopoly role of FTOs had greatly diminished, but they were not eliminated. Traders could sometimes choose to continue to deal with an FTO, which was likely to be a much smaller entity than before. Small foreign firms were most likely to deal with these FTOs, while larger firms increasingly chose to establish commercial or technical representation offices.

The decision to choose an FTO or separate representation was often made on the basis of where the most experienced local sales executives were employed. In many cases they moved from state FTOs to become private representatives. The most innovative and entrepreneurial made this move, often leaving the hard-liners in the command of the remaining FTOs. The decision whether or not to use an FTO could have other consequences. Contracting with a government owned enterprise or trading organization raises two important questions. First, is the entity entitled to raise sovereign immunity as a defense in litigation? Chapter 9 (sovereign immunity) discusses this defense and the important commercial activity and waiver exceptions. Explicit waiver in NME contracts may be the best way to assure that one will not face the issue.

The second problem is less easily avoided. It is illustrated by the *Czarnikow Ltd. v. Centrala Handlu Zagranicznego Rolimpex* case, [1979] A.C. 351, [1978] 2 All E.R. 1043 (H.L.)(hereafter *Rolimpex*). Rolimpex was given the Polish monopoly on sugar sales abroad and contracted to sell Polish sugar to Czarnikow, a foreign purchaser. Because of a reduction in the expected sugar crop in Poland there was insufficient sugar for the domestic market. The Polish government canceled export licenses, causing Rolimpex to be unable to deliver to Czarnikow. Czarnikow saw this as little other than one Polish government branch telling another not to do something, and thus not excusable under the *force majeure* clause of the contract. Many Polish jurists familiar with the case express amusement that one might think that the Polish government did not have absolute control over Rolimpex. But on the facts before the court, the House of Lords found Rolimpex sufficiently independent from the government not to be "an organ of the state", and therefore *force majeure* applied and Rolimpex was excused from performance. In a later English House of Lords decision, involving the application of the restrictive theory of sovereign immunity, Lord Wilberforce stated:

> State-controlled enterprises, with legal personality, ability to trade and to enter into contracts of private law, though wholly subject to the control of their state, are a well-known feature of the

modern commercial scene. The distinction between them, and their governing state, may appear artificial: but it is an accepted distinction in
the law of England and other states.... Quite
different considerations apply to a state-con-
trolled enterprise acting on government directions on the one hand, and a state, exercising
sovereign functions, on the other. *I Congreso del
Partido*, [1983] A.C. 244, 258.

The United States Supreme Court also has expressed support for separate legal personality of
enterprises organized by NME governments. The
Court has suggested that to ignore such separate
status might cause third parties to restrict credit to
such enterprises for fear that the assets of the
enterprise might be diverted to pay claims against
the state itself, and that it would frustrate NMEs in
creating state owned enterprises to promote economic development. *First National City Bank v.
Banco Para El Comercio Exterior De Cuba*, 462 U.S.
611 (1983)(hereafter *First National City Bank*). But
the Supreme Court does not seem to have the same
enthusiasm for acknowledging separate FTO status
that English courts disclose. The U.S. Supreme
Court in *First National City Bank* turned to "equitable principles" and adopted a kind of "disregard
of the corporate fiction" approach, noting that:

Giving effect to Bancec's [Cuban bank] separate
juridical status in these circumstances, even
though it has long been dissolved, would permit
the real beneficiary of such an action, the Government of the Republic of Cuba, to obtain relief in

our courts that it could not obtain in its own right without waiving its sovereign immunity and answering for the seizure of Citibank's assets—a seizure previously held by the Court of Appeals to have violated international law. We decline to adhere blindly to the corporate form where doing so would cause such an injustice. Id. at 632.

Whether the United States court would have applied equitable principles to a *Rolimpex* situation is unclear, but the uncertain relation between state as state and state as enterprise suggests addressing the issue in the contract.

CURRENCY ISSUES IN TRADING WITH NONMARKET ECONOMY NATIONS

When selling goods to buyers in NMEs, the question of price is often subservient to the question of obtaining payment in internationally traded ("hard") currencies. Like most developing nations, NMEs possess comparatively small amounts of hard currencies. But unlike most developing nations, NMEs have at times prohibited the removal of any domestic currency from the country. Thus a foreign seller is not permitted to obtain what that seller would have no use for anyway—the "soft" NME currency. Prohibiting the removal of currency allowed NMEs to control the exchange value of the currency for the limited international transactions which were permitted. But the value so established in such a case tends to be artificial, and creates another problem when the country begins a transition to a market economy. For example, the Cuban government has long rigidly controlled the Cuban peso, and prohibited its removal from the country. Many pesos are removed, however, and the currency has gained a nominal international value. While the Cuban government long attempted to maintain the peso at a value of slightly more than a dollar, in mid–1994 some 100–150 pesos were needed to obtain a single dollar on the black market. The ratio has since dropped by more than fifty percent. Artificial values lead to dual or multiple exchange rates. The official rate, at which commercial transactions must be negotiated, may change without warning and leave a foreign seller unable to obtain an amount of hard currency representing the value of the goods. Restrictions on the exchange of currencies change with equal lack of warning, and may leave that seller without *any* access to hard currency.

Shortages of hard currency are attributable to the traditionally limited contact NMEs maintained with the developed nations. Few exports and limited tourism (often discouraged), plus inability to borrow extensively (Poland an exception), resulted in access to considerably less hard currency than developing nations have been able to obtain. NME imports often had to pay their own way, in the form of countertrade, as discussed below.

Lacking a value against other currencies, and not welcome at international banks in exchange for hard currencies when removal is permitted, most

NME currencies thus are of little interest to foreign traders. Foreign sellers to NMEs are likely to demand cash-in-advance, or where that is not possible, use letters of credit issued or confirmed by a bank in a developed country, with the letter of credit assuring payment in a hard currency.

LETTERS OF CREDIT AND NONMARKET ECONOMY NATIONS

When the goods to be traded are high on the priority list of a NME nation's planners, the foreign exporter should be able to demand payment in hard foreign currency. In some cases this might mean cash payment in hard currency at the time of the sale. But more likely the sale will involve a standard letter of credit confirmed (if not issued) by a bank in the exporter's nation. But confirmation by a Western bank may be difficult to obtain if the issuing bank in the NME has a past history of delays in paying due to actual shortages of foreign currency, or government controls which overrule previously approved currency exchanges. As the priority of the goods sold to the NME diminishes, the foreign seller will not be able to obtain cash in advance. Probably not even a letter of credit. The seller may have to find local goods in the NME to accept in exchange for the goods to be sold to the NME. This is common barter, dressed in some new clothes under the name *countertrade*.

EXPORT CONTROLS AFFECTING SALE
OF GOODS TO NONMARKET
ECONOMIES

Selling goods or technology to some NMEs will involve the participation of the United States government in the form of export controls not applicable to most sales to market economies. Limitations on exports are based on either the nature of the good, or the country the goods are destined for, or a combination of the two. [Export controls are more thoroughly discussed in the International Trade and Investment Nutshell.] The Export Administration Act (50 U.S.C. § 240 et seq.) and the Export Administration Regulations (EAR) govern United States exports. The Export Administration Regulations play the major role where the United States *antiboycott* law applies, while the Department of Treasury's regulations administered by the Office of Foreign Assets Control (OFAC) play the major role where the United States *boycott* laws apply.

Exports to NMEs may be conditioned on obtaining a license from the Department of Commerce. The need for a license will depend on both the nature of the export and the identity of the purchasing nation. Many NMEs are included in country groups which mandate licenses. If the product is sold to a listed NME for nonmilitary or non-intelligence gathering purposes, but diverted to such uses, the United States law imposes severe sanctions on the exporter.

There has been considerable tension between the Departments of Commerce and Defense regarding exports to NMEs. The Department of Commerce is viewed as more favorable to business and pro-export. The Department of Defense, contrastingly, is viewed as extremely protective of any products or technology which might in any way be used to assist the military capacity of a NME. Although both changes to the EAR and executive declarations have relaxed controls on exports to many NMEs, especially those nations better referred to as former NMEs in transition, the Department of Defense continues to have the power to cause delays in performing its role of conducting reviews, whenever in its view there is a possibility that the export might be detrimental to national security. See *Daedalus Enterprises, Inc. v. Baldrige*, 563 F.Supp. 1345 (D.D.C.1983). Fortunately for many transitional nations trying to become market economies, the DOD has been exercising that power to delay less than in the past.

COUNTERTRADE

When goods proposed for export to an NME are actually not of a sufficient priority according to the state plan to merit government approval of payment in hard currency, or when the exporter is convinced by the NME that such is the case, the NME may allow payment for the foreign imported goods only by the acceptance of local NME goods. This is countertrade, which poses some interesting legal and economic problems. Countertrade has not been welcome in the West. Tax authorities worry that transactions not in currency will not appear in tax returns. The OECD fears that the pricing system is distorted. And those who view trade through the market oriented spectacles of the WTO and national trade laws are wary of this new mechanism which conflicts with carefully developed concepts of most favored nation and national treatment. Despite this reticence toward countertrade, trade statistics suggest that countertrade gained an important share of the trading market. That share is not limited to trade with NMEs. Countertrade is used in trading goods to many third world nations which have severely limited hard currency reserves.

The most common form of countertrade for an exporter of goods to a NME is *counterpurchase*, or *offsets*. The foreign seller agrees to accept goods which are unrelated to the sale. For example, an exporter of liquor to Ecuador has accepted bananas, and an exporter of commercial aircraft to Eastern Europe nations accepted in exchange hams, leather goods, cutting tools and crystal. Although the entire countertrade transaction may be included in one contract, the more common practice is to treat each side of the contract as separate, with currency payments for the exchange of the goods, and the use of letters of credit. A third linking contract or *protocol* makes the two otherwise unrelated transactions a countertrade arrangement. It is that third contract which includes provisions requiring both contracts to be executed for either to be valid, includes penalties if the foreign trader fails to find acceptable NME nation goods within a stated period of time, and allows the foreign trader to avoid performance of the countertrade agreement if the NME fails to fulfill its obligations.

Countertrade is referred to as *compensation* or *buyback* when the foreign party sells technology or even an entire plant (a "turnkey" sale) and agrees to be paid by a percentage of the production. For example, Occidental Petroleum constructed ammonia plants in the USSR and received payment in ammonia. Compensation deals are usually for far greater sums and longer durations than counterpurchase. The products are more easily disposed of by the foreign firm, since they relate to its line of business.

Other forms of countertrade have developed: import entitlement (foreign trader receives preference in receiving import licenses if it can show a record of exports), switch trading (use of an intermediary who finds third parties to enter a countertrade arrangement), and performance requirements (minimum export mandates for allowing foreign direct investment). Nearly any transaction which involves the exchange of products rather than currency may gain a countertrade label, but it is counterpurchase and compensation arrangements which have given countertrade an important place in international trade with NME and developing nations.

Objections to countertrade are often based on the poor quality of countertraded goods. Were the goods of acceptable quality they would stand on their own and not need the coercion of countertrade to enter the market. But some nations counter with the argument that markets are often closed, and countertrade tends to force them open. They argue that once traded, these products prove their merit. With this division of opinion, it is clear that as in the case of mandated joint ventures, much countertrade is involuntary in the sense that it is accepted by the developed nation party only because there is no other alternative to trading with the NME or developing nation. As NMEs began to assume market economy characteristics in the late 1980s, some of them indicated that they would reduce their demands for countertrade. While that has been the case, countertrade continues to be used for many transactions. It is much less significant than in the 1970s and 1980s, but it remains essential to understand.

IMPORTING GOODS FROM NONMARKET ECONOMIES

In contrast to where the United States or other developed nation party sells goods or services to a nonmarket economy nation, is where the United States or other developed nation party buys those goods. Although the trade in such direction is considerably less than purchases by nonmarket economies, MNEs do export a considerable amount directly that is not as a part of countertrade. These sales are usually documentary sales using letters of credit. Because the United States party is purchasing, it will pay in a hard currency and there ought to be no issues similar to those noted above about currency exchange. Of course, were the United States buyer trying to dispose of currency of the selling NME nation, which the buyer obtained for earlier sales not part of countertrade, the NME nation may reject accepting its own currency in payment, and demand hard currency.

What does affect purchases from NMEs are United States laws restricting trade with specific NME nations, such as Cuba. Trade is restricted not only by restricting exports as noted above, but by restricting or prohibiting imports as well. This is accomplished partly by restricting currency flows to certain nations, thus making it impossible to pay for the goods. Since currency is a subject of regulation by the Department of the Treasury, that department rather than the Department of Commerce administers currency regulations through its Office of Foreign Assets Control. The general regulations governing foreign assets control are followed by mostly country specific regulations. These all follow a general format, but vary depending upon the level of trade permitted with the specific countries. For example, the Cuban Assets Control Regulations are very strict, prohibiting nearly all transfers of money to Cuba.

THE COUNCIL FOR MUTUAL ECONOMIC ASSISTANCE (CMEA OR COMECON)

What the Marshall Plan and later the European Economic Community were to the West, COME-

CON became to the Soviet bloc and later to the NME nations as a whole. Less ambitious than the EEC, COMECON served as a negotiating framework for both annual and long-term trade agreements between and among the members. Long-term agreements usually attempted to balance trade evenly among members, since there was no multilateral payments system, a natural obstacle among nations with tightly controlled, nontraded currencies. COMECON also functioned as a multi-state "economic plan" for Eastern Europe, a plan often heavily skewed to favor Soviet economic interests. This severely limited trade with the West. Buying and selling goods was almost exclusively limited to trade among the COMECON nations. There were always attempts to sell goods to the West, in order to earn hard currency, but the poor quality of many goods, and the prohibitions on trade imposed by some market economies, kept this trade to a minimum. Purchases were occasionally made in the West, but they faced the limitations caused by the scarcity of hard currency and the same trading prohibitions which affected NME sales.

The COMECON market was not intended to create a larger market for non-members. A foreign exporter to Hungary, for example, did not thereby gain access to other nations of the COMECON. But a joint venture might gain that access. As the Eastern European nations and the USSR began to move away from NME characteristics, the future of COMECON was in doubt. By 1991 it had disintegrated, as formerly NME nations began to sign trade agreements with the West and as trade relations within the NME group began to be based on new agreements rather than old COMECON rules. The future of economic association is viewed to consist of links with the West, with the European Union and with membership in the WTO. COMECON has become part of the socialist Jurassic Park.

THE TRANSFER OF TECHNOLOGY AND DIRECT FOREIGN INVESTMENT

The sale of technology to NMEs duplicates some of the issues addressed above regarding the trading of goods or services. There may be problems involving (1) prohibitions or limitations on what technology may be exported to the particular NME, (2) the capacity of the NME to make payment for the technology in hard currency, and (3) demands for countertrade or taking products produced with the technology in lieu of payment (counterpurchase). Technology interjects an additional issue. Many nations which are less developed, including NMEs, reject the notion that technology is proprietary property and entitled to protection. They consider technology the property of mankind and often demand free access to it. But such demands have not been accepted in the developed market economies which are the sources of most current advanced technology. Technology is not transferred unless there is some assurance by the transferee's national intellectual property legislation that it will be protected. Many NMEs have now changed or moderated their earlier views and have adopted intellectual property laws intended to encourage technology transfers. Technology contracts to parties in NMEs must be carefully drafted. But even the most careful drafting will not overcome the absence of a national acceptance of the right to protect the interest in technology.

THE NONMARKET ECONOMY NATION AS A DEVELOPING NATION

There are no nonmarket economy nations which merit the label "developed". China falls far short, as did the USSR before its disintegration. Largeness ought not be equated with being developed. Thus in one sense all of the NMEs are developing nations. That may appear evident from this and the previous chapter. Each of the characteristics of a developing nation are present in a nonmarket economy nation. But they may appear in slightly different colors due to the overlay of NME status. For example, both have shortages of hard currency and often resort to currency exchange controls. But few developing nations which are not NMEs resort to such strict controls that the currency may not be exported, or that persons entering the nation are required to exchange so much hard currency for each day's stay. Both developing nations and NMEs usually have import controls. Such controls are usually the consequence of shortages of hard currency, but the import controls in NMEs may also be imposed to limit dealings with nations having an economic theory at odds with the NME. The NMEs often are unwilling to acknowledge that market economy nations produce better goods.

The movement away from being an NME to a market economy is view both as a change in fundamental theory, as well as one which offers a better opportunity to escape the "developing" label. Indeed, some NMEs have accepted some market economy characteristics, while reaffirming their commitment to socialist economic theory. The reasoning is that such acceptance may help speed the development process, and that the new openings to market theory are only temporary.

A characteristic of developing nations which tends not to be present in NMEs is an infrastructure of *laws* which govern features unique to market economies. That includes a corporation or company law, securities regulation and securities markets, antitrust laws, bankruptcy and advanced tax laws. Many NMEs must make significant changes to their constitutions to establish a basis for adopting market economy laws. Constitutional reform has been a stumbling block for several NMEs, when the demands of reformists clash with those intent on either preserving the status quo, or making only very small alterations in the NMEs structures.

THE PROCESS OF TRANSITION
FROM NME STATUS

After the failures of socialism in the USSR and Eastern Europe, many of the NME nations, new and old, have moved away from nonmarket theory. The rate of transition varies in each nation. In the former East Germany, reunification with West Germany thrust upon the former an instant capitalism. But that case is unique. Nations such as Hungary, Poland, the Ukraine, the progeny of Czechoslovakia (the Czech Republic and Slovakia), and others, have struggled with their identities. Movements sometimes are made towards market status urged by reformers, only to be held back by government officials suspicious of the consequences of the change. Changes decreed at the top often run into obstacles at the bottom, as vested interests in the old bureaucracies worry about their survival in a less subsidized future. Foreign parties engaged in trading in these nations are often frustrated with the delays seemingly endemic to doing business with an NME. They are also frustrated with crime and corruption, which has become in some nations a serious obstacle to a rapid transition. One characteristic of doing business in an NME in transition reflects the label "transition", the difficult of determining exactly where the country is along the path from NME to market economy.

Many observers of the process of disintegration of the USSR were amazed not that the system failed, but that the acknowledgements of the failure appeared so abruptly. However abrupt was the downfall of a system dedicated to socialist economic principles, the transition to market economy status has moved slowly in most nations. That is what has created so much frustration for foreign traders. Markets have opened and then closed, or opened and expanded, with little predictability. The astute foreign business person must become aware of the pace of transition, and the problems unique to the stages of transition. Many who have learned the system have profited by their commitment of time and effort.

CHAPTER EIGHT

DISPUTE SETTLEMENT: LITIGATION AND ARBITRATION

Dispute settlement should be dealt with when drafting the initial international business agreements between the parties, so that the dispute resolution process is known and understood before any actual dispute arises. The formal process chosen in the contract is most commonly either litigation or arbitration. Many international contracts require that mediation be used before any formal process is used, and mediation is the process preferred by many parties, especially Asian businesses. Whichever process is chosen, the contract should also choose the forum or tribunal and the governing law.

In addition, since a long-term international agreement is likely to generate "interpretative differences" from time to time, a contract should institutionalize in advance a quick and simple informal mechanism for resolving such differences. For example, it may be helpful to agree that the contract parties shall meet informally at least once every six months to discuss any interpretative matters which may arise.

Faced with a dispute, parties may seek access to dispute solving international tribunals or to courts in one or more countries. This Chapter discusses some considerations associated with access to international and national courts before discussing the widespread and increasing preference which merchants, investors and host countries have for arbitration.

INTERNATIONAL COURT OF JUSTICE

The International Court of Justice (ICJ) sits at The Hague, the Netherlands, and is comprised of fifteen judges drawn from all of the world's major legal systems. It is one of the principal organs of the United Nations and is the statutory, successor court to the former Permanent Court of International Justice of the League of Nations. The Statute of the ICJ delimits the Court's jurisdiction, and only allows States (countries) to be parties (have standing) before the Court in a contentious proceeding. The Court gives judgments in favor or against contesting States.

If a host country violates international law as against an investor, the State of which the investor is effectively a national may take up the grievance before the ICJ in a suit against the host country. However, an action before the ICJ is available only if the investor is complaining of official or governmental conduct, not merely conduct by private parties, and if the investor's own State seeks redress on the investor's behalf. The investor's State has complete discretion as to whether to espouse the claim, and need not (except as its own law may provide) pay the investor any judgment proceeds awarded by the Court.

Article 36 of the Statute of the ICJ contains the Court's principal jurisdictional mandate and provides, in part, that the jurisdiction of the ICJ comprises all the cases which States refer to it, and "all matters specially provided for" in treaties, or in the U.N. Charter. States may recognize that the ICJ has compulsory jurisdiction, on a reciprocal basis, for interpretation of a treaty or a question of international law; whether a particular fact establishes a breach of an international obligation; and the appropriate remedy for any breach of an international obligation. Such recognition of compulsory jurisdiction may be made either unconditionally, or conditioned upon reciprocal recognition of ICJ jurisdiction by other States. The ICJ, moreover, has the power to decide issues concerning its own jurisdiction.

In accepting ICJ jurisdiction over a particular case or over all cases which may arise, a State may decline nevertheless to consent that the Court shall have jurisdiction over a matter which lies within the State's "domestic jurisdiction," as determined by the Court or perhaps by that State.

ICJ judgments may include provisions for money damages and for injunctive relief and, if need be, may be enforced by reference to the United Nations Security Council for further appropriate action, including military action, against a noncompliant party (see UN Charter, Articles 39–51 and 94.2). From its beginning in 1945, the Court has shown an inclination to write opinions which contribute to a careful, considered, international jurisprudence.

In deciding cases submitted to it, Article 38(1) of the ICJ Statute directs it to use:

    a.   international conventions, whether general or particular, establishing rules expressly recognized by the contesting states;

    b.   international custom, as evidence of a general practice accepted as law;

    c.   the general principles of law recognized by civilized nations;

    d.   subject to the provisions of Article 59, judicial decisions and the teachings of the most highly qualified publicists of the various nations, as subsidiary means for the determination of rules of law.

Under Article 38(2), the ICJ also has the power "to decide *ex aequo et bono* [according to what is good and just], *if the Parties agree thereto*" (emphasis added), but has not used this power. There is substantial legal commentary, including commentary by the court, about the meanings of the words in Article 38(1).

TREATIES AND DISPUTE
SETTLEMENT

Since "international conventions" (treaties) are a source to which the Court refers and to which frequent reference is made in this Nutshell book, the reader may wish to consult the Vienna Convention on the Law of Treaties (see 63 A.J.I.L. 875 (1969)) which summarizes international law regarding treaties.

In short, a treaty (convention, international agreement) resembles an international contract between States. A treaty between two States is bilateral; one among three or more States is multilateral. A State is bound in international law by the treaties to which it is a "party", and it becomes a party by "ratifying", "approving", "accepting", "acceding" or "adhering" to the treaty pursuant to authority granted by the State's internal constitutional processes. For example, the United States becomes party to a treaty after it has been signed by the President (or his representative), has received the advice and consent of the U.S. Senate, and has been ratified and proclaimed by the President.

A distinction is drawn in international law between the international legal obligations of a State which is party to a treaty and a State which is a "signatory" to a treaty. States may participate in negotiations leading to the formation of a treaty and may, at the close of negotiations, sign the treaty without becoming fully bound in international law by the provisions of the treaty. The Vienna Convention (Article 18) takes the position that a signatory State to a treaty is obligated to refrain from acting in a way which would defeat the object and purpose of the treaty.

A State cannot invoke its internal law (including its Constitution) as an international legal justification for failing to perform its obligations under a treaty (see Vienna Convention Article 27). However, courts within a State may disregard a relevant treaty in favor of applying some other law if the law of the State permits such a result. Nevertheless, such action does not excuse the State from its international legal obligations.

Under Article 31 of the Vienna Convention, the terms of the treaty are to be given their ordinary meaning, and interpreted in the light of the objective and purpose of the treaty. As aids to interpretation, the court may use the treaty's text, "including its preamble and annexes," and any other related agreement made between all the parties at the conclusion of the treaty and also any contemporaneous instrument accepted by the parties as related to the treaty. Subsequent agreements between the parties, and subsequent practices establishing such agreements, may also be used as interpretative aids.

DISPUTE SETTLEMENT IN NATIONAL COURTS

A dispute between a foreign investor and a person in the host country may qualify for adjudication by a court within the host country, by a court within the investor's country of nationality, or by a court within an unanticipated third country notwithstanding the existence of law in many countries similar to the Doctrines of Act of State and Sovereign Immunity in the United States. See Chapters 9 and 10. For example, in the United States the Alien Tort Statute (28 U.S.C.A. § 1350) permits the noncitizen to sue another noncitizen in Federal District Court with respect to a claimed tort which has occurred outside of the United States but which has been "committed in violation of the law of nations or a treaty of the United States".

Recourse to a local court may lead to some surprises for a United States investor. For example, courts in some countries may not be as impermeable to political persuasion as are courts in the United States. The highest judicial appeal tribunal may be the country's chief political personality in some countries. In some countries the appropriate tribunal to hear an international commercial dispute may be a specialized court, such as a "commercial" court, or another kind of adjudicatory tribunal, perhaps called a "foreign investment grievances board".

Aside from the time and expense expended in getting a dispute aired thoroughly within local courts, difficulties may arise in securing persons or documents that are outside the country but are required by the litigation rules of the forum. Local court recognition of certain foreign public documents may be facilitated by the 1960 Convention

Abolishing the Requirement of Legalization of Foreign Public Documents, which the U.S. joined in 1981. TIAS 10072, 21 *Int'l Legal Mat.* 357. The Convention permits certification by the designated "competent authority" in the State from which the document comes.

Party litigants in a local court may have difficulty in working with the forum rules regarding notice and proof of applicable foreign law. The 1979 European Convention on Proof of and Information on Foreign Law, with additional Protocol, illustrates the "notice and proof" problem and modern efforts to deal with it. See 17 *Int'l Legal Mat.* 797 et seq.

Service of judicial documents upon a person in another country may be facilitated by the 1965 Convention on the Service Abroad of Judicial and Extra Judicial Documents in Civil and Commercial Matters (20 U.S.T. 361 et seq.; TIAS 6638), supplemented for the United States by the 1977 Department of Justice Instructions for Serving Foreign Judicial Documents and for Processing Requests for Serving American Judicial Documents Abroad. See 16 *Int'l Legal Mat.* 1331. It applies in all civil or commercial cases in which a judicial or extrajudicial document must be served abroad. Under it, each Contracting State designates a "Central Authority" which is available to other Contracting States to receive requests for service.

Parties who desire the taking of evidence abroad may receive some assistance from the 1970 Hague Convention on the Taking of Evidence Abroad in

Civil or Commercial Matters (23 U.S.T. 2555 et seq.; TIAS 7444), which has a framework similar to the 1965 Convention regarding service of judicial documents. One court in Germany has held that the Convention on Taking of Evidence Abroad does not permit an applicant to use it for "fishing expedition" discovery purposes. See 20 *Int'l Legal Mat.* 1025.

Where this treaty is not applicable, U.S. law provides foreign parties with broad evidence gathering opportunities under 28 U.S.C.A. §§ 1781–1782, but a U.S. party seeking evidence abroad may be hindered. Court orders sent abroad, purporting to use compulsory process to summon a non-citizen to appear as a witness, may be ineffective. *FTC v. Compagnie De Saint–Gobain–Pont–a–Mousson,* 636 F.2d 1300 (D.C.Cir.1980). Further, civil law countries view the taking of evidence as a judicial function and generally believe that gathering evidence within their territory, but without their consent, threatens their sovereignty. If the country does consent and participate in the evidence gathering, the evidence may be supplied in a form which is unusable in U.S. courts. In addition, a U.S. court order for production of evidence held abroad may conflict with "blocking statutes" or other non-disclosure laws of the foreign country.

The 1970 Hague Evidence Convention provides three alternative methods for gathering evidence abroad. First, a party may ask the U.S. court to send a "Letter of Request" to the "Central Authority" in the foreign country where the evidence is located. That Central Authority forwards the Request to the appropriate foreign court, which then holds the evidentiary proceeding, and will hold it under procedures specified by the U.S. court, unless they contravene the law of the foreign court. Second, a party to litigation in a U.S. court may ask that a U.S. diplomatic or consular officer accredited to a foreign country take evidence in that foreign country. And third, a party may request that a specially appointed commissioner take evidence abroad. Of these three methods, the Request is the most useful, for the others are noncompulsory proceedings. However, the Convention gives foreign judicial authorities substantial latitude in determining what evidence shall be transmitted back to a U.S. court, especially in discovery of documents. See *Pain v. United Technologies Corp.*, 637 F.2d 775 (D.C.Cir.1980).

If a foreign person is a party to litigation before a U.S. court, and the U.S. court has jurisdiction over that person, the U.S. court will apply its own procedural rules to that litigation—and to the foreign party. The U.S. court therefore has the power to compel that foreign party to produce evidence which is located abroad. *United States v. First Nat. City Bank*, 396 F.2d 897 (2d Cir.1968). Further, the 1970 Hague Evidence Convention is not the exclusive, or even the primary, method of obtaining evidence from abroad, and does not preclude the use of U.S. discovery and procedural rules to obtain evidence from foreign parties which are subject to the jurisdiction of U.S. courts. *Societe Nationale*

Industrielle Aerospatiale v. United States, 482 U.S. 522 (1987). U.S. courts are admonished to "consider international comity" before proceeding outside the Convention. Failure to produce evidence located abroad may be excused, after good faith efforts, if local law prohibits its release. *Societe Internationale Pour Participations Industrielles Et Commerciales, S.A. v. Rogers,* 357 U.S. 197 (1958). But see *In re Uranium Antitrust Litigation,* 617 F.2d 1248 (7th Cir.1980)(production of evidence ordered despite good faith and comity concerns in face of blocking statutes—default judgments rendered).

Problems can arise in gathering evidence abroad, even under the Convention. For example, there is not even agreement as to the meaning of the terms defining the scope of the Convention, as illustrated by a report of a meeting on the Convention, reprinted in 72 Am.J.Int'l L. 633 (1978):

> There exists no agreement on the scope of the Convention, i.e., on the meaning of the term "civil and commercial matters" as used in the caption and in Article 1 of the Convention. United States practice under the Convention, concurred in by the United Kingdom expert, is to consider any legal proceeding that is not criminal as "civil or commercial" (including an administrative proceeding). French practice, concurred in by the Swiss observer, excludes from "civil and commercial matters" legal proceedings that are criminal and fiscal. Japanese practice excludes all administrative matters. The German observer offered the opinion that under German practice, in

addition to criminal matters, proceedings involving the enforcement of public law (as distinguished from "private law") would be excluded. Finally, Egyptian practice excludes family law from the purview of "civil and commercial matters," since disputes involving family relations belong to the religious courts of that country.

RECOGNITION AND ENFORCEMENT OF FOREIGN JUDGMENTS

Americans are used to recognition and enforcement of the judgments of one state of the U.S. by any other state of the U.S. Sometimes they forget that this recognition and enforcement is due to the "full faith and credit" clause of the U.S. Constitution, and that the courts of most legal systems do not recognize judgments from other jurisdictions. For example, in nearly two thirds of the countries of the world, judgments of U.S. courts either are not enforceable at all or are enforceable only if certain conditions are met. As to foreign judgments brought to the U.S., the "full faith and credit" clause does not apply to make them enforceable—but there is no rule prohibiting enforcement. The result is that the courts have been left to their own analyses to develop policies and rules.

The common law rule in England was that a foreign court's judgment for money was only *prima facie* evidence of the subject matter that it purported to decide—but no more than that. It was not conclusive on the merits of the dispute and did not act as either res judicata or collateral estoppel to actions in English courts by the loser in the foreign court.

The U.S. Supreme Court adopted a different approach in *Hilton v. Guyot,* 159 U.S. 113 (1895). The Court denied enforcement of a French judgment, announcing that it followed a rule of "comity," which required the opportunity for a "fair trial abroad before a court of competent jurisdiction," "regular proceedings," citation or appearance of the defendant, "a system of ... impartial administration of justice," and without "prejudice" or fraud. The Court did not fault French justice on any of the above grounds, but it found that French courts did not recognize U.S. court judgments. Thus, the French judgment was denied conclusive effect, not because "comity" was lacking, but because "mutuality and reciprocity" were lacking. *Hilton* is still the leading federal law decision on the subject.

However, *Hilton* is rarely controlling, for most attempts to enforce foreign judgments will depend upon state law, not federal law, and state courts have felt free to pursue their own policies and doctrines. For example, the New York Court of Appeals, stating that it was not bound by *Hilton,* did give conclusive effect to a French court judgment, despite the known lack of reciprocity. *Johnston v. Compagnie Generale Transatlantique,* 242 N.Y. 381, 152 N.E. 121 (1926).

A state court, in determining its own policies, has several options. It may reject the judgment of the foreign court and accord no effect to it, requiring a *de novo* trial on the merits in its own courts. Alternatively, it may accept the foreign court's judgment as its own and "enforce" it in the same manner as a domestic judgment. Or, it may "recognize" the judgment by deciding that there are issues which do not need to be relitigated, even though the court will only "enforce" domestic judgments. Where courts only "recognize" foreign judgments, the party with a foreign court judgment must use it to obtain a domestic court judgment, which can then be enforced in the jurisdiction. Direct enforcement of foreign judgments is unusual; recognition of such judgments is more common.

Finally, there are courts which grant conditional recognition to foreign judgments. The conditions may relate to reciprocity of recognition between the two judicial systems involved (*Hilton*), or to "comity between nations" (e.g., *Johnston*). Where comity is the criterion, U.S. courts have tended to examine (1) the jurisdiction of the foreign court over both the persons and the subject matter involved, (2) the adequacy of the notice given, (3) the possibility of fraud in the decision, and (4) whether any public policy of the U.S. will be harmed by enforcement of the foreign judgment. Some U.S. courts seem to classify foreign legal systems as either favored or not favored, and judgments from favored systems are not investigated in detail. See, e.g., *Hunt v. BP Exploration Co. (Libya) Ltd.*, 492 F.Supp. 885 (N.D.Tex.1980).

Many states have little or no caselaw on this issue, so the National Conference of Commissioners on Uniform State Laws drafted the Uniform Foreign Money–Judgments Recognition Act, which has been enacted by twenty-eight states, the District of Columbia and the Virgin Islands. Under it, recognition is given only to foreign judgments which are final and enforceable where rendered. Further, only judgments for sums of money are eligible for recognition, not injunctions or specific performance decrees. The Uniform Act does not require reciprocity for recognition of foreign judgments, but does require an examination of the criteria and issues generally associated with "comity."

If a foreign judgment is given in a foreign currency, how should a state court design its award? In many states, a court's judgment must be in U.S. dollars. Although this should not induce a court to refuse recognition, it does raise issues of the proper time for computing currency conversion. The Uniform Foreign Money Claims Act, enacted in five states, allows the court to issue a judgment in a foreign currency, gives three criteria for doing so, and requires any conversion to be computed on the date of payment.

Countries have tried to facilitate the enforcement of judgments by bilateral treaty (e.g., the 1980 draft United Kingdom–United States Convention on Recognition and Enforcement of Judgments). Efforts to facilitate the enforcement of foreign judgments have been also the subject of multilateral treaties, such as the 1968 [EC] Common Market Convention on

Jurisdiction and the Enforcement of Judgments and the 1979 Inter–American [OAS] Convention on Extraterritorial Validity of Foreign Judgments and Arbitral Awards. See 18 *Int'l Legal Mat.* 1224.

CONTRACT PROVISIONS ABOUT DISPUTE FORUM AND GOVERNING LAW

Because of uncertainties surrounding international dispute settlement, two contract clauses to which lawyers, and increasingly nonlawyer negotiators, give close attention are the Forum Selection Clause and the Choice of Law Clause.

THE FORUM SELECTION CLAUSE

There are no universally accepted rules regarding jurisdiction of a particular court over the parties or subject matter of a dispute. Thus, when a dispute arises out of an international transaction, the parties to that dispute, if they seek litigation, are capable of bringing an action on that dispute in the courts of many different countries. Further, the substantive rules that may be used to resolve the dispute may be different in the different courts. Even the choice of law rules may be different, producing divergent results which depend only upon the court selected to hear the litigation. Attempting to obtain such a tactical advantage through court selection is international "forum shopping," and creates uncertainty in the resolution of disputes under the transaction.

The parties to an international transaction are well-advised to seek to avoid this uncertainty by resolving the issue of which forum shall have jurisdiction to hear disputes arising out of the transaction before any such disputes arise. This means that during the initial drafting of the contract the parties should decide which court shall have jurisdiction, and then specify that court in a Forum Selection Clause. That Clause should both specify the court which has jurisdiction and state that that court has exclusive jurisdiction to preclude other courts from entertaining the case.

A court which wishes to hear a case, despite a choice of forum clause which vests exclusive jurisdiction elsewhere, may construe the clause to resolve ambiguities against giving such an effect to the clause. See *Keaty v. Freeport Indonesia, Inc.*, 503 F.2d 955 (5th Cir.1974). A clause providing that "the District Court of Luanda should be considered the sole court competent to adjudicate to the exclusion of all others," has been construed to permit litigation in England on the ground that, subsequent to the clause's drafting, a revolution in the former Portuguese Angola resulted in the present District Court in Luanda not being the Court to which the contract parties had referred. See *Carvalho v. Hull, Blythe (Angola Ltd.)*, (1979) 1 W.L.R. 1228 (C.A.). Moreover, one court has disregarded a forum selection clause's effectiveness as to part of a counterclaim because of "judicial economy ... [and] to insure that complete justice is done." *Bankers*

Trust Co. v. Worldwide Transportation Services, Inc., 537 F.Supp. 1101 (E.D.Ark.1982).

At common law, choice of forum clauses were ineffective, since they were perceived as attempts to interfere with judicial administration by depriving a competent court of jurisdiction. The attitudes of U.S. courts have changed because of the U.S. Supreme Court's decision in *M/S Bremen v. Zapata Off–Shore Co.,* 407 U.S. 1 (1972). In that case, the Court upheld a Forum Selection Clause in which the parties had chosen, not the courts of one of their own countries, but the courts of London—a neutral forum which had no other relationship to the transaction. "[I]n the light of present day commercial realities and expanding international trade we conclude that the forum clause should control absent a strong showing that it should be set aside."

Although *Bremen* involved an international transaction and a decision in admiralty, the lower federal courts have extended its "more hospitable attitude" toward Forum Selection Clauses to include non-admiralty cases and cases involving domestic transactions. These cases can arise in two different contexts. First, when the parties approach the chosen forum, there may be an issue as to whether that court will accept jurisdiction over the action. The second, and more usual, context arises when one of the parties attempts to bring the action in a court outside the chosen forum.

Although Forum Selection Clauses are presumed to be valid, they will not be enforced if they deny one party an effective remedy, cause substantial inconvenience, are the product of fraud or unconscionable conduct, or contravene U.S. public policy. Thus, where a case involved factual disputes about the performance of a casting plant built in the U.S. by a Pennsylvania firm, the court refused to enforce the contract's selection of West Germany as the forum. The court characterized the clause as unreasonable and the German courts as substantially inconvenient, since the witnesses—the people involved in both the construction and the operation of the plant, as well as its customers—were all in the U.S. Further, all these witnesses spoke English, which would require translation "with its inherent inaccuracy." *Copperweld Steel Co. v. Demag–Mannesmann–Boehler*, 347 F.Supp. 53 (W.D.Pa.1972), affirmed 578 F.2d 953 (3d Cir.1978).

Many of these grounds for resisting application of a Forum Selection Clause are analyzed by the courts under the rubric of "reasonableness." "Mere inconveniences or additional expense is not the test of unreasonableness". *Gordonsville Indus., Inc. v. American Artos Corp.*, 549 F.Supp. 200, 205 (W.D.Va.1982). Moreover, where contract parties have agreed upon a Forum Selection Clause, a court in that forum may be disinclined later to consider a *forum non conveniens* motion; "In short, by their own exercise of discretion in agreeing upon a forum, the parties themselves [have] obviated considerations of inconvenience." *Arthur Young & Co. v. Leong*, 53 A.D.2d 515, 383 N.Y.S.2d 618 (1976).

Forum non conveniens is a doctrine which allows a court to refuse to accept jurisdiction over a case, so that the case may be tried in an alternative forum. Such decisions are almost entirely at the court's discretion, except that the party seeking a *forum non conveniens* decision must submit to the effective jurisdiction of the alternative forum. The factors that courts generally consider in making such decisions include the law applicable to the dispute, the location of witnesses, exhibits and documents, the language of the witnesses and documents, and the citizenship of the claimants.

It had been thought that courts would refuse to enforce Forum Selection Clauses which are found in contracts of adhesion, or in the fine print boiler plate printed clauses in a contract involving parties of unequal bargaining power, especially if counsel has not been consulted. However, in *Carnival Cruise Lines, Inc. v. Shute,* 499 U.S. 585 (1991), the United States Supreme Court upheld a Forum Selection Clause which was not bargained for and was contained in the middle of 25 paragraphs of boiler plate on a ticket form which was received after the conclusion of the transaction. The Court found the clause "reasonable" because it saved "judicial resources" and might lead to lower ticket prices, but the court noted that a domestic, not an alien, forum had been selected.

Congress attempted to overrule the *Carnival Cruise Lines* decision in a low visibility statutory amendment in 1992, but then changed the statutory language back to its original form in 1993. Compare Pub.L.No. 102–587, § 3006, 106 Stat. 5068 (1992), with Pub.L.No. 103–206, § 309, 107 Stat. 2425 (1993). Presumably, *Carnival Cruise Lines* survives all these amendments undisturbed. It may, however, still be true that a Forum Selection Clause written in a language the party is known not to understand may not be enforced. But an allegation of fraud in the transaction will not necessarily void a Forum Selection Clause, unless the inclusion of the clause was a product of fraud.

In addition, there may be a doctrine of nonenforcement of Forum Selection Clauses due to "changed circumstances" developing out of cases involving Iran–U.S. transactions. At least, U.S. courts have refused to enforce clauses selecting a forum in Iran for a variety of reasons, such as, no adequate remedy or "difficult and inconvenient." See, e.g., *McDonnell Douglas Corp. v. Islamic Republic of Iran*, 758 F.2d 341 (8th Cir.1985).

There are many pronouncements that the public policy of the U.S. may be violated where the selection of a foreign forum contravenes "mandatory law" of the U.S. However, the caselaw does not substantiate these pronouncements. The public policy of the state of Hawaii that cases concerning the insurance of risks located in Hawaii be tried there was not sufficient to invalidate a clause selecting a foreign forum. *Lien Ho Hsing Steel Enterprise Co. v.*

Weihtag, 738 F.2d 1455 (9th Cir.1984). A forum selection clause was upheld in a potential securities fraud case even where it was assumed that the chosen forum would not apply U.S. securities law. *AVC Nederland B.V. v. Atrium Investment Partnership*, 740 F.2d 148(2d Cir.1984).

The Carriage of Goods by Sea Act (COGSA), 46 U.S.C.A. App. § 1300–1315, has long been considered the archetype of "mandatory law." The Second Circuit held invalid a contract clause in a bill of lading subject to COGSA which selected a foreign forum. *Indussa Corp. v. S.S. Ranborg*, 377 F.2d 200 (2d Cir.1967)(en banc). The circuit court held that use of the foreign forum would put too high a hurdle on plaintiff's ability to enforce liability, and that the United States courts could not be certain that a foreign court would enforce United States mandatory law. This position is probably of doubtful validity now, however, because of the Supreme Court rulings in *Carnival Cruise Lines* (above), and *Vimar Seguros y Reaseguros, S.A. v. M/V Sky Reefer*, 515 U.S. 528 (1995). (See discussion under "Dispute Settlement by Arbitration," below.) Although *M/V Sky Reefer* involved an arbitration clause, the court stated that such clauses were merely a subset of foreign Forum Selection Clauses, and in dicta openly questioned the rationale of *Indussa*.

One difference between arbitration clauses and Forum Selection Clauses, however, is that the former are enforced under a treaty and a federal statute, thus presenting a federal question. Forum Selection Clauses are not. Thus, it is not clear whether a federal court sitting in diversity should follow the *Bremen* approach toward Forum Selection Clauses, or whether *Erie* requires application of state law. The U.S. Supreme Court has held that the decision to transfer a case from one district court to another within the United States is a matter of federal law under 28 U.S.C.A. § 1404(a), but *not* a federal question under *Bremen*. Each motion for such a transfer must be decided on a case-by-case basis, in which a Forum Selection Clause is a "central" consideration, but not a "dispositive" one. *Stewart Organization, Inc. v. Ricoh Corp.*, 487 U.S. 22 (1988). Thus, the *Bremen* approach does not control a court's determination, even where a U.S. forum is selected. If a foreign forum is selected, 28 U.S.C.A. § 1404(a) is not applicable, and state law would seem to apply.

In the European Union, the 1968 Convention on the Jurisdiction of Courts and the Enforcement of Judgments in Civil and Commercial Matters (Brussels Convention) provides in Article 17 that parties to a contract which is either a written agreement or an oral agreement evidenced in writing may confer exclusive jurisdiction upon a court . There does not need to be any objective connection between the legal relationship and the court designated. In varying degrees, Forum Selection Clauses in contracts have been treated as presumptively valid in Austria, England, France, Germany, Italy, Latin America and the Scandinavian countries. In some countries (e.g., Luxembourg) the clause must be signed specifically by the parties; the signing of the contract as a whole does not suffice. See EEC Court of Justice Case No. 784/79.

THE CHOICE OF LAW CLAUSE

Because the validity of a contractual Forum Selection Clause may turn on its validity under the law which governs the contract, the validity of the Choice of Law Clause assumes an added importance. *Smith, Valentino & Smith, Inc. v. Superior Court,* 17 Cal.3d 491, 131 Cal.Rptr. 374, 551 P.2d 1206 (1976). Broadly put, in common law and in European civil law jurisdictions, parties may choose the law which they wish to govern their contract relationship, as long as the law chosen is that of a place which has a substantial relationship to the parties and to the international business transaction, and is not contrary to a strong public policy of the place where suit is brought.

Where the validity of the Choice of Law Clauses is determined by statute, there seem to be two different approaches. The Uniform Commercial Code (§ 1–105) permits the parties to choose the law governing the contract, as long as the transaction bears "a reasonable relation" to the jurisdiction providing the governing law. Thus, "party autonomy" is permissible, but only within "reasonable" limits. That is not helpful to the merchants in a U.S.–German transaction who wish to use neither U.S. nor German law, but wish to use the law of some "neutral" country, such as England.

However, at least one federal circuit court has taken the Forum Selection concepts of *Bremen* and applied them to a Choice of Law Clause, which would uphold the stated law of the contract, without limitation. *Milanovich v. Costa Crociere, S.p.A.*, 954 F.2d 763 (D.C.Cir.1992). Likewise, the 1980 Convention on Contracts for the International Sale of Goods (Article 6), when applicable, permits the parties to "derogate," or choose some other law to govern the contract, without limitation. Thus, CISG permits unlimited party autonomy, and the merchants in the U.S.–German transaction could choose English law, if CISG were applicable. (For further discussion of the applicability of CISG in such cases, see Chapter 2, supra). In the EU, the 1980 Convention on the Law Applicable to Contractual Obligations (Article 3) also allows unlimited party autonomy. In sum, the legislative trend seems to favor fewer limits on party autonomy, and none in international transactions.

However, courts can still refuse to enforce a Choice of Law Clause because it is found to violate public policy, "a vague and variable phenomenon." In countries taking their legal heritage from Roman Law, laws expressing strong public policy may be called *jus cogens*—fundamental or "mandatory" rules of law, the operation of which parties may not contract away. These mandatory rules which are used to limit party autonomy may be either statutory or judicially-created, and will vary from country to country. Thus, they can create legal problems as to whether the parties may submit different aspects of a contract to different laws (*depecage*), or whether the courts of one country should recognize and apply the mandatory rules of a different country, regardless of the contract's Choice of Law or Forum Selection Clauses.

A forum court's notions of strong public policy may be expressed by a court conceding the *prima facie* applicability of a Choice of Law Clause but deciding that the clause, as drafted, does not preclude application of the forum's law to the circumstances of the parties' dispute. A holding in favor of application of the forum court's public policy (rule of law) may be accomplished also by holding that the dispute does not fall within the meaning of a Choice of Law Clause which has a clear meaning (*Hoes of America, Inc. v. Hoes,* 493 F.Supp. 1205, 1207 (C.D.Ill.1979)); or that the parties have drafted a Choice of Law Clause which requires considerable interpretation for its meaning to be clearly understood.

Moreover, "choice of law" rules of the chosen jurisdiction may permit a forum court to use its own law. Such a result may be possible because the chosen jurisdiction's entire law (whole law) including its "choice of law rules" ("private international law"), requires that the law of the forum be applied. Contra, *Siegelman v. Cunard White Star Ltd.,* 221 F.2d 189, 194 (2d Cir.1955). Thus, application of the choice of law rules of the chosen jurisdiction leads to application of a rule identical to the forum tribunal's rule, because the point in issue is one of first impression in the chosen jurisdiction.

MANDATORY PROVISIONS AND AN INTERSECTION BETWEEN FORUM SELECTION AND CHOICE OF LAW CLAUSES

Choice of Law Clauses and Forum Selection Clauses may be manipulated *inter sese;* for example, a forum court may use a Choice of Law Clause's referral to another, chosen jurisdiction's law to determine the validity of a Forum Selection Clause which purports to exclude litigation at the forum court. See *Smith, Valentino & Smith, Inc. v. Superior Court,* 17 Cal.3d 491, 131 Cal.Rptr. 374, 551 P.2d 1206 (1976). Moreover, mandatory (*jus cogens*) rules of law may operate to determine the effectiveness of a Choice of Law or Forum Selection Clause as well as the validity of a legal rule to which a choice of law clause may lead. One must consider mandatory rules both in the forum jurisdiction and in the chosen jurisdiction. For example, countries differ about whether Forum Selection and Choice of Law Clauses should be honored if contained within a standard form or an adhesion contract or when contrary to strong, public policy favoring the forum or application of its law. What emerges for the contract drafter is a probability calculus; one may succeed only in *reducing* potential choice of forum and choice of law surprises by taking care in the drafting of such clauses.

Although parties to an international commercial agreement may not be able to prevent a court from disregarding a contractual choice of forum or choice of law, the risk may be lessened in a negotiated agreement which states why the choices of forum and of law are considered reasonable in light of the planned transaction.

DISPUTE SETTLEMENT
BY ARBITRATION

Uncertainty about identity of the country and the court in which a dispute may be heard, about procedural and substantive rules to be applied, about the degree of publicity to be given the proceedings and the judgment, about the time needed to settle a dispute, and about the efficacy which may be given to a resulting judgment all have combined to make arbitration the preferred mechanism for solving international commercial disputes. Some Western European countries long have been accustomed to arbitration (e.g., see English Arbitration Act of 1889 and English Arbitration Act of 1950, as amended by Arbitration Act of 1979); the London Court of Arbitration, a private arbitration institution, has existed since 1892. The United States has had a Federal Arbitration Act since 1947 (9 U.S.C.A. § 1 et seq.). Arbitration in international commercial contracts is favored by the Peoples Republic of China, if mediation and conciliation fails, either through the Chinese Foreign Economic and Trade Arbitration Commission (FETAC) or the Chinese Maritime Arbitration Commission (MAC). Most of the nations of the former Soviet Union also favor arbitration, and have organizations similar to the Chinese FETAC and MAC. The Japan Commercial Arbitration Association has been active since

1953. Virtually all countries in Africa have arbitration statutes. Latin America, historically disadvantaged in many arbitral awards, increasingly is accepting arbitration. For example, the 1975 Inter–American Convention on International Commercial Arbitration (see 14 *Int'l Legal Mat.* 336) provides, in part, that "The Governments of the Member States of the Organization of American States ... have agreed that ... an agreement in which parties undertake to submit to arbitral decision any differences ... with respect to a commercial transaction is valid." The 1979 Inter–American Convention on Extraterritorial Validity of Foreign Judgments and Arbitral Awards expands upon the scope of the 1975 Convention.

The ultimate "Forum Selection Clause" is one that chooses no court at all, but selects an alternate dispute resolution mechanism, such as an arbitration tribunal. For a long period of time, the courts resisted validating such clauses, holding that they deprived the parties of due process of law (a reaction one might expect toward a competitor). However, legislatures were far more sympathetic to arbitration, and around the turn of the century began to enact statutes validating arbitration clauses. The issue now is firmly settled. In addition to arbitration, there are many other even less formal alternative dispute resolution mechanisms in use, such as the "mini-trial" or the use of "conciliation." The mini-trial, for example, comes in a variety of packages, each with a different impact on resolution of the dispute. It can be nonbinding if used with a "neutral advisor"; it can be semi-binding if its results are admissible in later proceedings; or it can be binding before a court appointed master. For a review of the variety of such alternative dispute resolution mechanisms, see Nelson, "Alternatives to Litigation of International Disputes," 23 *Int'l Lawyer* 187 (1989).

Arbitration provisions may appear in Treaties of Friendship, Commerce and Navigation. The purpose of such treaty provisions is to ensure the enforcement of arbitration clauses in commercial contracts between nationals of the Contracting States to the treaty. The treaty provisions will also require the courts of each Contracting State to enforce the awards of arbitral tribunals rendered under such arbitration clauses. Thus, the treaty provision may require the courts of each Contracting State to enforce such arbitration clauses and subsequent arbitration awards, even though the place of arbitration is not located within the Contracting States and the arbitrators are not nationals of the Contracting States.

Many lower federal courts had held that "mandatory laws" could not be the subject matter of arbitration, because of both the public interest indicated by the legislative intent underlying the enactment of mandatory law and the public policy favoring judicial enforcement of such law. However, the Supreme Court has now rejected that doctrine. In *Scherk v. Alberto–Culver Co.*, 417 U.S. 506 (1974), the Court held that Securities and Exchange Commission law issues arising out of an international contract are subject to arbitration under the Federal Arbitration Act (9 U.S.C.A. § 1 et seq.), despite the public interest in protecting the United States investment climate. In *Mitsubishi Motors Corp. v. Soler Chrysler–Plymouth, Inc.*, 473 U.S. 614 (1985), the Court held that antitrust claims arising out of an international transaction were arbitrable, despite the public interest in a competitive national economy, and the legislative pronouncements favoring enforcement by private parties. In *Vimar Seguros y Reaseguros, S.A. v. M/V Sky Reefer*, 515 U.S. 528 (1995), claims that the foreign arbitrators would not apply the United States mandatory law (COGSA) were rejected, on the ground that the U.S. could "review" the arbitral award at the award-enforcement stage. That power may, however, be very narrow under the 1958 United Nation's Convention on the Recognition and Enforcement of Foreign Arbitral Awards. (See further discussion, below.)

ENFORCEMENT OF ARBITRAL AWARDS: THE 1958 CONVENTION

In over eighty countries, the enforcement of arbitral awards is facilitated by the 1958 United Nations Convention on the Recognition and Enforcement of Foreign Arbitral Awards, 21 U.S.T. 2518, T.I.A.S. No. 6997, 330 U.N.T.S. 38, implemented in the United States by 9 U.S.C.A. §§ 201–208. "[T]he principal purpose underlying American ... implementation ... was to encourage the recognition and enforcement of commercial arbitration agreements in international contracts and to unify the standards by which agreements to arbitrate are observed and arbitral awards are enforced in the signatory countries." *Scherk v. Alberto–Culver Co.,* 417 U.S. 506, 520 n. 15 (1974). In an abbreviated procedure, under 9 U.S.C.A. §§ 203, 208, Federal district courts entertain motions to confirm or to challenge a foreign award.

The Treaty commits the courts in each Contracting State to recognize and enforce arbitration clauses and separate arbitration agreements for the resolution of international commercial disputes. Where the court finds an arbitral clause or agreement, it "*shall* ... refer the parties to arbitration, unless it finds that the said agreement is null and void, inoperative, or incapable of being performed" (emphasis added). The Treaty also commits the courts in each Contracting State to recognize and enforce the awards of arbitral tribunals under such clauses or agreements, and also sets forth the limited grounds under which recognition and enforcement may be refused. Under the Treaty, grounds for refusal to enforce include: (1) incapacity or invalidity of the agreement containing the arbitration clause "under the law applicable to" a party to the agreement, (2) lack of proper notice of the arbitration proceedings or the appointment of the arbitrator, (3) failure of the arbitral award to restrict itself to the terms of the submission to arbitration, or decision of matters not within the scope of that subdivision, (4) composition of the arbitral tribunal not according to the arbitration agreement or applicable law, and (5) non-finality of the arbitral award under applicable law.

In addition to the above grounds for refusal, recognition or enforcement may also be refused if it would be contrary to the public policy of the country in which enforcement is sought; or if the subject matter of the dispute cannot be settled by arbitration under the law of that country. Courts in the United States have taken the position that the "public policy limitation on the Convention is to be construed narrowly [and] to be applied only where enforcement would violate the forum state's most basic notions of morality and justice." *Fotochrome, Inc. v. Copal Co., Ltd.,* 517 F.2d 512 (2d Cir.1975). Recourse to other limitations of the Convention, in order to defeat its applicability, has been greeted with judicial caution. *Parsons & Whittemore Overseas Co., Inc. v. Societe Generale De L'Industrie Du Papier (RAKTA),* 508 F.2d 969 (2d Cir.1974).

As has been discussed above, in both *Mitsubishi Motors* and *M/V Sky Reefer*, the Court determined that issues arising out of international transactions and involving U.S. mandatory law were arbitrable. However, in *dictum* at the end of the *Mitsubishi* opinion, the Court stated that U.S. courts would have a second chance to examine whether the arbitral tribunal "took cognizance of the antitrust claims and actually decided them." It would seem to be difficult to fit any examination by the U.S. courts properly into the structure of the Treaty, by enforcing the arbitration clause and referring disputes to arbitration; but then by conditioning recognition and enforcement of the subsequent award on the basis of the antitrust subject matter. It is not clear whether *Mitsubishi* invites the U.S. courts merely to examine whether the arbitrators state that they considered the antitrust issues, or also invites them to examine whether the arbitrators considered these issues *correctly* (review on the merits). The former can be evaded by a mechanical phrase; the latter can harm the arbitral process, especially if the parties have chosen non–U.S. law. Compare Park, "Private Adjudicators and the Public Interest: The Expanding Scope of International Arbitration," 3 *Brook. J. Int'l Law* 629 (1986) with Lowenfeld, "The *Mitsubishi* Case: Another View," 2 *Arbitration J.* 178 (1986).

In either case, arbitrators' enforcement of U.S. antitrust laws may not be to the standards of U.S. courts, and the status of recognition and enforcement of arbitral awards involving antitrust issues is not yet clear—even after *Mitsubishi*. However, under the 1958 U.N. Convention on Recognition and Enforcement of Foreign Arbitral Awards, a mere "misunderstanding," or error in interpretation, of a mandatory law by an arbitral tribunal has generally not been held to "contravene public policy." The cases are split as to whether even a "manifest disregard" of United States law constitutes such a violation of public policy. Awards have been upheld which violate the U.S. Vessel Owner's Limitation of Liability Act, previously considered mandatory law.

Thus, it is not certain, under the Treaty, that United States courts retain the review powers assumed by the Court to be available at the "award-enforcement stage" of the proceedings.

Cases in the United States have pointed out that parties cannot refer a dispute to a court while an arbitration is in progress (*Siderius, Inc. v. Compania de Acero del Pacifico, S.A.,* 453 F.Supp. 22 (S.D.N.Y.1978)) or block enforcement of an award in the United States in reliance upon the fact that the award, although binding in the country where rendered, is under appeal there. *Fertilizer Corp. of India v. IDI Management, Inc.,* 517 F.Supp. 948 (S.D.Ohio 1981). After the arbitration is concluded, a party may not be able to block enforcement of the award in reliance upon the United States Foreign Sovereign Immunities Act (see *Ipitrade International, S.A. v. Federal Republic of Nigeria,* 465 F.Supp. 824 (D.D.C.1978)), but a court may decline to enforce in reliance upon the Act of State Doctrine. *Libyan American Oil Co. v. Socialist People's, etc.,* 482 F.Supp. 1175 (D.D.C.1980). One court has granted enforcement, under the Convention, of a New York award rendered in favor of a non-citizen claimant against a non-citizen defendant. *Bergesen v. Joseph Muller Corp.,* 548 F.Supp. 650 (S.D.N.Y. 1982).

ARBITRATION RULES AND LOCAL LAW

Centers for international arbitration include Geneva, London, New York, Paris, and Stockholm;

arbitration associations at such places have adopted fairly settled rules for conducting arbitrations. In these countries, the law provides limitations upon the power of persons to specify for themselves what rules should govern their contractual relationship (including aspects of dispute settlement). As between two contracting parties, many provisions of their law may be excluded from usual applicability to a commercial relationship (such "excludable" legal rules are called "jus dispositivum"), but the applicability of certain legal rules may not be excluded by the parties (such "non-excludable" legal rules are called "jus cogens").

The "jus cogens"/"jus dispositivum" dichotomy is found in the law of many European countries. It is also found in the United States Uniform Commercial Code and lies underneath the rationales of United States cases which had held that issues of antitrust liability cannot be arbitrated. See discussion of *Mitsubishi Motors Corp. v. Soler Chrysler–Plymouth,* above. The dichotomy's relevance to arbitration results in a conclusion that any arbitration rules chosen by parties to govern their dispute may not be honored if such rules contravene a "non-excludable" provision of the local law. For example, notwithstanding that parties may desire otherwise, it has been a "non-excludable" rule that "when there are several arbitrators, one of them shall be chairman of the tribunal".

An arbitration may be held if the parties specify the location of the arbitration even though (subject to overriding jus cogens) the parties have specified that some procedural rules different from those of the tribunal should apply, or have specified that the substantive law of another forum should govern the resolution of a dispute. To the extent that issues of substantive law may raise further "conflict of laws" (choice of law) issues, a "choice of law clause" drafted by the parties will be given effect. If the parties have not drafted such a clause into their contract, the conflict of laws rules of the forum will determine the applicable substantive law.

ELEMENTS OF AN AGREEMENT TO ARBITRATE

Some considerations should be weighed for inclusion in any agreement to arbitrate regardless of the rules or locale chosen for the arbitration. Such considerations include:

(1) the locale for arbitration (whether visas can be obtained easily, physical facilities for arbitration are available, and communications facilities are good),

(2) the jus cogens problem,

(3) choice of governing substantive rules.

Other considerations include:

(4) scope of the arbitral clause—some countries may not consider a clause about arbitration to apply in futuro unless it is made expressly applicable to existing and to future disputes. Some countries may give effect only to an arbitration clause that relates to a particular relationship,

such as "all differences that may arise out of or in connection with this Agreement" between the parties. The clause should include a reference to any actions by a party that constitute a waiver of the right to invoke the clause, and also should include, if desired, reference to conciliation efforts that must occur before arbitration becomes appropriate.

(5) selection of arbitrators—a minimum number of three may be required; an odd number usually is required. Countries, such as the Peoples Republic of China, may require that all arbitrators be drawn from an approved list of arbitrators who are nationals of that country if one party litigant is a national of China while other countries may prohibit more than one arbitrator of the same nationality as a party litigant. Some countries list factors which disqualify an arbitrator from service (e.g., certain financial connections with a party litigant). Because parties often cannot agree upon procedures for choosing arbitrators, some countries provide that an "appointing authority" shall intervene, as appropriate, to effect the selection. Parties may define, in advance, the circumstances which warrant intervention.

(6) payment of arbitrator fees—in some instances arbitrators are paid a flat fee or per diem fee, while in other instances arbitrators are paid a fee based upon a percentage of the value of the dispute. It should be made clear who, and under which circumstances, has an obligation to pay

which arbitrator(s) and whether arbitrators are due reimbursement for costs in addition to fees.

(7) language to be used—common languages for arbitrations are English and French. If interpreters are to be used, their payment and their number should be settled. The authoritative language of documentary evidence and of the arbitral award should be specified.

(8) nature of the proceedings—In the People's Republic of China arbitration proceedings are public, while in other countries they are private. In some countries the proceedings may not last longer than a specific time, unless extended for good reason, after which the authority to conduct the proceeding will be considered to have lapsed. In many countries parties may be represented by counsel.

(9) procedure to be followed—In some places the arbitration is decided customarily upon submission of documents without a hearing. Other places permit hearings, allow oral testimony (including testimony under oath), allow cross examination, allow limited "discovery", issue subpoenas, take written submissions from counsel, permit arbitrators to make personal investigations or to introduce evidence, and permit a written record of the proceedings to be taken. The law governing procedural issues should be specified by the parties. If ex parte representations by counsel to the tribunal are not desired, they should be prohibited. Countries differ about

whether an arbitration proceeding can take place in the absence of all of the arbitrators.

(10) ex aequo et bono—In some countries, the arbitrators may not decide a dispute ex aequo et bono (according to what is just and good) unless the parties empower the arbitrators to act on that basis.

(11) the award—the agreement to arbitrate should specify that an arbitrator's written award shall be given unless the dispute is settled amicably at an earlier time. Countries differ about whether an award must be accompanied by reasons, whether an award requires the unanimous consent of all arbitrators and whether the losing party pays all costs of the arbitration (including counsel fees and the costs of stenographers, "facility use" costs, and costs of expert witnesses). The award should be made as final and binding as applicable law allows, recognizing that in some countries substantive legal questions arising during an arbitration may be reviewed subsequently by a court of law and that in other countries part or all of the procedure and merits of the dispute may be reviewed by a court. It may be useful to agree specifically to exclude judicial review of the validity of the award. The agreement to arbitrate should specify that the award shall be enforceable in any competent court of law and in accordance with the 1958 Convention on the Recognition and Enforcement of Arbitral Awards. If a record is to be kept of the award, the place of its retention should be specified.

(12) severability—It may be desirable to indicate whether an invalidity of part(s) of the provisions concerning arbitration is intended to affect the validity of all provisions dealing with arbitration or other parts of the contract in which such arbitral provisions may appear. However, the consequences of including a severability provision should be calculated with care.

(13) the trigger clause—when the agreement calls for mediation and conciliation, or even just "friendly consultations" as many Chinese contracts do, prior to arbitration, a "trigger clause" is essential so that the parties will know when they have a right to go to arbitration. The Chinese, for example, prefer not to trigger arbitration whenever "there is a prospect of amicable settlement." Foreign parties to contracts with the PRC prefer a more certain, if not an absolute, right to arbitrate disputes.

INTERNATIONAL ARBITRAL RULES: UNCITRAL, ICSID AND OTHERS

The factors considered above are incorporated in Model International Commercial Arbitration Rules (see 15 *Int'l Legal Mat.* 701 (1978)). It was issued in 1976 by the United Nations Commission on International Trade Law (UNCITRAL) following ten years of study. The UNCITRAL Rules are intended to be acceptable in all legal systems and in all parts of the world. Rapidly developing countries favor the Rules because of the care with which they have been drafted, and because UNCITRAL was one forum for developing arbitration rules in which their concerns would be heard. The Arbitral Institute of the Stockholm Chamber of Commerce has been willing to work with the UNCITRAL Rules, as has the London Court of Arbitration. The Iran–United States Claims Tribunal has used the UNCITRAL Rules in dealing with claims arising out of the confrontation between the two countries in 1980. The UNCITRAL Rules are not identified with any national or international arbitration organization.

Among other things, UNCITRAL rules provide that an "appointing authority" shall be chosen by the parties or, if they fail to agree upon that point, shall be chosen by the Secretary–General of the Permanent Court of Arbitration at the Hague (comprised of a body of persons prepared to act as arbitrators if requested).

In addition to its 1976 Model Arbitration Rules, UNCITRAL has also promulgated a 1985 Model Law on International Commercial Arbitration. 2 B.D.I.E.L. 993 (1985). The Model Law has been enacted in Australia, Bahrain, Bermuda, Bulgaria, Canada, Cypress, Egypt, Germany, Guatemala, Hong Kong, Hungary, India, Iran, Ireland, Kenya, Lithuania, Malta, Mexico, New Zealand, Nigeria, Oman, Peru, Russia, Singapore, Sri Lanka, Tunisia, Ukraine, Zimbabwe and Scotland. It has also been enacted as state law by several states of the U.S., including California, Connecticut, Georgia, Oregon and Texas. There seems to be no competing federal law which would pre-empt the application of these enactments.

Under the UNCITRAL Model Law, submission to arbitration may be *ad hoc* for a particular dispute, but is accomplished most often in advance of the dispute by a general submission clause within a contract. Under Article 8 of the Model Law, an agreement to arbitrate is specifically enforceable. Although no specific language will guarantee the success of an arbitral submission, UNCITRAL recommends the following model submission clause:

> Any dispute, controversy or claim arising out of or relating to this contract, or the breach, termination or invalidity thereof, shall be settled by arbitration in accordance with the UNCITRAL Arbitration Rules as at present in force.

These considerations are also incorporated in the text of the Arbitration Rules adopted under the 1966 Convention on the Settlement of Investment Disputes Between States and Nationals of Other States (TIAS 6090), to which over eighty countries are parties as of 1983. The Convention is implemented in the United States by 22 U.S.C. § 1650 and § 1650a. An arbitral money award, rendered pursuant to the Convention, is entitled to the same full faith and credit in the United States as is a final judgment of a court of general jurisdiction in a State of the United States. 22 U.S.C.A. § 1650a.

The 1966 Convention provides for the establishment of an International Center for the Settlement of Investment Disputes (ICSID), as a non-financial organ of the World Bank (the International Bank for Reconstruction and Development). ICSID is designed to serve as a forum for conciliation and for arbitration of disputes between private investors and host governments. It provides an institutional framework within which arbitrators, selected by the disputing parties from an ICSID Panel of Arbitrators or from elsewhere, conduct an arbitration in accordance with ICSID Rules of Procedure for Arbitration Proceedings. Arbitrations are held in Washington D.C. unless agreed otherwise.

Under the 1966 Convention (Article 25), ICSID's jurisdiction extends only "to any legal dispute arising directly out of an investment, between a Contracting State or . . . any subdivision . . . and a national of another Contracting State, which the parties to the dispute consent in writing to submit to the Centre. Where the parties have given their consent, no party may withdraw its consent unilaterally." Thus, ICSID is an attempt to institutionalize dispute resolution between States and non-State investors. It therefore always presents a "mixed" arbitration.

If one party questions such jurisdiction (predicated upon disputes arising "directly out of" an investment, between a Contracting Party and the national of another, and written consent to submission), the issue may be decided by the arbitration tribunal (Rule 41). A party may seek annulment of any award by an appeal to an ad hoc committee of persons drawn by the Administrative Council of ICSID from the Panel of Arbitrators under the

Convention (Article 52). Annulment is available only if the Tribunal was not properly constituted, exceeded its powers, seriously departed from a fundamental procedural rule, failed to state the reasons for its award, or included a member who practiced corruption.

The Convention's 1966 jurisdictional limitations have prompted the ICSID Administrative Counsel to establish an Additional Facility for conducting conciliations and arbitrations for disputes which do not arise directly out of an investment and for investment disputes in which one party is not a Contracting State to the Convention or the national of a Contracting State. The Additional Facility is intended for use by parties having long-term relationships of special economic importance to the State party to the dispute and which involve the commitment of substantial resources on the part of either party; the Facility is not designed to service disputes which fall within the 1966 Convention or which are "ordinary commercial transaction" disputes. ICSID's Secretary General must give advance approval of an agreement contemplating use of the Additional Facility. Because the Additional Facility operates outside the scope of the 1966 Convention, the Facility has its own arbitration Rules.

There are also other frameworks for arbitration provided by Treaties (e.g., the 1961 European Convention on International Commercial Arbitration [484 UNTS 364] and the 1975 Inter–American Convention on International Commercial Arbitration (14 *Int'l Legal Mat.* 336)). Additionally, parties may use the Rules of the Court of Arbitration of the International Chamber of Commerce at Paris or of one of its national committees, such as the international commercial panel of the American Arbitration Association. The Court's rules are modern and are used often in international arbitration.

Parties who wish to refer any dispute to the London Court of Arbitration may use the following model clause:

> The validity, construction and performance of this contract (agreement) shall be governed by the laws of England and any dispute that may arise out of or in connection with this contract (agreement), including its validity, construction and performance, shall be determined by arbitration under the Rules of the London Court of Arbitration at the date hereof, which Rules with respect to matters not regulated by them, incorporate the UNCITRAL Arbitration Rules. The parties agree that service of any notices in reference to such arbitration at their addresses as given in this contract (agreement)(or as subsequently varied in writing by them) shall be valid and sufficient.

The Court of Arbitration of the ICC in Paris recommends use of the following model clause to engage its rules:

> All disputes arising in connection with the present contract shall be finally settled under the Rules of Conciliation and Arbitration of the International Chamber of Commerce by one or more

arbitrators appointed in accordance with the said
Rules....

Differences in length and in specificity between
the London model clause and the Paris model
clause reflect typical differences in successful contract drafting in the Common Law, on the one
hand, and in the Civil Law, on the other hand;
proper selection of assisting foreign counsel can
mitigate possible drafting pitfalls.

CHAPTER NINE

IMMUNITY OF STATES IN COMMERCIAL TRANSACTIONS

United States sellers and buyers who engage in international commercial transactions sometimes entering contracts with a foreign state, or an agency or instrumentality of a foreign state. If the contract is breached, or the United States party injured, litigation may be initiated in a court in the United States. For example, an Oregon company importing rhesus monkeys under a contract with the government of Bangladesh brought suit against Bangladesh in a United States court when the contract was unexpectedly terminated. Florida residents who purchased a package tour to the Dominican Republic, but upon landing were denied entry by that government as undesirables and returned to Florida at their own expense, sued the Dominican Republic state owned airlines in a United States court. Americans who purchased dollar-denominated certificates of deposit from a privately owned Mexican bank which was nationalized by the Mexican government, sued the state-owned bank in a United States court after the bank unilaterally converted the certificates from dollar to peso obligations. Persons engaging in commercial transactions who suffer losses because of actions of a foreign government often choose to bring suit in the United States rather than the foreign nation. But they usually are quickly confronted with two separate defenses presented by the foreign state intended to terminate that litigation. Both of the defenses are based on theories linked to sovereignty. First is the defense that the sovereign state cannot be held liable for its acts because of sovereign immunity (the subject of this chapter); the second is that according to the act of state doctrine a United States court should not sit in judgment of an act of a foreign nation which occurred in the territory of that foreign nation (the subject of the following chapter). While the first legal concept, sovereignty immunity, has been codified by the enactment of the Foreign Sovereign Immunities Act of 1976, the second, the act of state, remains a legal doctrine found in the pages of numerous court decisions, from its English origins in the 1674 decision, *Blad v. Bamfield*, 36 Eng.Rep. 992, 3 All E.R. 616, to its United States adoption and development in the 19th century.

The immunity of a foreign state from *jurisdiction* is a longstanding doctrine of state and international law. When the circumstances for its application are present, the court rejects or relinquishes jurisdiction to adjudicate or enforce over the foreign state. Because state immunity, in its characterization as state law, is influenced by each state's own concept of separation of powers, and notions of comity, state immunity theory assumes different forms in different nations. A nation's contours of state immunity may be found in case law, or in statutes or treaties.

Somewhat paradoxically, the source of law of the doctrine of state immunity in several common law tradition nations is statutory law, codified after struggling for scores of years with conflicting judicial opinions unable to fashion an acceptable theory. Contrastingly, the source of law of the doctrine in most civil law tradition nations is case law, with little attention given until recently of codification of the theory.

State immunity theory in the United States developed in case law from its origins in an 1812 Supreme Court decision until the enactment of the Foreign Sovereign Immunities Act of 1976 (28 U.S.C.A. §§ 1330, 1602–1611). The experience in the United Kingdom is a near mirror image, years of opinions unable to deal with the developing concept of a restrictive theory of sovereign immunity, and concluding with the enactment of the UK State Immunity Act of 1978. On the continent, the theory remains in case law, but may change for most European nations under the European Convention on State Immunity and Additional Protocol 1972. Furthermore, the United Nations International Law Commission prepared draft articles on jurisdictional immunities of states and their property, guided by the European Convention. Discussion of the draft articles continues in the ILC, as does the intention to ultimately conclude a convention.

HISTORY AND RATIONALE

L'état, c'est moi expresses the early relationship of the individual sovereign who personified the state. Peace endured often because of mutual recognition and respect between and among sovereigns. If courtesy and equality of states were insufficient reasons for respecting sovereignty, then practical necessity was. But the governments of sovereign nations began to expand their activities beyond public duties, extending them into the marketplace. In the 19th century the early theory of absolute immunity of a sovereign state began to give way to a restrictive theory which denied immunity to states engaged in commercial activities. Acceptance as well as definition of a restrictive theory evolved slowly over the past century and a half. Many nations, including the United States, found the transition from the absolute to the restrictive theory to be a struggle. The struggle involved complex questions of judicial deference to the executive, reaching an appropriate definition of commercial activity, and determining what forms of commercial activity ought to be governed by the restrictive rather than the absolute theory.

The roots of United States state immunity theory reach back to the Supreme Court decision in *The Schooner Exchange v. McFaddon*, 11 U.S. (7 Cranch) 116 (1812). Chief Justice Marshall stated that the courts of the United States lacked jurisdiction over a foreign state's (France) armed ship which had entered and was located in a United States port. When engaged in official acts *(jure imperii)* the sovereign (whether ancient prince or modern state):

[b]eing in no respect amenable to another; and being bound by obligations of the highest character not to degrade the dignity of his nation, by placing himself or its sovereign rights within the jurisdiction of another, can be supposed to enter a foreign territory only under an express license, or in the confidence that the [absolute] immunities belonging to his independent sovereign station, though not expressly stipulated, are reserved by implication, and will be extended to him. 7 Cranch at 137.

But Chief Justice Marshall was also aware of the logic of limits on immunity, acknowledging a distinction between the private property of a person who happens to be a prince, and the military force of a sovereign state. Had he been confronted with a case of commercial activity by a foreign state, the long struggle with state immunity theory in the United States might have been prevented.

Immunity of a foreign state was nevertheless consistently ruled by courts to be absolute, regardless of the nature of the activity. Although it may have appeared from *The Schooner Exchange* ruling that state immunity is domestic law, it is also an accepted principle of customary international law. See *Berizzi Brothers Co. v. The Pesaro*, 271 U.S. 562 (1926). Customary international law offered some support in the last few decades to nations (i.e., United Kingdom) confronting the absolute/restrictive debate, and searching for a justification to adopt the restrictive theory. But the evolution from absolute to restrictive theory was less influenced by international law than developing concepts within individual nations of the role of the state in modern society. As states increasingly became directly involved in commercial matters, especially as socialist economic theory caused states to expropriate and assume the ownership of nearly all of the means of production and distribution, the view of state immunity as absolute was challenged, at least by the developed market economies, as obsolete and inappropriate for modern societies.

Retention of the absolute theory of state immunity would have caused little difficulty had states engaged only in "sovereign acts". But the ancient principalities became modern states which engaged in many commercial transactions considered non-public in nature, even though the purpose of the transaction was to serve state objectives or interests. The doctrine of absolute and unqualified immunity grudgingly gave way to a restrictive theory which denied immunity when the state "descended" into the market place—where even Justice Marshall had said the sovereign should be treated equally as a private trader.

Beginning in the late 18th century many states entered fields of activities which if not exclusively identified as traditionally non-public spheres of activity, were generally agreed not to be activities identified with the public functions of a state. States began to engage in providing transportation, telegraph and telephone services, radio and television communications and the production of goods (extraction of natural resources, tobacco and matches, etc.). Such participation required participation in many common commercial sales and purchase agreements, construction contracts, and other activities more "business" than "governmental". These commercial transactions sometimes resulted in disputes which brought into the courts of one nation the state government or an agency or instrumentality of another, which had acted in a commercial capacity. National courts were slow to alter the absolute immunity doctrine, often fearful to offend a foreign sovereign, especially when that sovereign objected to the court's assumption of jurisdiction. Rather surprisingly, in civil law tradition nations on the Continent, an enlightened 19th century judiciary acknowledged the change and began to modify the absolute theory and lay down the foundations of contemporary restrictive theory. At the same time, in common law tradition nations such as the United States and England, the purportedly "law making" courts struggled with such evolution, and the restrictive theory only took root clearly with the enactment of legislation in the 1970s. As early as 1857 in Belgium, in *Etat du Pérou v. Krelinger*, P.B. 1857–II–348, restrictive theory began to take hold on the Continent. An Italian decision in 1882, *Morellet C. Governo Danese* (1882) Giu. It. 1883–I–125, continued the movement, as have Austrian and German courts in this century. The French development is less clear, but restrictive theory appears to have a foothold there as well. In the United States, judicial aversion to interference with political relations caused the courts to follow without much challenge the frequent and politically motivated "suggestions of immunity" from the Department of State, until the adoption of the Foreign Sovereign Immunities Act in 1976 established the restrictive theory as United States law. The United Kingdom also struggled with the conversion to the restrictive theory, the English courts only concluding that restrictive theory was part of UK law at the same time as the Parliament was adopting the restrictive theory with the passage of the State Immunity Act 1978.

The Department of State regularly requested immunity when friendly nations were sued in United States courts. But in 1952, the Department of State sent what became known as the "Tate Letter" to the Department of Justice, announcing that the Department of State's policy would be "to follow the restrictive theory of sovereign immunity in the consideration of request of foreign governments for a grant of sovereign immunity." 26 *Dept. of State Bulletin* 984 (1952). While the letter may have helped resolve one problem, it accentuated another. The letter stated:

It is realized that a shift in policy by the executive cannot control the courts but it is felt that the courts are less likely to allow a plea of sovereign immunity where the executive has declined to do so. There have been indications that at least some Justices of the Supreme Court feel that in this matter courts should follow the branch of the Government charged with responsibility for the conduct of foreign relations.

Although the Tate Letter announced an acceptance
of the restrictive theory of sovereign immunity, it
offered no guidelines or criteria to distinguish a
state's public acts from its private acts. Until the
passage of the Foreign Sovereign Immunities Act
24 years later, the application of the restrictive
theory proved troublesome. United States courts
almost always complied with "suggestions of immunity" from the Department of State, and foreign
sovereigns were often successful in urging the Department to support immunity for the kind of commercial acts for which the restrictive theory was
intended to deny immunity. But even when state
immunity was codified in the 1976 FSIA, it was
uncertain to what degree separation of powers
principles would induce a judicial caution about
embarrassing the executive branch in its role as
the primary organ of international policy. Moreover, and "[p]erhaps more importantly, in the
chess game that is diplomacy only the executive
has a view of the entire board and an understanding of the relationship between isolated moves".
Spacil v. Crowe, 489 F.2d 614, 619 (5th Cir.1974).
Although the FSIA did offer a welcome resolution
of some of the inconsistencies following the issuance of the Tate Letter, the Act has generated a
very substantial body of often strongly criticized
judicial decisions. A number of these decisions involved frustrated attempts to sue foreign states not
for commercial acts, but for acts quite clearly not
the subject of exemptions in the FSIA as enacted
in 1976, such as violations of human rights. An

amendment to the FSIA in 1997, which added an exemption for various acts which must be included within a broad definition of human rights (i.e., torture, extrajudicial killing, hostage taking), extended the scope of permissible actions against foreign sovereigns to encompass many of the earlier rejected actions.

Not all nations welcomed the development of a restrictive theory of state immunity. Socialist law (and some developing nation) jurists have argued that state immunity is absolute, that it attaches to a foreign state whenever such theory is part of the *domestic* law of the sovereign state. They argue that a fundamental principle of international law allocates to each state the right to declare whether or not that state may be sued in the courts of foreign states. This view rejects the more commonly accepted theory that state immunity is at least partly governed by principles of *customary* international law. These jurists argue that where, as in some of the nonmarket economies, the state decides to engage in what in most market economy nations would clearly be private, commercial acts, it is not for the courts of those other nations to decide whether the acts are *jure imperii* or *jure gestionis*. The characterization as *jure imperii* attached by the state to its own actions ought not be altered by foreign courts. This theory has not met with much success outside the nonmarket nations, and it appears to be diminishing in use in those nations as they commence the transition to market economies and wish to adopt market economy characteristics and legal theories. As the English courts have noted, the restrictive theory is based on the interests of justice and "does not involve a challenge to or inquiry into any act of sovereignty or governmental act of that state. It is ... neither a threat to the dignity of that state, nor any interference with its sovereign functions." *I Congreso del Partido*, (1981) 2 All E.R.1064, 1070 (H.L.)(Lord Wilberforce)(hereafter *I Congreso*). In the earlier appeal in *I Congreso* Lord Denning had written:

> When the government of a country enters into an ordinary trading transaction, they cannot afterwards be permitted to repudiate it and get out of their liabilities by saying that they did it out of high government policy or foreign policy or any other policy. They cannot come down like a god on to the stage, the deus ex machina, as if they had nothing to do with it beforehand. They started as a trader and must end as a trader. They can be sued in the courts of law for their breaches of contract and for their wrongs just as any other trader can. *I Congreso del Partido*, (1979) 1 All E.R. 1092, 1104 (C.A.).

National courts are often asked to define immunity consequences of a state's acting through other legal persons such as instrumentalities or agencies owned by the state, engaging in a venture which is commercial (whether in nature or in purpose), committing tortious (delictual) or criminal wrongs, breaching certain kinds of agreements, initiating suit in the foreign court, raising counterclaims to an existing action, or waiving immunity (expressly or impliedly by words or by conduct). Moreover, the attention of courts has also been drawn to questions about the proper procedure for bringing a foreign state before a court, and about execution against a state's assets. The results have not been very consistent, and the process of codification of state immunity theory in its many facets has attempted to bring some reason and uniformity to this important legal theory.

THE 1976 FOREIGN SOVEREIGN IMMUNITIES ACT

The enactment of the Foreign Sovereign Immunities Act in 1976 in the United States was urged by the Department of State, and was at least partly intended to relieve the government from diplomatic pressures, "thereby eliminating the role of the State Department in such questions and bringing the United States into conformity with the immunity practice of virtually every other country." *Martropico Compania Naviera S.A. v. Perusahaan Pertambangan Minyak Dan Gas Bumi Negara (Pertamina)*, 428 F.Supp. 1035, 1037 (S.D.N.Y.1977). The FSIA additionally illustrated to litigants that sovereign immunity decisions would be made on legal rather than political grounds. The judicial acceptance of the much used "suggestion of immunity" made by the executive was abrogated by the FSIA. *Republic of Philippines v. Marcos*, 665 F.Supp. 793 (N.D.Cal. 1987). In adopting the restrictive theory, the FSIA established legal standards applicable to claims of immunity made by foreign states, whether the litigation was initiated in a state or federal court in the United States. But the FSIA also guarantees foreign states the right to remove civil actions from a state court to a federal court, thus allying fears of "local" treatment and contemplating the development of a fairly uniform body of law in the federal courts. That body has proven to be less than uniform, one court has described it as a "statutory labyrinth that, owing to the numerous interpretive questions engendered by its bizarre structure ... has ... been a financial boon for the private bar but a constant bane of the federal judiciary". *Gibbons v. Udaras na Gaeltachta*, 549 F.Supp. 1094, 1105 (S.D.N.Y.1982). A further goal addressed in enacting the FSIA was to provide a procedure for service of process and obtaining *in personam* jurisdiction, thus avoiding the past practices of plaintiffs seizing property of foreign states to force an appearance. Finally, the FSIA allows *execution* upon certain essentially commercial assets of the foreign state, although the requirements for execution differ from and are stricter than those for jurisdiction to adjudicate.

Central to the FSIA are its categories of actions for which foreign states are *not* entitled to claim state immunity in United States courts. These exceptions are contained not in the sections which describe the grounds on which jurisdiction may be obtained, however, but are phrased as substantive acts for which foreign states may be held responsible. This effects an identity between substance and procedure in the FSIA, which means that a court faced with a claim of immunity from *jurisdiction* must engage ultimately in a close examination of the underlying cause of action to decide whether the plaintiff may obtain jurisdiction over the foreign state defendant. State immunity is not just a substantive defense under the Act; proof of the absence of entitlement to immunity by the presence of one of the exceptions is a jurisdictional requirement. *Yessenin-Volpin v. Novosti Press Agency*, 443 F.Supp. 849 (S.D.N.Y.1978)(hereafter *Yessenin-Volpin*). If a basis for jurisdiction is alleged, the burden of proof rests on the foreign state to demonstrate that immunity should be granted.

WHO IS A SOVEREIGN?

State immunity is a defense that is the patrimony of foreign states. A "foreign state" includes "a political subdivision of a foreign state or an agency or instrumentality of a foreign state." 28 U.S.C.A. § 1603(a). An "agency or instrumentality of a foreign state" is any entity:

(1) which is a separate legal person, corporate or otherwise, and

(2) which is an organ of a foreign state or political subdivision thereof, or a majority of whose shares or other ownership interest is owned by a foreign state or political subdivision thereof, and

(3) which is neither a citizen of a State of the United States [as defined in the Act], ... nor

created under the laws of any third country. 28 U.S.C.A. § 1603(b).

The distinction between a foreign state and agency or instrumentality is important—a foreign state is not liable for the acts of its agencies or instrumentalities in the absence of piercing the corporate veil. There is a presumption that the foreign state is separate from its instrumentalities. That presumption may be overcome by showing (1) that the corporate entity was so controlled that there was a principal/agent relationship, or (2) that allowing the distinction would work fraud or injustice. *First National City Bank v. Banco Para El Comercio Exterior De Cuba*, 462 U.S. 611 (1983).

The House Report preceding the FSIA offers some help by way of suggestions of defining a foreign state and agency or instrumentality. Numerous cases have addressed the issue. The Vatican has been held to be a foreign state. The PLO has been denied such status. Foreign trade organizations of nonmarket nations have usually been held to be instrumentalities, as have state owned corporations engaged in a wide variety of activities, such as airlines, mining, shipping, banking and production such as steel. The time for the determination of the status as a foreign state is the time the underlying conduct occurred, with some minority support for the time of the filing of the complaint.

It has often been difficult to determine whether a nonmarket or socialist entity qualifies as a foreign state. An early decision noted that "It is evident that all legal entities in the Soviet Union are government enterprises though organized on a commercial basis." *Yessenin-Volpin* at 854. That view was subject to considerable doubt. Moreover, the legal situation at the time in the Soviet Union was not duplicated precisely enough in other nonmarket economy nations "to characterize virtually every enterprise operated under a socialist system as an instrumentality of the state under the terms of the" Act. *Edlow Int'l Co. v. Nuklearna Elektrarna Krsko*, 441 F.Supp. 827, 831 (D.D.C.1977). To broadly classify a system of the ownership of the means of production and distribution as the means to determine the status as an agency or instrumentality was not intended by the FSIA. Id. at 832. Changes in the economic and political structures in nonmarket economies have diminished the frequency of trying to make these distinctions.

The FSIA does not address the status of international organizations as foreign states. Courts have denied such status to the OPEC, granted it to the British West Indies Central Labour Organization, and in other cases suggested that it did not have to reach a decision because immunity would exist (or not exist) whether absolute or restrictive theory applied.

A head of state is not given immunity under the FSIA, although the word "sovereign" in the title might so imply. Head of state immunity is a separate concept, as is diplomatic immunity. The United Kingdom State Immunity Act, however, does encompass head of state immunity, although its title "State Immunity Act" might suggest otherwise.

JURISDICTIONAL ISSUES

The FSIA is federal law. Subject matter jurisdiction is conferred by § 1330(a) to permit a nonjury civil action against a foreign state not entitled to immunity. If the court has subject matter jurisdiction under § 1330(a), and if service of process is made in accordance with § 1608, and if constitutional due process requirements are met, then the court has personal jurisdiction over the foreign state under § 1330(b). But, as noted, this jurisdiction is effective only when the foreign state is not entitled to immunity. The principal focus of the FSIA is to *confer* immunity upon a defendant foreign state, reaffirming the generally accepted theory that states are immune from foreign suit. But the FSIA would have been unnecessary to adopt were it not for the exceptions, which when established deny immunity to the foreign state. A court clearly lacks jurisdiction unless one of the exceptions applies. It should thus be apparent that "(u)nder the analytic structure of the Act, the existence of subject matter and personal jurisdiction, the requisites for service of process, and the availability of sovereign immunity as a defense are intricately coordinated inquiries." *Velidor v. L/P/G Benghazi*, 653 F.2d 812, 817 (3d Cir.1981).

Understanding the congressional pattern of subject matter and personal jurisdiction under the

FSIA requires one additional essential comment, that the "Act cannot create personal jurisdiction where the Constitution forbids it. Accordingly, each finding of personal jurisdiction under the FSIA requires, in addition, a due process scrutiny of the court's power to exercise its authority over a particular defendant." *Texas Trading & Milling Corp. v. Federal Republic of Nigeria*, 647 F.2d 300, 308 (2d Cir.1981)(hereafter *Texas Trading*). The FSIA "is designed to embody the 'requirements of minimum jurisdictional contacts and adequate notice.'" *East Europe Domestic Int'l Sales Corp. v. Terra*, 467 F.Supp. 383, 387 (S.D.N.Y.1979).

SERVICE OF PROCESS

Prior to the passage of the FSIA, suits against sovereigns were generally cast as *quasi in rem* actions, and service was effected by attaching some property interest belonging to the sovereign. During a visit of Pope Paul VI to the United States, one complainant tried to attach the motor vehicle scheduled to carry the Pope to official functions. In another instance, attachment was attempted on a ship belonging to the Soviet Union as it transited the Panama Canal. In the FSIA, Congress sought to facilitate and regulate service, and insure that the foreign sovereign received notice. Section 1608(a) provides that service on a state may be made by special arrangement, by arrangement pursuant to an applicable treaty, by a mailing to the head of the ministry of foreign affairs of the sovereign concerned, or by a mailing to the United States Department of State for transmission through diplomatic channels to the sovereign. Service on an agency or instrumentality of a sovereign is governed by § 1608(b), and may be sent to the person appointed or authorized to receive service or may be mailed, by signed receipt method, to the agency or instrumentality. The service of process rules of the FSIA have roots in Rule 4(i) of the Federal Rules of Civil Procedure, but the cases applying Rule 4 to foreign states illustrate inconsistencies justifying clarification.

Section "1330(b) ... (of the FSIA) satisfies the due process requirement of adequate notice by prescribing that proper service be made under section 1608." *Bankers Trust Co. v. Worldwide Transportation Services, Inc.*, 537 F.Supp. 1101, 1106 (E.D.Ark.1982). But actual notice received may be adequate even though the precise steps in § 1608 were not followed. *Harris Corp. v. National Iranian Radio and Television*, 691 F.2d 1344 (11th Cir.1982)(hereafter *Harris Corp.*) The court noted, however, that there "is no excuse for departure from the dictates of the statute." *Harris Corp.*, fn. 16 at 1352.

As noted earlier in this chapter, substantive due process requirements must also be satisfied. "To determine whether maintenance of this suit in the United States courts is consistent with due process, we must apply the 'minimum contacts' standard established by *International Shoe*". *Harris Corp.* at 1352. Courts differ about the relevant geographic entity (forum) against which "contacts" are to be measured. "Since service was made under § 1608, the relevant area in delineating contacts is the entire United States." *Texas Trading* at 314. "The Ninth Circuit [has] explicitly stated that it has not decided whether aggregation of national contacts is proper." *Meadows v. Dominican Republic*, 542 F.Supp. 33,34 (N.D.Cal.1982).

EXCEPTIONS TO SOVEREIGN IMMUNITY: WAIVER

A foreign state is not immune in any case "in which [it] has waived its immunity either explicitly or by implication, notwithstanding any withdrawal of the waiver ... except in accordance with the terms of waiver". 28 U.S.C.A. § 1605(a)(1).

Implied waivers are not easily established. A foreign state does not waive its state immunity by entering into a contract with another nation. That contract may give rise to a *commercial exception* issue, but a waiver must be intentional and knowing. *Transamerican Steamship Corp. v. Somali Democratic Republic*, 767 F.2d 998 (D.C.Cir.1985). How a foreign state responds to a complaint is important to determining the existence of an implicit waiver. Entering a general appearance may constitute a waiver, but not by failing to appear altogether. *Practical Concepts, Inc. v. Republic of Bolivia*, 811 F.2d 1543 (D.C.Cir.1987). Failing to timely answer or file motions, such as a motion to dismiss, will not automatically waive immunity.

Agreements to arbitrate may constitute an implied waiver, certainly where the agreement is to arbitrate in the United States, or to apply the law of the United States. But where the agreement is to arbitrate in another nation, or to apply the law of a third party nation, there may not be an implied waiver. *Verlinden B.V. v. Central Bank of Nigeria*, 488 F.Supp. 1284 (S.D.N.Y.1980); aff'd on other grounds, 647 F.2d 320 (2d Cir.1981), rev'd on other grounds, 461 U.S. 480 (1983). The same conclusion may be reached where the agreement is to arbitrate before an international organization, even though located in the United States. *Maritime Int'l Nominees Establishment v. Republic of Guinea*, 693 F.2d 1094 (D.C.Cir.1982).

Explicit waivers are more readily identifiable, such as those found in treaties. For example, the United States has waived immunity with respect to commercial and other activities in some of its treaties of friendship, commerce and navigation. The language used in the waiver is important—a commonly used provision in friendship treaties that immunity shall not be claimed from "suit, execution or judgment or other liability", is not an explicit waiver from prejudgment *attachment. Libra Bank Ltd. v. Banco Nacional de Costa Rica, S.A.*, 676 F.2d 47 (2d Cir.1982)(hereafter *Libra*). A statement in a trade agreement which prohibited State owned parties from "claim[ing] or enjoy[ing] immunities or execution of judgment or other liability," was not an explicit waiver for prejudgment attachment because the waiver had no bearing on the issue of prejudgment attachment. *S & S Machinery Co. v. Masinexportimport*, 706 F.2d 411 (2d Cir.1983). Prejudgment attachments are often viewed as provisional remedies beyond the scope of explicit waivers where there is no direct reference to prejudgment attachment.

A second source of explicit waivers is in private agreements. For example, language in loan documents providing that "The borrower can sue and be sued in its own name and does not have any right of immunity from suit with respect to the Borrower's obligations under this Letter or the Notes", and that the borrower "waives any right or immunity from legal proceedings including suit judgment and execution on grounds of sovereignty" has been held to be an explicit waiver of a right to raise the defense of state immunity for a prejudgment attachment. *Libra* at 49. Another decision held that a foreign state owned bank's reference to the use of the Uniform Customs and Practices for Documentary Credits (UCP) of the ICC in a letter of credit issued by the bank did not constitute an explicit waiver, when the bank was sued for dishonoring the letter of credit. *ICC Chemical Corp. v. Industrial & Commercial Bank of China*, 886 F.Supp. 1 (S.D.N.Y. 1995). There was no reference in the letter of credit to a waiver, and the UCP contains no provisions regarding immunities or provisional remedies.

The use of carefully drafted explicit waivers is of particular importance when one considers the narrow interpretation given by the courts to the commercial exception.

EXCEPTIONS TO SOVEREIGN IMMUNITY: COMMERCIAL ACTIVITY

The commercial activity exception is the reason the FSIA was enacted, and the most important aspect of the Act for this book. Law prior to the passage of the Act was unclear about whether a restrictive theory of sovereign immunity excluded acts which were commercial in *nature* or commercial in *purpose*. The FSIA chooses those commercial in *nature*, by defining "commercial activity" as:

either a regular course of commercial conduct or a particular commercial transaction or act. The commercial character of an activity shall be determined by reference to the nature of the course of conduct or particular transaction or act, rather than by reference to its purpose. 28 U.S.C.A. § 1603(d).

Determining what activity of the foreign state is alleged to be commercial is obviously a precondition to determining whether that activity is commercial and whether it fits into one of the three classes of commercial activity which deny immunity to the foreign state. The FSIA defines those three classes as:

A foreign state shall not be immune from the jurisdiction of courts of the United States or of the States in any case ... in which the action is based upon a commercial activity carried on in the United States by the foreign state; or upon an act performed in the United States in connection with a commercial activity of the foreign state elsewhere; or upon an act outside the territory of the United States in connection with a commercial activity of the foreign state elsewhere and that act causes a direct effect in the United States. 28 U.S.C.A. § 1605(a)(2).

The legislative history of the FSIA suggests that a commercial activity is one which an individual might customarily carry on for profit. If the activity is one which normally could be engaged in by a private party, it is commercial and a foreign state is not immune, but if the activity is one in which only a state can engage, it is noncommercial under the FSIA. The focus is not on whether the defendant generally engages in commercial activities, but on the particular conduct giving rise to the action. *Brazosport Towing Co., Inc. v. 3,838 Tons of Sorghum Laden on Board*, 607 F.Supp. 11 (S.D.Tex. 1984). The legislative history offers some help:

> [A] contract by a foreign government to buy provisions or equipment for its armed forces or to construct a government building constitutes a commercial activity. The same would be true of a contract to make repairs on an embassy building. Such contracts should be considered to be commercial contracts, even if their ultimate object is to further a public function.... Activities such as a foreign government's sale of a service or a product, its leasing of property, its borrowing of money, its employment or engagement of laborers, clerical staff or public relations or marketing agents, or its investment in a security of an

American corporation, would be among those included within the definition. (H.R. Rep. No.1487,
94th Cong., 2d Sess. 16 (1976)).

The concern being the *nature* of the activity rather
than its *purpose*, a distinction difficult to make in
many cases, and seemingly ignored by some courts,
cases nevertheless have held commercial activity to
include fulfillment of public debt obligations by
Argentina, purchasing grain from a United States
company under a United States government program, a Republic of Ireland joint venture with two
United States citizens to manufacture plastic cos-
metic containers, a Turkish government owned gun
manufacturer selling in the United States, artistic
contracts for tours of USSR artists to the United
States and Great Britain, and a Polish government
owned company selling golf carts in the United
States. Noncommercial activities have included na-
tionalizing plaintiff's corporation, establishing
terms and conditions for removal of natural resources from its territory, and granting and revok-
ing a license to export a natural resource. The
Supreme Court has spoken rather clearly that the
definition of commercial activity excludes any interpretation based on the *purpose* of the activity. *Republic of Argentina v. Weltover, Inc.*, 504 U.S. 607
(1992). There is no very clear definition of commercial activity which can be drawn from the cases.
When one seems to have a consistent pattern outlined, a case is discovered which challenges if not
destroys that pattern.

Since considerable litigation against foreign states in the United States follows uncompensated nationalizations, the view that a "nationalization is the quintessentially sovereign act, never viewed as having a commercial character," obviously is a disappointment to many United States persons who have had their property expropriated. *Alberti v. Empresa Nicaraguense De La Carne*, 705 F.2d 250 (7th Cir. 1983). The exception contained in § 1605(a)(3), rights taken in violation of international law, may apply to some nationalizations, depending on the relation of the property located in the United States to the property nationalized. The "property tracing" feature of the FSIA severely limits the use of this alternative violation of international law provision of the FSIA. The FSIA is not a helpful statute to persons whose property has been expropriated by a foreign state.

The three part commercial activity test of § 1605(a)(2) requires the commercial activity to bear some relationship to the United States. The first part is "action based upon a commercial activity carried on in the United States by the foreign state." This is the easiest part of the test, and essentially involves how much commercial activity was done in the United States, and what is the link between the cause of action and the commercial activity. "Substantial contact" with the United States is sufficient. *Gemini Shipping, Inc. v. Foreign Trade Organization*, 647 F.2d 317 (2d Cir. 1981). The second part of the test deals with an "act performed in the United States in connection

with a commercial activity of the foreign state performed elsewhere". It is the least used of the three
parts since many of the acts complained of occur
outside the United States. When they do occur in
the United States the matter is often considered
under or in combination with part one of the test. It
is the third part of the test which is most often
subject to interpretation. That part covers an "act
outside ... the United States in connection with a
commercial activity of the foreign state and that act
causes a direct effect in the United States". Since
many acts do occur abroad, the direct effect language is often the focus of attention. The federal
circuit courts split on what constitutes a direct
effect. Some followed the view that it must be
"substantial and foreseeable", drawing upon the
Restatement of Foreign Relations section, seemingly approved by the House Report, on jurisdiction to
prescribe. *Maritime Int'l Nominees Establishment v.
Republic of Guinea*, 693 F.2d 1094 (D.C.Cir.1982).
Other circuits rejected this view and held that the
direct effect requirement was satisfied where there
was some financial loss. *Texas Trading & Milling
Corp. v. Federal Republic of Nigeria*, 647 F.2d 300
(2d Cir.1981). The Supreme Court accepted the
latter view, ruling that an effect is direct if it
" 'follows as an immediate consequence of the defendant's ... activity' ". *Republic of Argentina v.
Weltover, Inc.*, 504 U.S. 607 (1992)(citing *Texas
Trading*). The most recent debate regarding the
"direct effect in the United States" language, is
whether the act must be "a legally significant act"

in the United States, causing a split among the circuit courts.

EXCEPTIONS TO SOVEREIGN IMMUNITY: VIOLATIONS OF INTERNATIONAL LAW

Rights in property taken in violation of international law may preclude the defense of sovereign immunity if

that property or any property exchanged for such property is present in the United States in connection with a commercial activity carried on in the United States by the foreign state; or that property or any property exchanged for such property is owned or operated by an agency or instrumentality of the foreign state and that agency or instrumentality is engaged in a commercial activity in the United States. 28 U.S.C.A. § 1605(a)(3).

This section may be used to respond to noncompensated nationalizations of property, but the decisions have restricted the provisions beyond what many thought the FSIA intended to reach. The obvious case would be a foreign state expropriating the aircraft of a United States airline and then using those aircraft, or ones exchanged for them, to fly to the United States. It would also apply if the foreign airlines did other business in the United States. The more difficult, and more likely, case is where immovable properties, such as factories, are taken. If the products of the factory were to be sold in the United States, they might be reached, but that is probably just what the expropriating state will avoid doing.

SOVEREIGN IMMUNITY AND COUNTERCLAIMS

When the foreign state initiates a claim in the courts and is subjected to counterclaims, the foreign state may not be able to assert an immunity from such claims. Section 1607 of the FSIA provides that:

In any action brought by a foreign state, or in which a foreign state intervenes, in a court of the United States or of a State, the foreign state shall not be accorded immunity with respect to any counterclaims–

(a) for which a foreign state would not be entitled to immunity under section 1605 of this chapter had such claim been brought in a separate action against the foreign state; or

(b) arising out of the transaction or occurrence that is the subject matter of the claim of the foreign state; or

(c) to the extent that the counterclaim does not seek relief exceeding in amount or differing in kind from that sought by the foreign state.

The sovereign's filing of an unconditional, affirmative claim by way of a counterclaim will remove immunity. *In re Oil Spill by Amoco Cadiz Off Coast of France*, 491 F.Supp. 161 (N.D.Ill.1979). One court has held that the filing of a counterclaim, conditioned upon non-acceptance of the sovereign immunity defense, will not constitute a waiver. *In re Rio Grande Transport, Inc.*, 516 F.Supp. 1155 (S.D.N.Y. 1981).

EXECUTION OF A JUDGMENT

Prior to passage of the FSIA, courts long held that the assets of a state which was not immune from suit, nevertheless were immune absolutely from execution pursuant to a judgment. Section 1611 of the FSIA continues to accord absolute immunity to the property of an international organization, to the property of a foreign central bank or monetary authority held for its own account, and to property of a military character for use in certain connections with a military activity. Section 1610 of the FSIA, however, has changed prior law. Subject to certain conditions, property of a foreign state "used for a commercial activity in the United States" is no longer immune from attachment in aid of execution or from execution upon a judgment entered by a court of the United States or by one of its states. The FSIA provides also that, in such courts, property of a foreign state, used for a commercial activity within the United States, is not immune from attachment prior to the entry of judgment if the foreign state has explicitly waived its immunity from attachment prior to judgment and the purpose of the attachment is to secure satisfaction of an eventual judgment rather than to obtain jurisdiction over the foreign state.

CHAPTER TEN

THE ACT OF STATE DOCTRINE IN COMMERCIAL TRANSACTIONS

When a United States seller or buyer in a commercial transaction with a foreign state, upon a breach of that transaction agreement, brings suit against the foreign state, the defense of sovereignty immunity often is accompanied by a separate defense of "act of state". Either defense generates, if accepted, judicial abstention. But for different reasons. The sovereign immunity doctrine mandates that a foreign sovereign not be sued in the courts of other nations, thus focusing on who should or should not be sued. It is concerned with the status of the defendant. It is a question of the court finding *jurisdiction*. Contrastingly, the act of state doctrine suggests that courts of one nation should not sit in judgment of the acts of a foreign sovereign which occurred in the foreign state, thus focusing on what is or is not a issue for the court to address. It is concerned with the act of the defendant, and its location. It is a question of whether the court ought to go forward, not a question of jurisdiction. The act of state "operates as an issue preclusion device." *National American Corp. v. Federal Republic of Nigeria*, 448 F.Supp. 622, 640 (S.D.N.Y.1978), affirmed 597 F.2d 314 (2d Cir.1979). Sovereign immunity is jurisdictional in nature and, if sovereign immunity exists, the court lacks jurisdiction. But the act of state doctrine does not deprive a court of jurisdiction. Where the act of state doctrine is at issue, the court may have jurisdiction but chooses, for act of state reasons, not to go forward and decide the issue.

An example of how the act of state doctrine applies is where the law of a foreign state requires publishing each new law in the official daily of the nation within ten days of signing by the head of state. Assume in a given case someone in the United States is challenging the validity of an act of a foreign state because the state failed to follow the ten day publication requirement. The real dispute might be over an expropriation of the foreign person's property, or a cancellation of the foreign person's concession contract, either carried out under the belatedly published law. The act of state doctrine states that the United States court should not determine the legal validity of the publication under the law of the foreign state—it was a foreign state act undertaken, properly or not, by the foreign state and in the territory of that foreign state. Application of the act of state in such instance brings little criticism. But where the act of the foreign state is alleged to have violated international law, such as the act of expropriation itself, or the act of cancelling the concession contract, considerable variations of opinion arise.

From some rather humble origins, the act of state doctrine has assumed very grand proportions, partly due to the limitations on the use of the state immunity defense because of the Foreign Sovereign Immunities Act.

The two doctrines, sovereign immunity and act of state, are frequently confused because both may appear as defenses where the foreign state is alleged to have been engaged in commercial activity, and where some question of international law is present. Sovereign immunity in the United States is exclusively governed by the FSIA, which has exemption provisions for certain commercial activity, and for very limited violations of international law. Those two issues have not escaped the act of state doctrine, which has not been the subject of legislation such as the FSIA. Thus, when the act of state appears as a defense, business persons are often quick to argue for an exception based on a commercial activity, or a violation of international law.

The act of state doctrine in the United States is not governed by federal statute but rather by case law, with a few statutory exceptions where the act of state defense is not allowed, such as for some violations of international law and in enforcement proceedings of arbitral awards. A more recent example is the Cuban Liberty and Democratic Solidarity (Helms–Burton) Act, which in 22 U.S.C. § 6082(a)(6), prohibits the courts from using the act of state doctrine to decline to hear a case involving liability for trafficking in confiscated property. The Congress appears ready to deny use of the act of state doctrine if case law applies the act of state doctrine to limit actions by U.S. Citizens affected by foreign government actions. Nearly forty years ago, Congressional anger over *Banco Nacional de Cuba v. Sabbatino*, 376 U.S. 398 (1964)(hereafter *Sabbatino*), led to legislation mandating that courts not accept the act of state defense in some instances where there are alleged violations of international law (discussed infra). Whether the doctrine applies to bar a counterclaim, whether it applies to an act in violation of a treaty, uncertainty over the situs of an act of state, and most recently, whether it applies to motives rather than acts of foreign state officials, have been additional issues of importance to international business persons. But of most concern to those engaged in international business transactions is the debate regarding the existence of a commercial exception to the doctrine.

The growth of one of these two doctrines, state immunity and act of state, has affected the thinking regarding the other. After the adoption of the restrictive theory of sovereign immunity, some jurists have thought that act of state theory should follow suit, and include a commercial activity exception. The jury remains out on whether there is such an exception—it is a question in need of an answer from the Supreme Court.

HISTORY OF THE ACT OF STATE DOCTRINE

The act of state doctrine can be traced to the 1674 English case of *Blad v. Bamfield*, 36 Eng.Rep.

992 (applied in 1981 in *Buttes Gas and Oil Co. v. Hammer (No. 3)*, [1981] 3 All E.R. 616). It also exists in the jurisprudence of France, Germany, Greece, Italy, The Netherlands, Switzerland and other countries. American cases expressing ideas resembling the doctrine date to 1808 in *Hudson v. Guestier*, 8 U.S. (4 Cranch) 293, although the 1812 case, *The Schooner Exchange v. McFaddon*, 11 U.S. (7 Cranch) 116, is sometimes thought to be the United States origin of the doctrine. The initial important United States decision, and the one often cited as the true origin of the doctrine in the United States, is *Underhill v. Hernandez*, 168 U.S. 250 (1897)(hereafter *Underhill*). There the Supreme Court stated that:

> Every sovereign state is bound to respect the independence of every other state, and the courts of one country will not sit in judgment on the acts of the government of another, done within its own territory. Redress of grievances by reason of such acts must be obtained through the means open to be availed of by sovereign powers as between themselves. Id. at 252.

The *Underhill* litigation arose from claimed damages suffered by the plaintiff (Underhill) at the hands of a Venezuelan revolutionary army commander (Hernandez) during an alleged false arrest in Venezuela. The United States had subsequently recognized the revolutionary government.

The *Underhill* statement was reaffirmed unequivocally in cases involving expropriations during the

Mexican Revolution, *Oetjen v. Central Leather Co.*, 246 U.S. 297 (1918), and *Ricaud v. American Metal Co.*, 246 U.S. 304 (1918)(suggesting the doctrine was required by comity), and the Russian Revolution, *United States v. Belmont*, 301 U.S. 324 (1937). Other cases which involved the doctrine also supported *Underhill*. See e.g., *American Banana Co. v. United Fruit Co.*, 213 U.S. 347 (1909)(viewing it as a choice of law rule). The doctrine as expressed in *Underhill* was reaffirmed in the modern classic, *Sabbatino*.

ACT OF STATE AND THE EXPROPRIATION OF PROPERTY

Banco Nacional de Cuba v. Sabbatino began the contemporary history of the act of state doctrine and its applicability to expropriations. The case involved rights to property affected by the extensive Cuban nationalizations of property in 1960. Justice Harlan stated:

> [T]he Judicial Branch will not examine the validity of a taking of property within its own territory by a foreign sovereign, extant and recognized by this country at the time of suit, in the absence of a treaty or other unambiguous agreement regarding controlling legal principles, even if the complaint alleges that the taking violates customary international law. Id. at 428.

Justice White dissented, stating:

I do not believe that the act of state doctrine, as judicially fashioned in the Court, and the reasons underlying it, require American courts to decide cases in disregard of international law and of the rights of litigants to a full determination on the merits. Id. at 441.

The Supreme Court decision was not well received by many members of Congress. The Sabbatino Amendment to the Foreign Assistance Act was quickly passed, and stated:

Notwithstanding any other provisions of law, no court in the United States shall decline on the ground of the federal act of state doctrine to make a determination on the merits giving effect to the principles of international law in a case in which a claim of title or other right [to property] is asserted by any party including a foreign state ... based upon ... a confiscation or other taking ... by an act of that state in violation of the principles of international law, including the principles of compensation and the other standards set out in this subsection: *Provided*, that this subparagraph shall not be applicable ... (2) in any case with respect to which the President determines that application of the act of state doctrine is required in that particular case by the foreign policy interests of the United States and a suggestion to this effect is filed on his behalf in that case with the court. 22 U.S.C. § 2370(e)(2)(bracketed words added in 1965 to clarify that the doctrine continued to apply to acts not involving the taking of property).

This Sabbatino Amendment (also called the Second Hickenlooper Amendment) led to a reversal of the *Sabbatino* decision on remand, Cuba being found to have violated international law. But in the years that followed, the courts have not applied very enthusiastically this hurriedly adopted reversal of a doctrine adopted and long approved by the judicial branch. The Second Circuit has strictly interpreted the Sabbatino Amendment as applicable only where the expropriated property has in some manner found its way into the United States. *Empresa Cubana Exportadora De Azucar y Sus Derivados v. Lamborn & Co., Inc.*, 652 F.2d 231 (2d Cir.1981)(hereafter *Empresa*). But the D.C. Circuit has suggested that the Sabbatino Amendment was not intended to be limited only to expropriated personal property which found its way into the United States. The court reasoned that the statute referred to personal property only to diminish fears that the statute might be misread to create a new class of jurisdiction allowing a right to challenge all foreign expropriations in United States courts, even when there was no attachable property present. *Ramirez de Arellano v. Weinberger*, 745 F.2d 1500 (D.C.Cir.1984, vacated for other reasons, 471 U.S. 1113 (1985). Resolution of this conflict awaits clarifying legislation or a future decision of the Supreme Court. The *Ramirez* view certainly represents the side favored by international business persons. That view is quite moderate when compared to some of the thinking behind the Helms–Burton Act in 1996. If the President so allows, that Act would permit

United States persons, including persons not citizens at the time of the taking (i.e., then Cuban citizens), to bring suit in United States courts against any foreign party trafficking in property in Cuba expropriated by the Castro government. The assumption is that any such judgment could be satisfied out of any assets owned by that foreign party in the United States. If such suits are allowed, they would challenge the view towards the act of state doctrine defense expressed in many cases subsequent to the enactment of the *Sabbatino* decision. Those cases did not accurately reflect the sense of the Congress when it passed the Sabbatino Amendment. For that reason, the Helms–Burton Act prohibits the application of the act of state doctrine in trafficking cases. Given further opportunities to lodge a blow against the act of state doctrine, Congress is not likely to be very kind to it, especially when it conflicts with United States business interests. Nor is Congress likely to be fully sympathetic to the view of the Restatement, discussed next below.

The Restatement (Third) of Foreign Relations, § 443, adopted after much debate, states, "[C]ourts in the United States will generally refrain from examining the validity of a taking by a foreign state of property within its own territory, or from sitting in judgment on other acts of a government character done by a foreign state within its own territory and applicable there." That reflects the *Sabbatino* decision, and neither the sense of the Sabbatino Amendment nor the above noted Helms–Burton

Act. Section 444 does provide "[T]he act of state doctrine will not be applied in a case involving a claim of title or other right to property, when the claim is based on the assertion that a foreign state confiscated the property in violation of international law." The President may recommend otherwise. This may be a more a narrow version of the intent of the Sabbatino Amendment than Congress meant, reflecting less the *Ramirez de Arellano* decision than *Empresa Cubana*. Perhaps the Congress will not have to be so concerned with the application of the doctrine where there are violations of international law. There may be some softening of that judicial reluctance to find an international law exception, particularly in cases involving terrorism or violations of human rights.

ACT OF STATE ENCOUNTERS SOME LIMITS

The act of state doctrine, subsequent to the formation of many of its contemporary characteristics in expropriation cases, was for several years expanded in scope. Many observers, and certainly many international business persons, were confused at how extensively it was applied to limit judicial resolution of conflicts. But in 1990 the broad use of the doctrine was abruptly brought to a halt by a new decision of the United States Supreme Court, *W.S. Kirkpatrick & Co. v. Environmental Tectonics Corp., Int'n.*, 493 U.S. 400 (1990)(hereafter *Kirkpatrick*). It remains unclear what the impact of *Kirk-*

patrick will be on the extensive use of the act of state doctrine in future years.

The cases in the past two decades which seemed to most frequently turn to the act of state as a defense often involved various complaints regarding violations of the United States antitrust law by foreign defendants. The possible severe financial consequences of treble damages led many foreign defendants in antitrust actions to claim that any injury to the plaintiff was caused by the foreign state's actions, rather than any act or conspiracy by the foreign defendant. Some courts applied the act of state without inquiring whether the foreign state's actions were urged or *compelled* by the defendant. See *Hunt v. Mobil Oil Corp.*, 550 F.2d 68 (2d Cir.1977), cert. denied 434 U.S. 984 (1977). Thus, the act of state became enmeshed with the *foreign compulsion* doctrine. In view of the *Kirkpatrick* decision the application of the act of state doctrine in antitrust and other cases, where the government is at most a very minor participant, may diminish.

In the *Kirkpatrick* litigation Environmental Tectonics learned that the reason it had lost a proposed contract with Nigeria was that its competitor Kirkpatrick had bribed Nigerian government officials and obtained the contract for itself. Environmental Tectonics sought damages against Kirkpatrick, which raised the act of state doctrine in that proof of the bribe might require the court to consider an act of the foreign state, Nigeria. The circuit court declined to apply the act of state doctrine because the Department of State said that such inquiry would not cause embarrassment to United States foreign relations. This was reminiscent of cases prior to the enactment of the Foreign Sovereign Immunities Act, when alleged embarrassment to United States foreign relations was the justification for refusing jurisdiction in numerous cases. But the Supreme Court rejected the reasoning of the circuit court, refusing to apply the doctrine because it did not involve an inquiry into the lawfulness of an act of the foreign government, but merely the consideration of the motivations of foreign officials. For the act of state to apply the court must have to declare an official act of the foreign state invalid in resolving the case before the court. This test will need some refining. One can think of situations where judicial consideration of an *act* of a foreign state would cause little embarrassment, but inquiry into the *motives* of an act would cause great embarrassment to United States foreign relations. In the later Bhopal litigation, the Second Circuit refused to determine the validity of the Indian government's Bhopal Act for act of state reasons, but before it was willing to defer to that Act and only recognize claims presented by the Indian government, the court had little trouble discussing and evaluating the political and judicial systems of India, which might have been resented by the Indian government and embarrass United States/ Indian foreign relations had not the court concluded that India qualifies as a democracy, and therefore the Bhopal Act must be recognized. *Bi v. Union Carbide Chemicals & Plastics Co.*, 984 F.2d 582 (2d Cir.1993), cert. denied 510 U.S. 862 (1993)(hereafter *Bi*). Perhaps a better route would have been for the court to have directly applied the act of state doctrine to dismiss the suits, because recognizing the rights of individual Indian citizens to bring claims in the United States would require ruling that the Bhopal Act was in some way invalid, thus violating the act of state doctrine. The *Bi* decision was one of the first important decisions after *Kirkpatrick*, which it did not even mention, which might have helped develop the act of state in the post *Kirkpatrick* era.

Kirkpatrick is an extremely important decision, suggesting to lower federal courts a method by which the attempted expansion of the act of state doctrine to fill gaps left by the adoption of the Foreign Sovereign Immunities Act may be refuted, and considerably diminished in acceptability in future cases. But it does mean the end of the act of state doctrine. In a highly publicized case dealing with Swiss bank deposits of former Philippine President Marcos frozen by the Swiss government, the 9th circuit court applied the act of state doctrine in a case attempting to reach those assets, because the court believed it would require a determination of the lawfulness of an act of the Swiss government. Credit Suisse v. United States District Court, 130 F.3d 1342 (9th Cir.1997).

ACT OF STATE DOCTRINE AND THE SEPARATION OF POWERS

The act of state doctrine is punctuated by unclear contours, debatable exceptions and an unsympathetic Congressional response. The cases illustrate that the doctrine is deliberate but flexible. There is general agreement that the doctrine is grounded in self-imposed judicial restraint:

While historic notions of sovereign authority do bear upon the wisdom of employing the act of state doctrine, they do not dictate its existence.

That international law does not require application of the doctrine is evidenced by the practice of nations. . . .

The text of the Constitution does not require the act of state doctrine; it does not irrevocably remove from the judiciary the capacity to review the validity of foreign acts of state.

The act of state doctrine does, however, have "constitutional" underpinnings. It arises out of the basic relationships between branches of government in a system of separation of powers. It concerns the competency of dissimilar institutions to make and implement particular kinds of decisions in the area of international relations. The doctrine as formulated in past decisions expresses the strong sense of the Judicial Branch that its engagement in the task of passing on the validity of foreign acts of state may hinder rather than further this country's pursuit of goals both for itself and for the community of nations as a whole in the international sphere. *Sabbatino* at 421, 423.

The act of state doctrine rests upon considerations of international comity and separation of powers between the executive and judicial branches of the government. It is intended to avoid embarrassment in the conduct of the nation's foreign relations. There must be some role for the executive to have some assurance that United States foreign policy will not be dictated by an obscure rural court. One has only to envision a justice of peace court in a distant corner of the United States, proclaiming the illegality of actions taken in a foreign country by the highest officers of that government, to sense the international prudence of protecting and maintaining the act of state doctrine. See *DeRoburt v. Gannett Co., Inc.*, 548 F.Supp. 1370, 1380 (D.Hawai'i 1982). Thus, it:

> . . . would be not only offensive and unnecessary, but it would imperil the amicable relations between governments, and vex the peace of nations, to permit the sovereign acts or political transactions of states to be subjected to the examination of the legal tribunals of other states. *Underhill v. Hernandez*, 65 Fed. 577, 579 (2d Cir.1895).

"In short, . . . the validity of a foreign act of state in certain circumstances is a 'political question' not cognizable in our courts." *First National City Bank v. Banco Nacional de Cuba*, 406 U.S. 759, 787–788 (1972)(Brennan, J. dissenting), rehearing denied 409 U.S. 897 (1972).

The political branches of our government are able to consider the competing economic and political considerations and respond to the public will in order to carry on foreign relations in accordance with the best interests of the country as a whole. The courts, in contrast, focus on single disputes and make decisions on the basis of legal principles. The timing of our decisions is largely a result of our caseload and of the random tactical considerations which motivate parties to bring lawsuits and to seek delay or expedition. When the courts engage in piecemeal adjudication of the legality of the sovereign acts of states, they risk disruption of our country's international diplomacy. The executive may utilize protocol, economic sanction, compromise, delay, and persuasion to achieve international objectives. Ill-timed judicial decisions challenging the acts of foreign states could nullify these tools and embarrass the United States in the eyes of the world. *IAM v. OPEC*, 649 F.2d 1354, 1358 (9th Cir.1981).

The act of state doctrine's interface with the separation of powers, between the executive and judicial branches of the United States government, has been discussed by courts for over twenty years in large part because of *Bernstein v. N.V. Nederlandsche–Amerikaansche Stoomvaart–Maatschappij*, 210 F.2d 375 (2d Cir.1954)(hereafter *Bernstein*). In *Bernstein* the court was inclined to apply the act of state doctrine, but the Department of State urged the court to refrain and to proceed with an examination of the legal issues. The court concluded that:

[I]n the prior appeal in this case ... because of the lack of a definitive expression of Executive Policy, we felt constrained to follow ... [the act of state doctrine].... Following our decision, however, the State Department issued ... [a policy statement intended] ... to relieve American courts from any [such] restraint upon the exercise of their jurisdiction.... In view of this supervening expression of Executive Policy, we amend our mandate ... [that the act of state doctrine precludes judicial inquiry]. *Bernstein* at 375–376.

The validity of this "*Bernstein* exception" to the act of state doctrine was before the Supreme Court in *First National City Bank v. Banco Nacional de Cuba*, 406 U.S. 759 (1972), rehearing denied 409 U.S. 897 (1972)(hereafter *First National*). Reversing the lower court, three justices, as a plurality, wrote that:

[W]here the Executive Branch, charged as it is with primary responsibility for the conduct of foreign affairs, expressly represents to the Court that application of the act of state doctrine would not advance the interests of American foreign policy, that doctrine should not be applied by the courts. In so doing, we of course adopt and approve the so-called *Berstein* exception to the act of state doctrine. We believe this to be no more than an application of the classical common-law maxim that "[the] reason of the law ceasing, the law itself also ceases".... Our holding is in no sense an abdication of the judicial function of the Executive Branch. Id. at 768.

Two concurring Justices and four dissenting Justices disagreed, however, the latter writing that:

As six members of this Court recognize today, ... [it] is clear that the representations of the Department of State are entitled to weight for the light they shed on the permutation and combination of factors underlying the act of state doctrine. But they cannot be determinative....

The task of defining the contours of a political question such as the act of state doctrine is exclusively the function of this Court.... The *"Bernstein"* exception relinquishes the function to the Executive by requiring blind adherence to its requests that foreign acts of state be reviewed. Conversely, it politicizes the judiciary. Id. at 790.

Four years later, in *Alfred Dunhill of London, Inc. v. Republic of Cuba*, 425 U.S. 682, 725 (1976)(hereafter *Dunhill*), four dissenting Justices wrote:

[Six] members of the Court in *First National* ... disapproved finally the so-called *Bernstein* exception to the act of state doctrine, thus minimizing the significance of any letter from the Department of State ... the task of defining the role of the judiciary is for this Court, not the Executive Branch.

Constitutional effect aside, a *Bernstein* letter from the Department of State to a court may be quite persuasive in providing the court with a reason to avoid application of the doctrine. Lack of such a letter may not result in a reverse conclusion; in 1982, the Department of State advised the Solicitor

General that "courts should not infer from the silence of the Department of State that adjudication in ... (a pending) case would be harmful to the foreign policy of the United States." See 22 *Int'l Legal Mat.* 207.

The *Kirkpatrick* decision supports the view of *Dunhill* that it is the function of the judiciary rather than the executive to define the role of the judiciary in addressing acts of foreign states. The Supreme Court in *Kirkpatrick* did not reject any role for the executive, but clearly rejected the circuit court's giving "full, faith and credit" to the letter from the Department of State.

THE ACT OF STATE DOCTRINE AND SOME EXCEPTIONS

As in the case of the application of sovereign immunity, there are exceptions to the act of state doctrine. Those applicable to sovereign immunity are specifically included in the FSIA, but those which limit the act of state doctrine are for the most part found, as is the doctrine itself, in the pages of precedent. One exception, where the act violates international law, has been discussed above. It constitutes an exception partly framed in legislation, the Sabbatino Amendment, and partly in subsequent case law. Another exception found in legislation applies to the enforcement of arbitral agreements, confirmation of arbitral awards, and execution upon judgments based on orders confirming such awards. 9 U.S.C.A. § 15. Two other actions

which are debated as constituting exceptions are
waivers and commercial activities.

EXCEPTIONS TO THE ACT OF STATE
DOCTRINE: WAIVERS

A foreign sovereign may appear in an action
brought against the foreign state in a United States
court and expressly waive its right to raise the act
of state defense. That it would do so is unusual, but
it has the right. Less certain is whether the foreign
state, after having appeared and waived the defense, might retract that waiver. If the retraction
itself is revocable at any time during the proceeding
until the conclusion of the trial, the basic concept of
waiver seems week at best, or more accurately, it is
illusory.

If a foreign state does not expressly waive the act
of state defense, but does bring a counterclaim after
a suit is brought against it, does that constitute a
waiver? A majority of the Court in the *First National* decision suggested no, but as *dictum*, not as part
of the opinion. Where the counterclaim is not the
act of the foreign state in a suit against it, but is
initiated by the United States party after the foreign state has initiated suit, may the foreign state
raise the act of state doctrine as a defense to the
counterclaim? The foreign state is *not* stripped of its
right to invoke the act of state as a defense to a
counterclaim just because it thereby waives its right
to avoid a counterclaim on grounds of state immunity. See *Empresa* at 238. A clear and unambiguous

statement by a foreign state that it does not object to judicial scrutiny of a state act may influence a court, but other factors may also be considered. *Compania de Gas de Nuevo Laredo, S.A. v. Entex, Inc.*, 686 F.2d 322 (5th Cir.1982).

EXCEPTIONS TO THE ACT OF STATE DOCTRINE: COMMERCIAL ACTIVITY

Uncertainty also clouds the issue of the existence of a commercial activity exception to the act of state doctrine. The Supreme Court has stated that:

> [T]he concept of an act of state should not be extended to include the repudiation of a purely commercial obligation owed by a foreign sovereign or by one of its commercial instrumentalities.... In their commercial capacities, foreign governments do not exercise powers peculiar to sovereigns.... Subjecting them in connection with such acts to the same rules of law that apply to private citizens is unlikely to touch very sharply on 'national nerves.' *Dunhill* at 695, 704.

The *Dunhill* case has gained uncertain and perhaps unjustified status as constituting the "commercial exception" to the act of state doctrine, notwithstanding that only four justices joined in that part of the opinion, and that four other justices wrote that:

> [I]t does not follow that there should be a commercial act exception to the act of state doctrine....

The carving out of broad exceptions to the doctrine is fundamentally at odds with the careful case-by-case approach adopted in *Sabbatino*. *Dunhill* at 725.

However, Justice Stevens, who was not one of the four approving the idea of a commercial exception, seemed to believe that a breach of a commercial contract which was unrelated to some political or legislative purpose would not be a situation where the act of state would be accepted as a defense. The ambiguity of the Court has led to different views expressed in lower federal courts. One court has stated that:

consideration of the commercial nature of a given act is compelled if the doctrine is to be applied correctly. In this connection, attention is owed not to the purpose of the act but to its nature. The goal of the inquiry is to determine if denial of the act of state defense. In the case under consideration will thwart the policy concerns in which the doctrine is rooted. *Sage Int'l, Ltd. v. Cadillac Gage Co.*, 534 F.Supp. 896, 905 (E.D.Mich.1981).

But another court has observed that:

While purely commercial activity may not rise to the level of an act of state, certain seemingly commercial activities will trigger act of state considerations.... When the state *qua* state acts in the public interest, its sovereignty is asserted. The Courts must proceed cautiously to avoid an affront to that sovereignty.... [W]e find that the act of state doctrine remains available when such caution is appropriate regardless of any commercial component of the activity involved. *IAM v. OPEC*, 649 F.2d 1354, 1360 (9th Cir.1981).

If a commercial exception is not to be granted, determining that the situs of the activity (commercial or not) is not in the foreign state may cause judicial rejection of the doctrine. This has proven important to the international debt issue. If nonpayment is held to have occurred at the office of the lending bank in the United States, the doctrine may be rejected as a defense. See *Allied Bank Int'l v. Banco Credito Agricola de Cartago*, 757 F.2d 516 (2d Cir.1985), cert. denied 473 U.S. 934 (1985).

With the Eleventh Circuit added to those denying a commercial activity exception, the split among lower courts continues. It is an area in need of direction from the Supreme Court.

CONCLUSION

The *Underhill* pronouncement that the "courts of one country will not sit in judgment on the acts of the government of another, done within its own territory," remains the foundation of the act of state doctrine in the United States. Governments undertake many acts. Where a government act constitutes the taking of property of foreign persons, which was not the case in *Underhill*, the foundations of the act of state doctrine begin to tremble. Such a tremble followed the massive expropriations of foreign property by the government of Cuba in the early 1960s. While the Supreme Court in the

Sabbatino case would not fashion an exception to the act of state doctrine for violations of international law in expropriating property, the United States Congress quickly established that exception in the Sabbatino Amendment. But subsequent judicial decisions read that legislative response more strictly than Congress appeared to intend. The Amendment did alter the presumption attendant to a court ruling on a foreign state act. The pre-Sabbatino presumption that *any* adjudication of unlawfulness of a foreign act would embarrass United States foreign relations unless the President stated otherwise, became a presumption that such adjudication would not embarrass the President unless he stated that it would. In the *Kirkpatrick* decision the United States Supreme Court made it quite clear that what the President states regarding going ahead will do or not do in embarrassing the United States foreign policy, is to be accepted *or* rejected by the court depending on other circumstances of the case. Exceptions carved out of the doctrine are likely to moderate if not nullify "suggestions of executive embarrassment" coming from the President. The full impact of *Kirkpatrick* is yet to be determined. As is the full extent of Congresses willingness to prohibit the application of the act of state in situations it addresses, such as in the Helms–Burton Act.

The act of state doctrine is important to actions other than the taking of property, and actually has been recently more often used as a defense by private individuals rather than foreign states. In such cases as private suits based on violations of the antitrust laws, an effective defense has been "the foreign government made me do it," the doctrine of foreign compulsion integrated with the doctrine of act of state. The act of state thus becomes part of the idea that there should be no infringement or nullification of the sovereignty of a nation by judicial rulings of another state which extend extraterritorially.

INDEX

-D-

-L-

-P-

-R-

-S-

-U-